current procedural terminology

cpt®
2010
Changes

An Insider's View

AMA
AMERICAN
MEDICAL
ASSOCIATION

Contents

Foreword

The American Medical Association is pleased to offer *CPT® Changes 2010: An Insider's View*. Since this book was first published in 2000, it has served as the definitive text on additions, revisions, and deletions to the CPT code set.

In developing this book, it was our intention to provide CPT users with a glimpse of the logic, rationale, and proposed function of CPT changes that resulted from the decisions of the CPT Editorial Panel and the yearly update process. American Medical Association (AMA) staff members have the unique perspective of being both participants in the CPT editorial process and users of the CPT code set. *CPT Changes* is intended to bridge understanding between clinical decisions made at the CPT Editorial Panel regarding appropriate service or procedure descriptions with functional interpretations of coding guidelines, code intent, and code combinations necessary for users of the CPT code set. A new edition of this book, like the codebook, is published annually.

To assist CPT users in applying new and revised CPT codes, this book includes clinical examples that describe the typical patient who might receive the procedure and detailed descriptions of the procedure. Both of these are required as a part of the CPT code change proposal process and are used by the CPT Editorial Panel in crafting language, guidelines, and parenthetical notes associated with the new or revised codes. In addition, many of the clinical examples and descriptions of the procedures are used in the AMA/Specialty Society RVS Update process for conducting surveys on physician work and in developing work relative value recommendations to the Centers for Medicare and Medicaid Services (CMS) as part of the Medicare Physician Fee Schedule (MPFS).

We are confident that the information contained in *CPT Changes* each year will prove to be a valuable resource to CPT users not only as they apply changes for the year of publication but also as a resource for frequent reference as they continue their education in CPT coding. The AMA makes every effort to be a voice of clarity and consistency in an otherwise confusing system of health care claims and payment, and *CPT Changes 2010: An Insider's View* demonstrates our continued commitment to assist users of the CPT code set.

Using This Book

This book is designed to serve as a reference guide to understanding the changes contained in *Current Procedural Terminology (CPT®) 2010* and is not intended to replace the CPT codebook. Every effort is made to ensure accuracy; however, if differences exist, you should always defer to the information contained in the *CPT 2010* codebook.

The Symbols

This book uses the same coding conventions that appear in the CPT nomenclature.

- ● Indicates that a new procedure number was added to the CPT nomenclature

- ▲ Indicates that a code revision has resulted in a substantially altered procedure descriptor

- ✛ Indicates a CPT add-on code

- ⊘ Indicates a code that is exempt from the use of modifier 51 but is not designated as a CPT add-on procedure/service

- ►◄ Indicate revised guidelines, cross-references, and/or explanatory text

- ⊙ Indicates a code that typically includes moderate sedation

- ⁄ Indicates a code for a vaccine that is pending FDA approval

- # Indicates a resequenced code

- ○ Indicates a reinstated or recycled code

Whenever possible, complete segments of text from the CPT codebook are provided, however, in some cases the text has been abbreviated.

The Rationale

After each change or series of changes is a rationale. The rationale is intended to provide a brief explanation as to why changes occurred but may not answer every question that may arise as a result of the changes.

Reading the Clinical Examples

The clinical examples and their procedural descriptions included in this text with many of the codes provide practical situations for which the new and/or revised codes in the *CPT 2010* codebook would be appropriately reported. It is important to note that these examples do not suggest limiting the use of a code but only represent the typical patient and service or procedure. They do not describe the universe of patients for whom the service or procedure would be appropriate. In addition, third-party payer reporting policies may differ.

The Tabular Review of the Changes

The table beginning on page 259 allows you to see all of the code changes at a glance. By reviewing the table you can easily determine the level to which your particular field of interest has been affected by the changes in the *CPT 2010* codebook.

CPT Codebook Text and Guidelines

In *CPT Changes 2010*, guideline and revised CPT codebook text appears in brown indented type. Any revised text, guidelines, and/or headings are indicated with the ►◄ symbols. This convention in *CPT Changes 2010* differs slightly from the CPT codebook. Within the codebook, symbols are placed at the beginning and end of a paragraph that contains a revision or revisions. *CPT Changes 2010* offers readers a more detailed view of the changes to the codes and guidelines. In this book, the revision symbols (►◄) are placed around each specific change.

Resequencing CPT® Codes:
An Initiative Implemented in 2010

In an effort to meet the growing demands for available numbers in CPT code sets while adhering to the principles of health information technology (HIT), the American Medical Association (AMA) has introduced a resequencing system to integrate new code concepts into existing code families regardless of the availability of sequential numbers. In other words, the numbers assigned to some CPT codes will not necessarily fit into the numerical order of some code families.

Resequencing utilizes the content within the code descriptor to determine placement and offers flexibility for code assignment beyond the capability of the traditional numbering convention. The resequencing approach for code placement is based on the principle that codes are deleted and a new number is established when the meaning of the code changes, or when other editorial policies apply (eg, a code conversion from Category III to Category I). Deletions to display related codes together in printed materials are not acceptable criteria for renumbering.

Adherence to the traditional numbering convention that inherently forces deletion and renumbering would compromise the long term maintenance and integrity of the CPT codes. Resequencing allows related concepts to be placed in an numerical sequence regardless of the availability of numbers for sequential numerical placement, extending the existence of the current five-digit numbering scheme, improving the growth and flexibility of CPT content, and the use of CPT codes in electronic products.

Technical Strategy for Resequencing

Effective 2010, the resequencing principle will be implemented as part of the CPT code sets' maintenance with the following approach.

The replacement of a resequenced code will be in sections in which the user would most conveniently find the procedure. Whenever possible, attempts will be made to assign code numbers that fall within a family of anatomically-related procedures or a subsection. If no code numbers are available within a subsection or family, the closest code number (limited to the section level, eg, Surgery) will be assigned.

A set of navigational alerts will be employed throughout the codebook to help users locate resequenced or out-of-sequence codes. These alerts include: (1) a "#" symbol (preceding any other symbols applied to the code) to denote a resequenced code and (2) references at the location where the code would have been found numerically (with the code number as a place holder) directing the user to the subsection where the resequenced code with the "#" symbol is located. As a result of resequencing, some code ranges will need to be expanded. Cross-references, parenthetical notes, and introductory notes with code ranges affected by resequenced codes will be more explicit. If a code range includes resequenced codes, the range will be broken down into individual codes listed in numeric order.

Further navigational assistance to users with this new resequencing concept is provided in the list of resequenced or out-of-sequence codes located in Appendix N of the *CPT® 2010* codebook. It is important to note that the Index for the CPT codebook will continue to list codes according to the current methodology and the code listings will not be modified due to resequencing.

Introduction

Introduction

To eliminate confusion, duplicative text was removed from the Special Report instructions at the beginning of each section of the CPT codebook.

Appendix M has been revised to include associated *CPT Assistant* references for deleted codes.

Evaluation and Management

The Evaluation and Management Services section includes extensive revisions to the guidelines for the Consultations, Office or Other Outpatient Consultations, Inpatient Consultations sections. Editorial revisions were made to the Nursing Facility Services codes and additional revisions were made to the guidelines of the Prolonged Services without Direct (Face-To-Face) Patient Contact subsection.

Evaluation and Management

Consultations

▶A consultation is a type of evaluation and management service provided by a physician at the request of another physician or appropriate source to either recommend care for a specific condition or problem or to determine whether to accept responsibility for ongoing management of the patient's entire care or for the care of a specific condition or problem.◀

A physician consultant may initiate diagnostic . . .

▶A "consultation" initiated by a patient and/or family, and not requested by a physician or other appropriate source (eg, physician assistant, nurse practitioner, doctor of chiropractic, physical therapist, occupational therapist, speech-language pathologist, psychologist, social worker, lawyer, or insurance company), is not reported using the consultation codes but may be reported using the office visit, home service, or domiciliary/rest home care codes as appropriate.

The written or verbal request for a consult may be made by a physician or other appropriate source and documented in the patient's medical record by either the consulting or requesting physician or appropriate source. The consultant's opinion and any services that were ordered or performed must also be documented in the patient's medical record and communicated by written report to the requesting physician or other appropriate source.◀

If a consultation is mandated . . .

Any specifically identifiable procedure . . .

If subsequent to the completion of . . .

▶To report services provided to a patient who is admitted to a hospital or nursing facility in the course of an encounter in the office or other ambulatory facility, see the notes for Initial Hospital Inpatient Care (page 16) or Initial Nursing Facility Care (page 24).◀

For definitions of key components and . . .

Rationale

The consultation definition included within the introductory notes under the Evaluation and Management (E/M) section subheading Consultations has been editorially revised to outline the two circumstances under which consultations provided at the request of another physician or appropriate source may be rendered: (1) to provide opinion/services for a specific condition or problem, or (2) to allow a determination to be made on whether to accept the ongoing management of the patient's entire care or for the care of a specific condition or problem (ie, transfer of care). *(See Rationale listed for Transfer of Care definition under the Evaluation and Management (E/M) Services Guidelines section).*

It has been emphasized that documentation of the written or oral request for a consultation can be made by either the consultant or by the requesting physician or other appropriate source.

Another editorial change was made under the Consultations subheading to direct users to see the instructions in the Initial Hospital Inpatient Care and Initial Nursing Facility Care sections to determine how to code circumstances in which a patient is admitted to the hospital or nursing facility in the course of an office or other ambulatory facility visit. These circumstances are described in a new paragraph added to the introductory notes for Inpatient Consultations. *(For further explanation, see Rationale following code 99251.)*

Office or Other Outpatient Consultations

NEW OR ESTABLISHED PATIENT

▶The following codes are used to report consultations provided in the physician's office or in an outpatient or other ambulatory facility, including hospital observation services, home services, domiciliary, rest home, or emergency department (see the preceding Consultation definition above). Follow-up visits in the consultant's office or other outpatient facility that are initiated by the physician consultant or patient are reported using the appropriate codes for established patients, office visits (99211-99215), domiciliary, rest home (99334-99337), or home (99347-99350). If an additional request for an opinion or advice regarding the same or a new problem is received from another physician or other appropriate source and documented in the medical record, the office consultation codes may be used again. Services that constitute transfer of care (ie, are provided for the management of the patient's entire care or for the care of a specific condition or problem) are reported with the appropriate new or established patient codes for office or other outpatient visits, domiciliary, rest home services, or home services.◀

99241   **Office consultation** for a new or established patient, which requires these 3 key components:

Rationale

A note has been added under the Office or Other Outpatient Consultations subsection to reference the use of other groups of codes (eg, new or established office or other outpatient visits (99241-99245), domiciliary, rest home services (99339-99340), or home services (99341-99350), when the services rendered are not consultative but performed under the direction or management of the provider rendering care for all the patient's care or for a specific condition or problem (ie, transfer of care services). *(See Rationale listed for Transfer of Care definition under the Evaluation and Management (E/M) Services Guidelines section.)*

Inpatient Consultations

NEW OR ESTABLISHED PATIENT

▶The following codes are used to report physician consultations provided to hospital inpatients, residents of nursing facilities, or patients in a partial hospital setting. Only one consultation should be reported by a consultant per admission. Subsequent services during the same admission are reported using subsequent hospital care codes (99231-99233) or subsequent nursing facility care codes (99307-99310), including services to complete the initial consultation, monitor progress, revise recommendations, or address a new problem. Use subsequent hospital care codes (99231-99233) or

    ⊘=Modifier 51 Exempt   ⊙=Moderate Sedation ✚=Add-on Code ✗=FDA approval pending

subsequent nursing facility care codes (99307-99310) to report transfer of care services (see page 25, Concurrent Care and Transfer of Care definitions).

When an inpatient consultation is performed on the date that a patient is admitted to a hospital or nursing facility, all evaluation and management services provided by the consultant related to the admission are reported with the inpatient consultation service code (99251-99255). If a patient is admitted after an outpatient consultation (office, emergency department, etc), and the patient is not seen on the unit on the date of admission, only report the outpatient consultation code (99241-99245). If the patient is seen by the consultant on the unit on the date of admission, report all evaluation and management (E/M) services provided by the consultant related to the admission with either the inpatient consultation code (99251-99255) or with the initial inpatient admission service code (99221-99223). Do not report both an outpatient consultation and inpatient consultation for services related to the same inpatient stay. When transfer of care services are provided on a date subsequent to the outpatient consultation, use the subsequent hospital care codes (99231-99233) or subsequent nursing facility care codes (99307-99310).◄

99251   **Inpatient consultation** for a new or established patient, which requires these 3 key components:

✍ Rationale

An instructional note referencing the Transfer of Care and Concurrent Care definitions found in the Evaluation and Management (E/M) Services Guidelines section has been added to the opening paragraph under the Inpatient Consultation subsection (*See Rationale listed for Transfer of Care definition under the Evaluation and Management (E/M) Services Guidelines section*). This note also directs the use of subsequent hospital care codes (99231-99233) or subsequent nursing facility care codes (99307-99310) for reporting any transfer of care services that occur in the hospital setting following the initial hospital or nursing facility care services.

A new paragraph has been added to the introductory notes for Inpatient Consultations, which in summary instructs the following:

If an inpatient consultation service is provided on the date of hospital or nursing facility admission by a consultant, all evaluation and management (E/M) services related to the admission that may be performed by the consultant are to be reported with the inpatient consultation service code (99251-99255). However, when admission services are provided on the same date as the inpatient consultation by the same provider, in the inpatient setting, the provider may report either the inpatient consultation code (99251-99255) or the initial inpatient admission service code (99221-99233), but not both codes. This is dependent on whether the consultant has admitting privileges.

Two more statements for clarification have also been added to this new paragraph to indicate: (1) reporting both an outpatient and inpatient consultation related to the same inpatient stay is not appropriate; and (2) when transfer of care services are provided in the inpatient setting, whether hospital or nursing home, and a consultation service by the same provider was already performed in the outpatient setting, use the subsequent hospital care codes (99231-99233) or subsequent nursing facility care codes (99307-99310).

Nursing Facility Services

Initial Nursing Facility Care

NEW OR ESTABLISHED PATIENT

When the patient is admitted to . . .

Hospital discharge or observation discharge services . . .

(For nursing facility care discharge, see . . .

▲99304   Initial nursing facility care, per day, for the evaluation and management of a patient, which requires these 3 key components:

■ **A detailed or comprehensive history;**

■ **A detailed or comprehensive examination; and**

■ **Medical decision making that is straightforward or of low complexity.**

Counseling and/or coordination of care with other providers or agencies are provided consistent with the nature of the problem(s) and the patient's and/or family's needs.

Usually, the problem(s) requiring admission are of low severity. Physicians typically spend 25 minutes at the bedside and on the patient's facility floor or unit.

▲99305   Initial nursing facility care, per day, for the evaluation and management of a patient, which requires these 3 key components:

■ **A comprehensive history;**

■ **A comprehensive examination; and**

■ **Medical decision making of moderate complexity.**

Counseling and/or coordination of care with other providers or agencies are provided consistent with the nature of the problem(s) and the patient's and/or family's needs.

Usually, the problem(s) requiring admission are of moderate severity. Physicians typically spend 35 minutes at the bedside and on the patient's facility floor or unit.

▲99306   Initial nursing facility care, per day, for the evaluation and management of a patient, which requires these 3 key components:

■ **A comprehensive history;**

■ **A comprehensive examination; and**

■ **Medical decision making of high complexity.**

Counseling and/or coordination of care with other providers or agencies are provided consistent with the nature of the problem(s) and the patient's and/or family's needs.

Usually, the problem(s) requiring admission are of high severity. Physicians typically spend 45 minutes at the bedside and on the patient's facility floor or unit.

Subsequent Nursing Facility Care

All levels of subsequent nursing facility care include reviewing the medical record and reviewing the results of diagnostic studies and changes in the patient's status (ie, changes in history, physical condition, and response to management) since the last assessment by the physician.

▲99307   Subsequent nursing facility care, per day, for the evaluation and management of a patient, which requires at least 2 of these 3 key components:

■ **A problem focused interval history;**

■ **A problem focused examination;**

■ **Straightforward medical decision making.**

Counseling and/or coordination of care with other providers or agencies are provided consistent with the nature of the problem(s) and the patient's and/or family's needs.

Usually, the patient is stable, recovering, or improving. Physicians typically spend 10 minutes at the bedside and on the patient's facility floor or unit.

▲99308   Subsequent nursing facility care, per day, for the evaluation and management of a patient, which requires at least 2 of these 3 key components:

■ **An expanded problem focused interval history;**

■ **An expanded problem focused examination;**

■ **Medical decision making of low complexity.**

Counseling and/or coordination of care with other providers or agencies are provided consistent with the nature of the problem(s) and the patient's and/or family's needs.

Usually, the patient is responding inadequately to therapy or has developed a minor complication. Physicians typically spend 15 minutes at the bedside and on the patient's facility floor or unit.

▲99309   Subsequent nursing facility care, per day, for the evaluation and management of a patient, which requires at least 2 of these 3 key components:

■ **A detailed interval history;**

■ **A detailed examination;**

■ **Medical decision making of moderate complexity.**

Counseling and/or coordination of care with other providers or agencies are provided consistent with the nature of the problem(s) and the patient's and/or family's needs.

Usually, the patient has developed a significant complication or a significant new problem. Physicians typically spend 25 minutes at the bedside and on the patient's facility floor or unit.

▲99310   Subsequent nursing facility care, per day, for the evaluation and management of a patient, which requires at least 2 of these 3 key components:

■ **A comprehensive interval history;**

■ **A comprehensive examination;**

■ **Medical decision making of high complexity.**

Counseling and/or coordination of care with other providers or agencies are provided consistent with the nature of the problem(s) and the patient's and/or family's needs.

The patient may be unstable or may have developed a significant new problem requiring immediate physician attention. Physicians typically spend 35 minutes at the bedside and on the patient's facility floor or unit.

Other Nursing Facility Services

▲99318   Evaluation and management of a patient involving an annual nursing facility assessment, which requires these 3 key components:

- **A detailed interval history;**

- **A comprehensive examination; and**

- **Medical decision making that is of low to moderate complexity.**

Counseling and/or coordination of care with other providers or agencies are provided consistent with the nature of the problem(s) and the patient's and/or family's needs.

Usually, the patient is stable, recovering, or improving. Physicians typically spend 30 minutes at the bedside and on the patient's facility floor or unit.

🖎 Rationale
Codes 99304, 99305, 99306, 99307, 99308, 99309, 99310, and 99318 were editorially revised to include terminology that is consistent with the description of unit/floor time that has been established to include the time spent at the patient's bedside and/or on the patient's facility floor or unit. The time component for nursing home facility codes first appeared in the CPT codebook 2008.

Prolonged Services

Prolonged Physician Service Without Direct (Face-To-Face) Patient Contact

▶Codes 99358 and 99359 are used when a physician provides prolonged service not involving direct (face-to-face) care that is beyond the usual non-face-to-face component of physician service time.

This service is to be reported in relationaddition to other physician services, including evaluation and management services at any level. This prolonged service may be reported on a different date than the primary service to which it is related. For example, extensive record review may relate to a previous evaluation and management service performed earlier and commences upon receipt of past records. However, it must relate to a service or patient where direct (face-to-face) patient care has occurred or will occur and relate to ongoing patient management. A typical time for the primary service need not be established within the CPT code set.

Codes 99358 and 99359 are used to report the total duration of non-face-to-face time spent by a physician on a given date providing prolonged service, even if the time spent by the physician on that

⊘=Modifier 51 Exempt   ⊙=Moderate Sedation   ✚=Add-on Code   ⋈=FDA approval pending

date is not continuous. Code 99358 is used to report the first hour of prolonged service on a given date regardless of the place of service. It should be used only once per date.◄

Prolonged service of less than 30 minutes total duration on a given date is not separately reported.

Code 99359 is used to report each additional 30 minutes beyond the first hour regardless of the place of service. It may also be used to report the final 15 to 30 minutes of prolonged service on a given date.

Prolonged service of less than 15 minutes beyond the first hour or less than 15 minutes beyond the final 30 minutes is not reported separately.

►Do not report 99358-99359 for time spent in medical team conferences, on-line medical evaluations, care plan oversight services, anticoagulation management, or other non-face-to-face services that have more specific codes and no upper time limit in the CPT code set. Codes 99358-99359 may be reported when related to other non-face-to-face services codes that have a published maximum time (eg, telephone services).◄

▲99358   **Prolonged evaluation and management service** before and/or after direct (face-to-face) patient care first hour

+▲99359   each additional 30 minutes (List separately in addition to code for prolonged physician service)

Rationale

Revisions have been made to the guidelines of the Prolonged Physician Services Without Direct (Face-To-Face) Patient Contact and to codes 99358 and 99359. In addition, the add-on code status has been removed from Prolonged Services code 99358, allowing its use on a separate date from an Evaluation and Management (E/M) service or other CPT coded procedure or service performed.

Revisions to the guidelines include clarification that prolonged services without direct (face-to-face) patient contact codes are to be reported for prolonged services that are beyond the usual non-face-to-face component of physician service time. Also, with the removal of the add-on code status from code 99358, the guidelines clarify that the prolonged services may now be reported on a different date than the primary service to which it is related. Codes 99358 and 99359 are no longer restricted to use on the same date as the related service. However, the guidelines specify that the prolonged service must relate to a service or patient in which direct face-to-face patient care has occurred or will occur, and relate to ongoing patient management. The primary service to which the prolonged service is related does not need to have a typical time established in the CPT code set. Additional language states that code 99358 should be used only once per date.

New language added to the guidelines also gives instruction not to report codes 99358 and 99359 for non-face-to-face services that already have specific CPT codes such as medical team conferences, on-line medical evaluations, care plan oversight services, anticoagulation management, or other non-face-to-face services that have more specific codes and no upper time limit in the CPT code set. When related to other non-face-to-face services that have a published maximum time (eg, telephone services), codes 99358 and 99359 may be reported. In support of the revised guidelines, the parenthetical note following code 99359 has been deleted.

Coinciding with the removal of the add-on code status from code 99358, the descriptors of codes 99358 and 99359 were revised with the deletion of the standard add-on code language. The examples of prolonged services were also removed from codes 99358 and 99359.

⊘=Modifier 51 Exempt   ⊙=Moderate Sedation   ✚=Add-on Code   ⚡=FDA approval pending

Anesthesia

The Anesthesia section acquired only one code deletion due to its low reporting volume.

Anesthesia

01630 Anesthesia for open or surgical arthroscopic procedures on humeral head and neck, sternoclavicular joint, acromioclavicular joint, and shoulder joint; not otherwise specified

(01632 has been deleted. To report, see 01630, 01638)

01634 shoulder disarticulation

 Rationale

Code 01632 has been deleted for 2010 because of the low volume of shoulder procedures for which code 01630 was reported (ie, 23220, 23221, 23222). Codes 23221 and 23222 have also been deleted for 2010 for the same reason (low reporting volumes). Code 23220 remains in the CPT code set, although it has been revised for 2010. See the Musculoskeletal System section within the Surgery section for further information regarding this revision. A cross-reference note has been added following code 01630 instructing users to see codes 01630 and 01638 for reporting anesthesia for procedures performed on the shoulder.

Surgery

Significant changes were made to the Surgery section, some of which are the following:

- Extensive revisions to the Musculoskeletal System section include language added to the introductory guidelines related to excision of subcutaneous soft tissue tumors, excision of fascial or subfascial soft tissue tumors, radical resection of soft tissue tumors, and radical resection of bone tumors services. In addition, numerous additions, revisions and deletions have been made to the soft tissue tumor and bone tumor codes (41 new codes, 53 revised codes, 7 deleted codes, and new parenthetical and instructional notes). This section has been expanded to achieve greater granularity, consistency, and standardization for these services.

- The most notable changes made in the Digestive System are within the Anus section, particularly the Excision subsection where nearly all of the codes were editorially revised with a few codes resequenced to allow proper placement of the related concepts.

- Many changes were made in the Introduction/Injection of Anesthetic Agent (nerve Block), Diagnostic or Therapeutic section to allay confusion regarding facet joint and facet joint nerve injections. The paravertebral facet joint or facet joint nerve injection codes 64470-64476 have been deleted and a new subheading was added for Paravertebral Spinal Nerves and Branches with 6 new codes for reporting paravertebral facet joint injections with image guidance (fluoroscopy or CT) specified in the code descriptors to be inclusive components.

Surgery

General

10021   Fine needle aspiration; without imaging guidance

10022   with imaging guidance

►(For placement of percutaneous localization clip during breast biopsy, use 19295)◄

(For radiological supervision and interpretation, see 76942, 77002, 77012, 77021)

 Rationale

A cross-reference has been added following code 10022 to direct the use of code 19295 for percutaneous placement of a localization clip during breast biopsies.

Integumentary System

Skin, Subcutaneous, and Accessory Structures

EXCISION—BENIGN LESIONS

►The closure of defects created by incision, excision, or trauma may require intermediate or complex closure. Repair by intermediate or complex closure should be reported separately. For excision of benign lesions requiring more than simple closure, ie, requiring intermediate or complex closure, report 11400-11446 in addition to appropriate intermediate (12031-12057) or complex closure (13100-13153) codes. For reconstructive closure, see 15002-15261, 15570-15770. For excision performed in conjunction with adjacent tissue transfer, report only the adjacent tissue transfer code (14000-14302). Excision of lesion (11400–11446) is not separately reportable with adjacent tissue transfer. See page 58 for the definition of *intermediate* or *complex* closure.◄

11400   Excision, benign lesion including margins, except skin tag (unless listed elsewhere), trunk, arms or legs; excised diameter 0.5 cm or less

 Rationale

In accordance with the establishment of codes 14301 and 14302, the Excision— Benign Lesions guidelines have been revised to expand the code range and support the establishment of these services.

EXCISION—MALIGNANT LESIONS

►The closure of defects created by incision, excision, or trauma may require intermediate or complex closure. Repair by intermediate or complex closure should be reported separately. For excision of malignant lesions requiring more than simple closure, ie, requiring intermediate or complex closure, report 11600-11646 in addition to appropriate intermediate (12031-12057) or complex closure (13100-13153) codes. For reconstructive closure, see 15002-15261, 15570-15770. For excision performed in conjunction with adjacent tissue transfer, report only the adjacent tissue transfer code (14000-14302).

Excision of lesion (11600–11646) is not separately reportable with adjacent tissue transfer. See page 58 for the definition of *intermediate* or *complex closure.*◄

When frozen section pathology shows the . . .

11600   Excision, malignant lesion including margins, trunk, arms, or legs; excised diameter 0.5 cm or less

 Rationale

Similar to the preceding rationale for Excision–Benign Lesions, the Excision—Malignant Lesions guidelines have been revised to expand the code range and support the establishment of codes 14301 and 14302.

ADJACENT TISSUE TRANSFER OR REARRANGEMENT

For full thickness repair of lip . . .

►Codes 14000-14302 are used for excision (including lesion) and/or repair by adjacent tissue transfer or rearrangement (eg, Z-plasty, W-plasty, V-Y plasty, rotation flap, random island flap, advancement flap). When applied in repairing lacerations, the procedures listed must be performed by the surgeon to accomplish the repair. They do not apply to direct closure or rearrangement of traumatic wounds incidentally resulting in these configurations. Undermining alone of adjacent tissues to achieve closure, without additional incisions, does not constitute adjacent tissue transfer, see complex repair codes 13100-13160. The excision of a benign lesion (11400-11446) or a malignant lesion (11600-11646) is not separately reportable with codes 14000-14302.◄

Skin graft necessary to close secondary . . .

14000   Adjacent tissue transfer or rearrangement, trunk; defect 10 sq cm or less

►(14300 has been deleted. To report, see 14301, 14302)◄

● **14301**   Adjacent tissue transfer or rearrangement, any area; defect 30.1 sq cm to 60.0 sq cm

➕● **14302**   each additional 30.0 sq cm, or part thereof (List separately in addition to code for primary procedure)

►(Use 14302 in conjunction with 14301)◄

 Rationale

Code 14300 was identified as not accurately describing the work that was involved in this service and has been deleted. Codes 14301 and 14302 have been established to more accurately describe minimal and more extensive adjacent tissue transfer services. Code 14301 is reported for defects 30.1 to 60.0 square centimeters, and 14302 is an add-on code that should be reported for each additional 30.0 square centimeters or part thereof. These new codes will differentiate the physician work for procedures greater than 30 sq cm. An instructional parenthetical note has been added following code 14302 to direct users to report code 14302 in conjunction with code 14301.

The guidelines for Adjacent Tissue Transfer services have been revised to support the establishment of these services and to delineate that undermining alone of adjacent tissues to achieve closure, performed without additional incisions, does not constitute adjacent tissue transfer services. When performed, the complex repair codes 13100-13160 should be reported.

Clinical Example (14301)

A 63-year-old female presents with an excised basal cell carcinoma on the left medial cheek that has left a 9.0 sq cm defect through the subcutaneous plane. A cheek rotation flap that is 42.0 sq cm is raised adjacent to the defect. The flap is transposed into the defect to achieve closure. The donor site is closed primarily.

Description of Procedure (14301)

The lesion is excised and then oriented and marked with sutures for pathologic examination. Hemostasis is obtained. Care is taken to determine the availability of adjacent tissue for closure and the possibility of functional impairment or anatomic distortion of adjacent structures. A flap is designed on the adjacent cheek skin. The flap is incised and raised at the appropriate level. The flap is rotated into the defect. Tension is assessed and additional dissection is performed as necessary. The donor site is closed in layers. Drains are placed as necessary. The flap is sutured into position.

Clinical Example (14302)

A 63-year-old female presents with an excised squamous cell carcinoma on the left medial cheek that has left a 16.0 sq cm defect through the subcutaneous plane. A cervicofacial flap that is 72.0 sq cm is elevated adjacent to the defect. The flap is transposed into the defect to achieve closure. The donor site is closed primarily.

Description of Procedure (14302)

Additional lesion excision is carried out. Hemostasis is obtained. Continued care is taken to determine the availability of adjacent tissue for closure and the possibility of functional impairment or anatomic distortion of adjacent structures. The larger flap is incised and raised at the appropriate level. The larger flap is rotated into the defect. Tension is assessed and additional dissection is performed as necessary. The additional donor site is closed in layers. Drains may be placed. The larger flap is sutured into position.

FLAPS (SKIN AND/OR DEEP TISSUES)

▶(For adjacent tissue transfer flaps, see 14000-14302)◀

15570   Formation of direct or tubed pedicle, with or without transfer; trunk

15650   Transfer, intermediate, of any pedicle flap (eg, abdomen to wrist, Walking tube), any location

(For eyelids, nose, ears, or lips, see also anatomical area)

▶(For revision, defatting or rearranging of transferred pedicle flap or skin graft, see 13100-14302)◀

Rationale

In accordance with the establishment of codes 14301 and 14302, the cross-references preceding code 15570 and following code 15650 have been revised to expand the code range and support the establishment of these services.

OTHER FLAPS AND GRAFTS

▶Code 15740 describes a cutaneous flap, transposed into a nearby but not immediately adjacent defect, with a pedicle that incorporates an axial vessel into its design. The flap is typically transferred through a tunnel underneath the skin and sutured into its new position. The donor site is closed directly.

Neurovascular pedicle procedures are reported with 15750. This code includes not only skin but also a functional motor or sensory nerve(s). The flap serves to reinnervate a damaged portion of the body dependent on touch or movement (eg, thumb).◀

Repair of donor site requiring skin . . .

15740	Flap; island pedicle
15750	neurovascular pedicle

▶(For random island flaps, V-Y subcutaneous flaps and other flaps from adjacent areas, see 14000-14302)◀

 Rationale

New introductory guidelines for flap repairs and grafts have been added to provide clarification and appropriately define codes 15740 and 15750. A new cross-reference note was added following code 15750 to instruct the appropriate reporting of codes 14000-14302 for random island flaps and other flaps from adjacent areas.

OTHER PROCEDURES

15830	Excision, excessive skin and subcutaneous tissue (includes lipectomy); abdomen, infraumbilical panniculectomy

▶(Do not report 15830 in conjunction with 12031, 12032, 12034, 12035, 12036, 12037, 13100, 13101, 13102, 14000-14001, 14302)◀

 Rationale

The cross-reference following code 15830 has also been revised to support the establishment of codes 14301 and 14302.

Destruction

Destruction means the ablation of benign, . . .

Any method includes electrosurgery, cryosurgery, laser . . .

(For destruction of lesion(s) in specific . . .)

▶(For laser treatment for inflammatory skin disease, see 96920-96922)◀

(For paring or cutting of benign . . .)

(For sharp removal or electrosurgical destruction . . .)

⊘=Modifier 51 Exempt   ⊙=Moderate Sedation   ✚=Add-on Code   ✗=FDA approval pending

(For cryotherapy of acne, use 17340)

(For initiation or follow-up care of . . .)

(For shaving of epidermal or dermal . . .)

DESTRUCTION, BENIGN OR PREMALIGNANT LESIONS

17000   Destruction (eg, laser surgery, electrosurgery, cryosurgery, chemosurgery, surgical curettement), premalignant lesions (eg, actinic keratoses); first lesion

 Rationale

A cross-reference has been added to the Destruction Subsection to direct users to codes 96920-96922 for laser treatment for inflammatory skin disease.

Breast

INTRODUCTION

+▲19295   Image guided placement, metallic localization clip, percutaneous, during breast biopsy/aspiration (List separately in addition to code for primary procedure)

▶(Use 19295 in conjunction with 10022, 19102, 19103)◀

 Rationale

Code 19295 has been revised to include clip placement during fine needle aspiration, as described in code 10022. In accordance with the revision of code 19295, the instructional note following code 19295 has been revised to include code 10022, fine needle aspiration with imaging guidance.

Musculoskeletal System

Closed treatment specifically means that the fracture site is not surgically opened (exposed to the external environment and directly visualized). This terminology is used to describe procedures that treat fractures by three methods: (1) without manipulation; (2) with manipulation; or (3) with or without traction.

Open treatment is used when the fractured bone is either: (1) surgically opened (exposed to the external environment) and the fracture (bone ends) visualized and internal fixation may be used; or (2) the fractured bone is opened remote from the fracture site in order to insert an intramedullary nail across the fracture site (the fracture site is not opened and visualized).

Manipulation is used throughout the musculoskeletal . . .

▶***Excision of subcutaneous soft tissue tumors*** (including simple or intermediate repair) involves the simple or marginal resection of tumors confined to subcutaneous tissue below the skin but above the deep fascia. These tumors are usually benign and are resected without removing a significant amount of surrounding normal tissue. Code selection is based on the location and size of the tumor. Code selection is determined by measuring the greatest diameter of the tumor plus that margin required for complete excision of the tumor. The margins refer to the most narrow margin required to adequately excise the tumor, based on the physician's judgment. The measurement of the tumor plus margin is made at the time of the excision. Appreciable vessel exploration and/or neuroplasty should be reported separately. Extensive undermining or other techniques to close a defect created by skin excision may require a complex repair which should be reported separately. Dissection or elevation of tissue planes to permit resection of the tumor is included in the excision.

Excision of fascial or subfascial soft tissue tumors (including simple or intermediate repair) involves the resection of tumors confined to the tissue within or below the deep fascia, but not involving the bone. These tumors are usually benign, are often intramuscular, and are resected without removing a significant amount of surrounding normal tissue. Code selection is based on size and location of the tumor. Code selection is determined by measuring the greatest diameter of the tumor plus that margin required for complete excision of the tumor. The margins refer to the most narrow margin required to adequately excise the tumor, based on the physician's judgment. The measurement of the tumor plus margin is made at the time of the excision. Appreciable vessel exploration and/or neuroplasty should be reported separately. Extensive undermining or other techniques to close a defect created by skin excision may require a complex repair which should be reported separately. Dissection or elevation of tissue planes to permit resection of the tumor is included in the excision.

Digital (ie, fingers and toes) subfascial tumors are defined as those tumors involving the tendons, tendon sheaths, or joints of the digit. Tumors which simply abut but do not breach the tendon, tendon sheath, or joint capsule are considered subcutaneous soft tissue tumors.

Radical resection of soft tissue tumors (including simple or intermediate repair) involves the resection of the tumor with wide margins of normal tissue. Appreciable vessel exploration and/or neuroplasty repair or reconstruction (eg, adjacent tissue transfer[s], flap[s]) should be reported separately. Extensive undermining or other techniques to close a defect created by skin excision may require a complex repair which should be reported separately. Dissection or elevation of tissue planes to permit resection of the tumor is included in the excision. Although these tumors may be confined to a specific layer (eg, subcutaneous, subfascial), radical resection may involve removal of tissue from one or more layers. Radical resection of soft tissue tumors is most commonly used for malignant tumors or very aggressive benign tumors. Code selection is based on size and location of the tumor. Code selection is determined by measuring the greatest diameter of the tumor plus that margin required for complete excision of the tumor. The margins refer to the most narrow margin required to adequately excise the tumor, based on the physician's judgment. The measurement of the tumor plus margin is made at the time of the excision. For radical resection of tumors of cutaneous origin, (eg, melanoma) see 11600-11646.

Radical resection of bone tumors (including simple or intermediate repair) involves the resection of the tumor with wide margins of normal tissue. Appreciable vessel exploration and/or neuroplasty and complex bone repair or reconstruction (eg, adjacent tissue transfer[s], flap[s]) should be reported separately. Extensive undermining or other techniques to close a defect created by skin excision may require a complex repair which should be reported separately. Dissection or elevation of tissue planes to permit resection of the tumor is included in the excision. It may require removal of the entire bone if tumor growth is extensive (eg, clavicle). Radical resection of bone tumors is usually performed for malignant tumors or very aggressive benign tumors. If surrounding soft tissue is removed during these procedures, the radical resection of soft tissue tumor codes should not be reported separately. Code selection is based solely on the location of the tumor, **not on** the size of the tumor or whether the tumor is benign or malignant, primary or metastatic.◄

✎ Rationale

For CPT 2010, the Musculoskeletal System subsection has been expanded to include new guidelines to define procedures related to excision of subcutaneous soft tissue tumors, excision of fascial or subfascial soft tissue tumors, radical resection of soft tissue tumors, and radical resection of bone tumors services. In addition, extensive changes have been made to the soft tissue tumor and bone tumor codes, including 41 new codes, 53 revised codes, 7 deleted codes, new parenthetical notes and new references directing the users to the placement of resequenced (out-of-numerical-sequence) codes. (See page xi for information on the CPT code resequencing principle.) These numerous and extensive changes occur throughout the head, neck and (soft tissues) thorax, back and flank, abdomen, shoulder, humerus (upper arm) and elbow, forearm and wrist, hand and fingers, pelvis and hip joint, femur (thigh region) and knee joint, leg (tibia and fibula) and ankle joint, and foot and toes subsections sections.

This effort was undertaken to address the significant advancements made in the treatment of bone and soft tissue tumors during the past 10 years. Additionally, the expansion of this section has been undertaken to achieve greater granularity, consistency, and standardization when reporting the soft tissue tumor and bone tumor services.

New guidelines in the Musculoskeletal System subsection (1) define procedures related to excision of subcutaneous soft tissue tumors, excision of fascial or subfascial soft tissue tumors, radical resection of soft tissue tumors, and radical resection of bone tumors services, (2) explain the most appropriate method for code selection (eg, code selection is based on size and location of the tumor), (3) direct the user to report other services related to appreciable vessel exploration and/or neuroplasty and complex soft tissue repair or reconstruction (eg, adjacent tissue transfer[s], flap[s]), (4) clarify that the work of simple or intermediate repair is inherent in these services, (5) instruct the user to separately report extensive undermining or other techniques used to close a defect created by skin excision when it requires a complex repair, and (6) instruct that dissection or elevation of tissue planes to permit resection of the tumor is included in the excision.

The guidelines further clarify that code selection is based solely on the location of the tumor, not on the size of the tumor or whether the tumor is benign or malignant, primary or metastatic. Finally, the guidelines direct the user to report the excision of malignant lesion codes 11600-11646 for radical resection of tumors of cutaneous origin.

General

INCISION

20000   Incision of soft tissue abscess (eg, secondary to osteomyelitis); superficial

INTRODUCTION OR REMOVAL

20555   Placement of needles or catheters into muscle and/or soft tissue for subsequent interstitial radioelement application (at the time of or subsequent to the procedure)

▶(For interstitial radioelement application, see 77776-77778, 77785-77787)◀

 Rationale

In support of the deletion of code 77784, the cross-reference note following code 20555 has been revised to reflect the appropriate codes for reporting interstitial radioelement application.

Head

EXCISION

●**21011**   Excision, tumor, soft tissue of face or scalp, subcutaneous; less than 2 cm

●**21012**   2 cm or greater

●**21013**   Excision, tumor, soft tissue of face and scalp, subfascial (eg, subgaleal, intramuscular); less than 2 cm

●**21014**   2 cm or greater

▲**21015**   Radical resection of tumor (eg, malignant neoplasm), soft tissue of face or scalp; less than 2 cm

(To report excision of skull tumor for osteomyelitis, use 61501)

●**21016**   2 cm or greater

Rationale

Five codes have been established in the Head section: codes 21011 and 21012 describe excision of a subcutaneous soft tissue tumor of the face or scalp, less than or greater than 2 cm; codes 21013 and 21014 describe excision of a subfascial soft tissue tumor of the face or scalp, less than or greater than 2 cm; code 21016 describes radical resection of a soft tissue tumor of the face or scalp, greater than 2 cm. Code 21015 has been revised for standardization of the nomenclature to describe radical resection of a soft tissue tumor of the face or scalp, less than 2 cm.

Clinical Example (21011)

A 35-year-old female undergoes excision of a 1.5-cm tumor on her scalp.

Description of Procedure (21011)

An incision is made through the skin and subcutaneous tissue of the scalp. The tumor is identified and dissected free of surrounding structures and fascial attachments. The wound is inspected and irrigated. After ensuring complete hemostasis, the wound is closed in layers with interrupted sutures.

Clinical Example (21012)

A 35-year-old female undergoes excision of a 3.0-cm tumor on her forehead.

○=Modifier 51 Exempt   ⊙=Moderate Sedation   +=Add-on Code   ✎ =FDA approval pending

Description of Procedure (21012)

An incision is made through the skin and subcutaneous tissue of the forehead overlying the mass, taking care to follow relaxed skin tension lines. The tumor is identified and dissected free of surrounding structures and fascial attachments. Dissection is carried out at the level of the tumor capsule, with meticulous technique to avoid injury to neurovascular structures, including branches of the facial nerve. Any such structures within the operative field are identified and preserved. The wound is inspected and irrigated. After ensuring complete hemostasis, the wound is closed in layers with interrupted sutures.

Clinical Example (21013)

A 35-year-old female undergoes excision of a 1.5-cm submuscular tumor on her forehead.

Description of Procedure (21013)

An incision is made through the skin and subcutaneous tissue of the forehead overlying the mass, taking care to follow relaxed skin tension lines. The frontalis muscle is identified and incised. The tumor is identified and dissected free of surrounding structures and fascial attachments. Dissection is carried out at the level of the tumor capsule, with meticulous technique to avoid injury to neurovascular structures, including branches of the facial nerve. Any such structures within the operative field are identified and preserved. The wound is inspected and irrigated. After ensuring complete hemostasis, the wound is closed in layers with interrupted sutures.

Clinical Example (21014)

A 50-year-old male undergoes excision of a 6.5-cm tumor in the jaw musculature.

Description of Procedure (21014)

A curvilinear incision is made in relaxed skin tension creases anterior to the auricle, extending inferiorly and then anteriorly into the upper neck, 3 cm below and parallel to the lower edge of the mandible. A subplatysmal flap is elevated over the submandibular triangle, more superiorly at the level of the parotid fascia, to expose the submandibular and parotid glands. Peripheral branches of the facial nerve, including the buccal and marginal mandibular branches, are identified and preserved. The flap is further extended anteriorly over the masseter muscle. The muscle is split, and the tumor is excised from within the masseter muscle. The wound is inspected and irrigated. After ensuring complete hemostasis, a deep drain is placed, taking care to avoid contact with facial nerve branches. The wound is closed in layers with interrupted sutures.

Clinical Example (21015)

A 45-year-old male presents with a 1.5-cm sarcoma of the jaw muscles. At operation, the tumor and adjacent soft tissue are resected.

Description of Procedure (21015)

A curvilinear incision is made in relaxed skin tension creases anterior to the auricle, extending inferiorly and then anteriorly into the upper neck, 3 cm below and parallel to the lower edge of the mandible. A subplatysmal flap is elevated over the submandibular triangle, more superiorly at the level of the parotid fascia, to expose the submandibular and parotid glands. Peripheral branches of the facial nerve, including the buccal and marginal mandibular branches, are identified and preserved. The flap is further extended anteriorly over the masseter muscle to expose the tumor. The tumor is removed en bloc, including a wide margin of masseter muscle and any necessary surrounding structures, including skin at the previous biopsy site. The specimen is sent to pathology for frozen and permanent sections. The specimen is oriented for the pathologist, with direct communication between the surgeon and pathologist to ensure accurate pathologic interpretation. Frozen sections are taken from the surrounding tissue as indicated. Additional excision is carried out if necessary to obtain a clear margin. The wound is inspected and irrigated. A deep drain is placed taking care to avoid contact with facial nerve branches. The wound is closed in layers with interrupted sutures.

 Clinical Example (21016)

A 45-year-old male presents with a 6-cm sarcoma of the jaw muscles. At operation, the tumor and adjacent soft tissue are resected.

Description of Procedure (21016)

A curvilinear incision is made in relaxed skin tension creases anterior to the auricle, extending inferiorly and then anteriorly into the upper neck, 3 cm below and parallel to the lower edge of the mandible. A subplatysmal flap is elevated over the submandibular triangle, more superiorly at the level of the parotid fascia, to expose the submandibular and parotid glands. Peripheral branches of the facial nerve, including the buccal and marginal mandibular branches, are identified and preserved. The flap is further extended anteriorly over the masseter muscle to expose the tumor. The parotid gland and peripheral branches of the facial nerve are retracted, and the tumor is removed en bloc, including a wide margin of jaw musculature and any necessary surrounding structures, including skin at the previous biopsy site. The specimen is sent to pathology for frozen and permanent sections. The specimen is oriented for the pathologist, with direct communication between the surgeon and pathologist to ensure accurate pathologic interpretation. Frozen sections are taken from the surrounding tissue as indicated. Additional excision is carried out if necessary to obtain a clear margin. The wound is inspected and irrigated. A deep drain is placed taking care to avoid contact with facial nerve branches. The wound is closed in layers with interrupted sutures.

Neck (Soft Tissues) and Thorax

EXCISION

21550   Biopsy, soft tissue of neck or thorax

(For needle biopsy of soft tissue, use 20206)

21552   ▶Code is out of numerical sequence. See 21550-21632◀

21554   ▶Code is out of numerical sequence. See 21550-21632◀

⊘=Modifier 51 Exempt   ⊙=Moderate Sedation   ✚=Add-on Code   ✗=FDA approval pending

▲21555	Excision, tumor, soft tissue of neck or anterior thorax, subcutaneous; less than 3 cm
#●21552	3 cm or greater
▲21556	Excision, tumor, soft tissue of neck or anterior thorax, subfascial (eg, intramuscular); less than 5 cm
#●21554	5 cm or greater
▲21557	Radical resection of tumor (eg, malignant neoplasm), soft tissue of neck or anterior thorax; less than 5 cm
●21558	5 cm or greater

✍ Rationale

In the Neck (Soft Tissues) and Thorax section, two reference notes have been added to direct the user to the appropriate code range (21550-21632) for placement of out-of-sequence codes 21552 and 21554. Codes 21552 and 21554 appear with a number symbol (#) to indicate that these codes are out of numerical sequence. Code 21552 has been established to report excision of a subcutaneous soft tissue tumor of the neck or anterior thorax, 3 cm or greater. Code 21555 has been revised for standardization of the nomenclature to describe excision of a subcutaneous soft tissue tumor of the neck or anterior thorax, less than 3 cm.

Codes 21554 describes excision of a subfascial soft tissue tumor of the neck or anterior thorax, less than or greater than 5 cm. Code 21556 has been revised for standardization of the nomenclature to describe excision of a subfascial soft tissue tumor of the neck or anterior thorax, subfascial, less than 5 cm.

Code 21558 has been established to report radical resection of a soft tissue tumor of the neck or anterior thorax, greater than 5 cm. Code 21557 has been revised for standardization of the nomenclature to describe a radical resection of a soft tissue tumor of the neck or anterior thorax; less than 5 cm.

🩺 Clinical Example (21552)

A 30-year-old male undergoes excision of an enlarging 5-cm tumor of the anterior thorax near the anterior axillary line.

Description of Procedure (21552)

Under anesthesia, an oblique incision is made through the skin and subcutaneous tissue overlying the mass. The tumor is identified and dissected free along the tumor capsule, taking care not to traumatize surrounding structures. The tumor is removed and sent for permanent pathologic evaluation. The wound is inspected and irrigated. After ensuring complete hemostasis, the wound is closed in layers with interrupted sutures.

🩺 Clinical Example (21554)

A 45-year-old male undergoes excision of a 9-cm tumor deep in the posterior-lateral para-spinal region of the neck behind the sternocleidomastoid.

Description of Procedure (21554)

Under anesthesia, a longitudinal incision is made over the posterior-cervical triangle. The platysma is identified and split with the major portion retracted anteriorly. The posterior portion of the sternocleidomastoid and the interval between the sternocleidomastoid and the anterior trapezius is identified. Within that interval, great care is necessary to avoid injuring the spinal accessory nerve root that innervates the muscles. Dissection is carried deep between those two muscles. Sensory branches of the cervical nerves to the skin cross the posterior portion of the sternocleidomastoid muscle and are protected. The branch of the transverse cervical artery in the inferior portion of the wound has to be ligated and incised. The carotid sheath and jugular vein can be palpated anteriorly in the incision and are carefully retracted out of the field. Several perforating vessels off the jugular vein are also ligated and incised. As the interval is further explored, the mass is palpable deep within the wound. At this point, in the inferior portion of the incision, the omohyoid muscle is identified posteriorly, the levator scapula and the middle scalene muscles are identified in the proximal wound, and the anterior scalene identified in the proximal anterior wound. The mass itself is sitting directly between them and has spread them apart. The mass is then identified and appears to be consistent with the MRI, which showed homogenous mass consistent with a lipoma. Because it is a lipoma, a marginal resection will be performed. The mass is peeled off the anterior scalene muscle and the omohyoid and gradually retracted off the anterior portion of the wound. This is freed up from the back of the carotid sheath and the jugular vein.

Several small feeding vessels into the lipoma are ligated and incised. Inferior in the wound, the brachial plexus can be palpated deep in the interval between the anterior and middle scalene. It is directly underneath and adherent to the underside of the lipoma. The nerve roots are very carefully retracted, and the lipoma is carefully dissected off the major trunks of the brachial plexus in the bottom of the wound. Next to the brachial plexus, the take-off of the subclavian artery and vein can be seen. Several small perforating branches can be seen there, and these are retracted out of the way as well as the suprascapular artery coming off the base of the thyro-cervical trunk.

Once that area is identified, the rest of the lipoma is gently dissected off the brachial plexus and is removed en block. Because it is lipoma, frozen sections are not performed on the margins. The mass is handed off the field. The gloves and instruments are changed and the wound is copiously irrigated. Hemostasis is obtained. The top of the brachial plexus is inspected to make sure that there is no damage to any of the major nerve trunks. The spinal accessory nerve proximally in the wound can be seen as it goes underneath the sternocleidomastoid and trapezius, and that is also inspected to make sure there is no injury. A drain is placed with great care to make sure it is not on either the subclavian vessels or carotid sheath. This is brought out posteriorly. The posterior triangle also has several lymph nodes in the area, and the lymph chain here had to be carefully protected since there is no need to remove the lymph nodes in a lipoma. The muscles are allowed to retract back into their original location. The wound is closed in layers with interrupted sutures.

Clinical Example (21555)

A 25-year-old male undergoes excision of a 2.5-cm lipoma on his neck.

Description of Procedure (21555)

Under anesthesia, an incision is made through the skin and subcutaneous tissue of the neck overlying the mass. The tumor is identified and dissected free along the tumor capsule, taking care not to traumatize surrounding structures. The tumor is removed and sent for permanent pathologic evaluation. The wound is inspected and irrigated. After ensuring complete hemostasis, the wound is closed in layers with interrupted sutures.

Clinical Example (21556)

A 45-year-old male undergoes excision of a 3-cm tumor deep in the posterior-lateral para-spinal region of the neck behind the sternocleidomastoid.

Description of Procedure (21556)

Under anesthesia, a longitudinal incision is made over the posterior-cervical triangle. The platysma is identified and split with the major portion retracted anteriorly. The posterior portion of the sternocleidomastoid and the interval between the sternocleidomastoid and the anterior trapezius is identified. Within that interval, great care is necessary to avoid injuring the spinal accessory nerve root, which innervates the muscles. Dissection is carried deep between those two muscles. Sensory branches of the cervical nerves to the skin cross the posterior portion of the sternocleidomastoid muscle and are protected. The branch of the transverse cervical artery in the inferior portion of the wound has to be ligated and incised. The carotid sheath and jugular vein can be palpated anteriorly in the incision and are carefully retracted out of the field.

Several perforating vessels off the jugular vein are also ligated and incised. As the interval is further explored, the mass is palpable deep within the wound. At this point, in the inferior portion of the incision, the omohyoid muscle is identified posteriorly, the levator scapula and the middle scalene muscles are identified in the proximal wound, and the anterior scalene identified in the proximal anterior wound. The mass itself is sitting directly between them and has spread them apart.

The mass is then identified and appears to be consistent with the magnetic resonance imaging (MRI) scan, which showed homogenous mass consistent with a lipoma. Because it is a lipoma, a marginal resection will be performed. The mass is peeled off the anterior scalene muscle and the omohyoid and gradually retracted off the anterior portion of the wound. This is freed up from the back of the carotid sheath and the jugular vein. Several small feeding vessels into the lipoma are ligated and incised. Inferior in the wound, the brachial plexus can be palpated deep in the interval between the anterior and middle scalene. It is directly underneath and adherent to the underside of the lipoma. The nerve roots are very carefully retracted, and the lipoma is carefully dissected off the major trunks of the brachial plexus in the bottom of the wound. Next to the brachial plexus, the take-off of the subclavian artery and vein can be seen. Several small perforating branches can be seen there, and these are retracted out of the way, as well as the suprascapular artery coming off the base of the thyro-cervical trunk. Once that area is identified, the rest of the lipoma is gently dissected off the brachial plexus and is removed en block. Because it is lipoma, frozen sections are not performed on the margins. The mass is handed off the field. The gloves and instruments are changed, and the wound is copiously irrigated. Hemostasis is obtained. The top of the brachial plexus is inspected to make sure that there is no damage to any of the major nerve trunks. The spinal accessory nerve proximally in the wound can be seen as it goes underneath the sternocleidomastoid and trapezius and is inspected to make sure there is no injury. A drain is placed with great care to make sure it is not on either the subclavian vessels or carotid sheath. This is brought out posteriorly. The posterior triangle also has several lymph nodes in the area, and the lymph chain here had to be carefully protected, since there is no need to remove the lymph nodes in a lipoma. The muscles are allowed to retract back into their original location. The wound is closed in layers with interrupted sutures.

 Clinical Example (21557)

A 47-year-old male presents with a 3-cm sarcoma near the sternocleidomastoid muscle in the neck. At operation, the tumor and adjacent soft tissue are resected.

Description of Procedure (21557)

Under anesthesia, an incision is made along the sternocleidomastoid muscle encompassing the overlying skin from the biopsy site. Subplatysmal flaps are raised. The tumor, attached to the sternocleidomastoid muscle, is isolated. Medially and superiorly, the internal jugular vein, carotid artery, and vagus nerve are identified and retracted toward the midline. Laterally and posteriorly, the spinal accessory nerve is identified within the posterior triangle and dissected free of the sternocleidomastoid muscle anteriorly to the internal jugular vein, preserving the nerve. Transection of the superior aspect of the sternocleidomastoid muscle, already partially transected by following the spinal accessory nerve, is completed with a wide margin around the tumor. Inferior to the tumor, the sternocleidomastoid muscle is likewise transected with a wide margin, separating the muscle from the internal jugular vein and omohyoid muscle. The deep aspect of the tumor and sternocleidomastoid muscle are then dissected free of the fascia investing the deep neck musculature and brachial plexus, taking care not to traumatize these structures and taking a margin of fibrofatty tissue. The specimen is sent to pathology for frozen and permanent sections. The specimen is oriented for the pathologist, with direct communication between the surgeon and pathologist to ensure accurate pathologic interpretation. Frozen sections are taken from the surrounding tissue as indicated. Additional excision is carried out if necessary to obtain a clear margin. The wound is inspected and irrigated. A deep drain is placed. The wound is closed in layers with interrupted sutures.

 Clinical Example (21558)

A 45-year-old male undergoes excision of a 9-cm tumor deep in the posterior-lateral para-spinal region of the neck behind the sternocleidomastoid.

Description of Procedure (21558)

Under anesthesia, a longitudinal incision is made over the posterior-cervical triangle. The platysma is identified and split with the major portion retracted anteriorly. The posterior portion of the sternocleidomastoid and the interval between the sternocleidomastoid and the anterior trapezius are identified. Within that interval, great care is necessary to avoid injuring the spinal accessory nerve root, which innervates the muscles. Dissection is carried deep between those two muscles. Sensory branches of the cervical nerves to the skin cross the posterior portion of the sternocleidomastoid muscle and are protected. The branch of the transverse cervical artery in the inferior portion of the wound has to be ligated and incised. The carotid sheath and jugular vein can be palpated anteriorly in the incision and are carefully retracted out of the field.

Several perforating vessels off the jugular vein are also ligated and incised. As the interval is further explored, the mass is palpable deep within the wound. At this point, in the inferior portion of the incision, the omohyoid muscle is identified posteriorly, the levator scapula and the middle scalene muscles are identified in the proximal wound, and the anterior scalene identified in the proximal anterior wound. The mass itself is sitting directly between them and has spread them apart. The mass is then identified and appears to be consistent with the magnetic resonance imaging (MRI) scan, which showed homogenous mass consistent with a lipoma. Because it is a lipoma, a marginal resection will be performed.

The mass is peeled off the anterior scalene muscle and the omohyoid and gradually retracted off the anterior portion of the wound. This is freed up from the back of the carotid sheath and the jugular vein. Several small feeding vessels into the lipoma are ligated and incised. Inferior in the wound, the brachial plexus can be palpated deep in the interval between the anterior and middle scalene. It is directly underneath and adherent to the underside of the lipoma. Very carefully the nerve roots are retracted, and the lipoma is carefully dissected off the major trunks of the brachial plexus in the bottom of the wound. Next to the brachial plexus, the take-off of the subclavian artery and vein can be seen. Several small perforating branches can be seen there, and these are retracted out of the way, as well as the suprascapular artery coming off the base of the thyro-cervical trunk. Once that area is identified, the rest of the lipoma is gently dissected off the brachial plexus and is removed en block. Because it is lipoma, frozen sections are not performed on the margins. The mass is handed off the field. The gloves and instruments are changed, and the wound is copiously irrigated. Hemostasis is obtained. The top of the brachial plexus is inspected to make sure that there is no damage to any of the major nerve trunks. The spinal accessory nerve proximally in the wound can be seen as it goes underneath the sternocleidomastoid and trapezius, and that is also inspected to make sure there is no injury. A drain is placed with great care to make sure it is not on either the subclavian vessels or carotid sheath. This is brought out posteriorly. The posterior triangle also has several lymph nodes in the area, and the lymph chain here had to be carefully protected, as in a lipoma there is no need to remove the lymph nodes. The muscles are allowed to retract back into their original location. The wound is closed in layers with interrupted sutures.

Back and Flank

EXCISION

▲**21930**   Excision, tumor, soft tissue of back or flank, subcutaneous; less than 3 cm

●**21931**   3 cm or greater

●**21932**   Excision, tumor, soft tissue of back or flank, subfascial (eg, intramuscular); less than 5 cm

●**21933**   5 cm or greater

▲**21935**   Radical resection of tumor (eg, malignant neoplasm), soft tissue of back or flank; less than 5 cm

●**21936**   5 cm or greater

Rationale

In the Back and Flank section, code 21931 has been established to report excision of a subcutaneous soft tissue tumor of the back or flank, greater than 3 cm. Code 21930 has been revised for standardization of the nomenclature to describe excision of a subcutaneous soft tissue tumor of the back or flank, less than 3 cm.

Codes 21932 and 21933 have been established to report excision of a subfascial soft tissue tumor of the back or flank less than or greater than 5 cm. Code 21936 has been established to report radical resection of a soft tissue tumor of the back or flank, greater than 5 cm. Code 21935 has been revised for standardization of the nomenclature to describe radical resection of a soft tissue tumor of the back or flank, less than 5 cm.

Clinical Example (21930)

A 40-year-old female undergoes excision of a 2.5-cm spongy tumor on her back.

Description of Procedure (21930)

An incision is made through the skin and subcutaneous tissue over the lesion. Subcutaneous flaps are raised with electrocautery and hemostasis is controlled. The tumor is excised along with proper margin of tissue. Hemostasis is secured with electrocautery and sutures where needed. Small lymphatic channels are ligated. The wound is inspected and irrigated. The wound is closed in layers with interrupted sutures.

Clinical Example (21931)

A 50-year-old male undergoes excision of a 5-cm fatty tumor on his flank.

Description of Procedure (21931)

An incision is made through the skin and subcutaneous tissue over the lesion. Subcutaneous flaps are raised with electrocautery to expose the lesion, and hemostasis is controlled. The tumor is excised along with the proper margin of tissue. As the tumor is lifted out of the wound, small lymphatics and feeding blood vessels are ligated. Hemostasis is secured with electrocautery and sutures where needed. The wound is inspected and irrigated. The wound is closed in layers with interrupted sutures.

                ⊘=Modifier 51 Exempt   ⊙=Moderate Sedation   ✚=Add-on Code   ⋀=FDA approval pending

Clinical Example (21932)

A 60-year-old male undergoes excision of a 4-cm tumor in the paraspinal musculature of the back.

Description of Procedure (21932)

An incision is made through the skin and subcutaneous tissue over the lesion. Subcutaneous flaps are raised with electrocautery. The paraspinal muscle is exposed around the tumor. The tumor is excised along with surrounding muscle using electrocautery and dissection. As the tumor is lifted out of the wound, small lymphatics and feeding blood vessels are ligated. Hemostasis is secured with electrocautery and sutures where needed. The wound is inspected and irrigated. The devitalized muscle is debrided. Where possible, the muscle fascial defect is approximated. A Penrose drain is placed in the cavitary defect. The wound is closed in layers with interrupted sutures.

Clinical Example (21933)

A 60-year-old male undergoes excision of a 7-cm tumor in the flank musculature of the back.

Description of Procedure (21933)

An incision is made through the skin and subcutaneous tissue over the lesion. Subcutaneous flaps are raised with electrocautery. The musculature is exposed around the tumor. The fascia is incised, and part of it is included with the specimen in the dissection for proper margins. The tumor is excised along with surrounding muscle using electrocautery and dissection. As the tumor is lifted out of the wound, small lymphatics and feeding blood vessels are ligated. The deep fascia is inspected for involvement by the tumor, as are the ribs and intercostal muscles. If deep margins are involved, resection to the periosteum of the ribs is carried out. Hemostasis is secured with electrocautery and sutures where needed. The wound is inspected and irrigated. The devitalized muscle is debrided. Where possible, the muscle fascial defect is approximated. A Penrose drain is placed in the cavitary defect. The wound is closed in layers with interrupted sutures.

Clinical Example (21935)

A 60-year-old female presents with a 4-cm sarcoma in the trapezius on the back. At operation, the tumor and adjacent soft tissue are resected.

Description of Procedure (21935)

Under anesthesia, an incision is made over the trapezius. Medial and lateral subcutaneous flaps are raised. The overlying skin from the biopsy is excised with the tumor. The musculature is exposed around the tumor. The fascia is incised, and part of it is included with the specimen in the dissection for proper margins. The dissection removes a large portion of the trapezius including the fascia of the deep paraspinal muscles below it. The tumor is removed en bloc, including necessary surrounding structures. As the tumor is lifted out of the wound, small lymphatics and feeding blood vessels are ligated. Frozen sections are taken from the surrounding tissue. The deep fascia is inspected for involvement by the tumor, as are the ribs and intercostal muscles. If deep margins are involved, resection to the periosteum of the ribs is carried out. The specimen is then removed from the field and marked for anatomic orientation. (This is documented on the pathology request form along with appropriate history and needed information.) The surgeon then breaks scrub and carries the specimen to the pathology department while the anesthesiologist and other operative personnel remain with the patient. Prior to this, the surgeon assesses the stability of the operative field and discusses with the anesthesiologist the stability of the patient. In the pathology department, the surgeon examines the resected specimen with the attending pathologist and orients the pathologist to the specimen anatomy. The specimen is inked for margins, and any areas that are questionable are inspected by frozen section. If all margins appear satisfactory, the surgeon returns to the operating room, repeats preoperative scrub, and returns to the surgical field. Metallic clips are placed to mark the margins for possible postoperative radiotherapy guidance. The wound is inspected and irrigated. The devitalized muscle is debrided. A deep drain is placed. The wound is closed in layers with interrupted sutures.

Clinical Example (21936)

A 60-year-old female presents with a 10-cm sarcoma in the trapezius and paraspinal muscles. At operation, the tumor and adjacent soft tissue are resected.

Description of Procedure (21936)

Under anesthesia, an incision is made over the trapezius. Medial and lateral subcutaneous flaps are raised. The overlying skin from the biopsy is excised with the tumor. The musculature is exposed around the tumor. The fascia is incised and part of it is included with the specimen in the dissection for proper margins. The dissection removes a large portion of the trapezius including the fascia of the deep paraspinal muscles below it. The tumor is removed en bloc, including necessary surrounding structures. As the tumor is lifted out of the wound, small lymphatics and feeding blood vessels are ligated. Frozen sections are taken from the surrounding tissue. The deep fascia is inspected for involvement by the tumor, as are the ribs and intercostal muscles. If deep margins are involved, resection to the periosteum of the ribs is carried out. The specimen is then removed from the field and marked for anatomic orientation. (This is documented on the pathology request form along with appropriate history and needed information.) The surgeon then breaks scrub and carries the specimen to the pathology department while the anesthesiologist and other operative personnel remain with the patient. Prior to this, the surgeon assesses the stability of the operative field and discusses with the anesthesiologist the stability of the patient. In the pathology department, the surgeon examines the resected specimen with the attending pathologist and orients the pathologist to the specimen anatomy. The specimen is inked for margins, and any areas that are questionable are inspected by frozen section. If all margins appear satisfactory, the surgeon returns to the operating room, repeats preoperative scrub, and returns to the surgical field. Metallic clips are placed to mark the margins for possible postoperative radiotherapy guidance. The wound is inspected and irrigated. The devitalized muscle is debrided. A deep drain is placed. The wound is closed in layers with interrupted sutures.

Spine (Vertebral Column)

▶(For injection procedure for facet joints, see 64490-64495, 64622-64627)◄

(For needle or trocar biopsy, see 20220-20225)

INCISION

22010 Incision and drainage, open, of deep abscess (subfascial), posterior spine; cervical, thoracic, or cervicothoracic

 Rationale

The cross-reference following the heading, "Spine (Vertebral Column)" has been revised to include the appropriate codes to report injection procedures for facet joints.

VERTEBRAL BODY, EMBOLIZATION OR INJECTION

⊙▲**22520** Percutaneous vertebroplasty, 1 vertebral body, unilateral or bilateral injection; thoracic

⊙▲**22521** lumbar

⊙**22526** Percutaneous intradiscal electrothermal annuloplasty, unilateral or bilateral including fluoroscopic guidance; single level

(Do not report codes 22526, 22527 in conjunction with 77002, 77003)

▶(For percutaneous intradiscal annuloplasty using method other than electrothermal, use 22899)◄

 Rationale

Codes 22520 and 22521 have been revised to include the conscious sedation symbol, as this is an inherent part of these procedures.

Following code 22526, the cross-reference note has been revised to direct the user to report code 22899 for percutaneous intradiscal annuloplasty using a method other than electrothermal.

Abdomen

EXCISION

▲**22900** Excision, tumor, soft tissue of abdominal wall, subfascial (eg, intramuscular); less than 5 cm

●**22901** 5 cm or greater

●**22902** Excision, tumor, soft tissue of abdominal wall, subcutaneous; less than 3 cm

●**22903** 3 cm or greater

●**22904** Radical resection of tumor (eg, malignant neoplasm), soft tissue of abdominal wall; less than 5 cm

---

22905 5 cm or greater

 Rationale

In the Abdomen section, code 22901 has been established to report excision of a subfascial soft tissue tumor of the abdominal wall, greater than 5 cm. Code 22900 has been revised for standardization of the nomenclature to describe excision of a subfascial soft tissue tumor of the abdominal wall, less than 5 cm.

Codes 22902 and 22903 have been established to report excision of a subcutaneous soft tissue tumor of the abdominal wall, less than and greater than 3 cm. Codes 22904 and 22905 have been established to report radical resection of a soft tissue tumor of the abdominal wall, less than and greater than 5 cm.

 Clinical Example (22900)

A 40-year-old male undergoes excision of a 4-cm lipoma of the external oblique muscle.

Description of Procedure (22900)

An incision is made through the skin and subcutaneous tissue over the lesion. Subcutaneous flaps are raised with electrocautery. The external oblique muscle is exposed around the tumor. The tumor is excised along with surrounding muscle using electrocautery and dissection. As the tumor is lifted out of the wound, small lymphatics and feeding blood vessels are ligated. Hemostasis is secured with electrocautery and sutures where needed. The wound is inspected and irrigated. The devitalized muscle is debrided. Where possible, the muscle fascial defect is approximated. A Penrose drain is placed in the cavitary defect. The wound is closed in layers with interrupted sutures.

Clinical Example (22901)

A 35-year-old female undergoes excision of a 9-cm lipoma of the external oblique muscle.

Description of Procedure (22901)

An incision is made through the skin and subcutaneous tissue over the lesion. Subcutaneous flaps are raised with electrocautery. The musculature is exposed around the tumor. The fascia is incised, and part of it is included with the specimen in the dissection for proper margins. The tumor is excised along with surrounding muscle using electrocautery and dissection. As the tumor is lifted out of the wound, small lymphatics and feeding blood vessels are ligated. The deep fascia is inspected for involvement by the tumor, as are the ribs and intercostal muscles. If deep margins are involved, resection to the periosteum of the ribs and/or peritoneum is carried out. Hemostasis is secured with electrocautery and sutures where needed. The wound is inspected and irrigated. The devitalized muscle is debrided. Where possible, the muscle fascial defect is approximated. A Penrose drain is placed in the cavitary defect. The wound is closed in layers with interrupted sutures.

 Clinical Example (22902)

A 40-year-old female undergoes excision of a 2-cm tumor on her abdominal wall.

⊘=Modifier 51 Exempt ⊙=Moderate Sedation ✚=Add-on Code ✗=FDA approval pending

Description of Procedure (22902)

An incision is made through the skin and subcutaneous tissue over the lesion. Subcutaneous flaps are raised with electrocautery, and hemostasis is controlled. The tumor is excised along with proper margin of tissue. Hemostasis is secured with electrocautery and sutures where needed. Small lymphatic channels are ligated. The wound is inspected and irrigated. The wound is closed in layers with interrupted sutures.

 Clinical Example (22903)

A 50-year-old male undergoes excision of a 5-cm spongy tumor on her abdominal wall.

Description of Procedure (22903)

An incision is made through the skin and subcutaneous tissue over the lesion. Subcutaneous flaps are raised with electrocautery to expose the lesion, and hemostasis is controlled. The tumor is excised along with proper margin of tissue. As the tumor is lifted out of the wound, small lymphatics and feeding blood vessels are ligated. Hemostasis is secured with electrocautery and sutures where needed. The wound is inspected and irrigated. The wound is closed in layers with interrupted sutures.

 Clinical Example (22904)

A 40-year-old male presents with a 3-cm sarcoma in the rectus abdominus muscle. At operation, the tumor and adjacent soft tissue are resected.

Description of Procedure (22904)

An incision is made over the trapezius. Medial and lateral subcutaneous flaps are raised. The overlying skin from the biopsy is excised with the tumor. The musculature is exposed around the tumor. The fascia is incised, and part of it is included with the specimen in the dissection for proper margins. The lateral border of the rectus abdominus is identified. The muscle is freed from the underlying oblique muscles, but the superficial portion of the oblique transverse abdominus is resected with the tumor. The tumor is removed en bloc, including necessary surrounding structures. As the tumor is lifted out of the wound, small lymphatics and feeding blood vessels are ligated. The surgeon then breaks scrub and carries the specimen to the pathology department while the anesthesiologist and other operative personnel remain with the patient. Prior to this, the surgeon assesses the stability of the operative field and discusses with the anesthesiologist the stability of the patient. In the pathology department, the surgeon examines the resected specimen with the attending pathologist and orients the pathologist to the specimen anatomy. The specimen is inked for margins, and any areas that are questionable are inspected by frozen section. If all margins appear satisfactory, the surgeon returns to the operating room, repeats preoperative scrub, and returns to the surgical field. The deep fascia is inspected for involvement by the tumor, as are the ribs and intercostal muscles. If deep margins are involved, resection to the periosteum of the ribs and/or peritoneum is carried out. Additional excision is carried out as necessary to obtain a clear margin. Metallic clips are placed to mark the margins for possible postoperative radiotherapy guidance. The wound is inspected and irrigated. The devitalized muscle is debrided. A deep drain is placed. The wound is closed in layers with interrupted sutures.

 Clinical Example (22905)

A 40-year-old male presents with a 9-cm sarcoma in the external oblique muscle of the abdominal wall. At operation, the tumor and adjacent soft tissue are resected.

Description of Procedure (22905)

An incision is made over the trapezius. Medial and lateral subcutaneous flaps are raised. The overlying skin from the biopsy is excised with the tumor. The musculature is exposed around the tumor. The fascia is incised, and part of it is included with the specimen in the dissection for proper margins. The lateral border of the rectus abdominus is identified. The muscle is freed from the underlying oblique muscles, but the superficial portion of the oblique transverse abdominus is resected with the tumor. The tumor is removed en bloc, including necessary surrounding structures. As the tumor is lifted out of the wound, small lymphatics and feeding blood vessels are ligated. Frozen sections are taken from the surrounding tissue. The deep fascia is inspected for involvement by the tumor, as are the ribs and intercostal muscles. If deep margins are involved, resection to the periosteum of the ribs and/or peritoneum is carried out. The surgeon then breaks scrub and carries the specimen to the pathology department while the anesthesiologist and other operative personnel remain with the patient. Prior to this, the surgeon assesses the stability of the operative field and discusses with the anesthesiologist the stability of the patient. In the pathology department, the surgeon examines the resected specimen with the attending pathologist and orients the pathologist to the specimen anatomy. The specimen is inked for margins and any areas that are questionable are inspected by frozen section. If all margins appear satisfactory, the surgeon returns to the operating room, repeats preoperative scrub, and returns to the surgical field. Metallic clips are placed to mark the margins for possible postoperative radiotherapy guidance. The wound is inspected and irrigated. The devitalized muscle is debrided. A deep drain is placed. The wound is closed in layers with interrupted sutures.

Shoulder

EXCISION

23065   Biopsy, soft tissue of shoulder area; superficial

23066   deep

(For needle biopsy of soft tissue, use 20206)

23071   ▶Code is out of numerical sequence. See 23065-23220◀

23073   ▶Code is out of numerical sequence. See 23065-23220◀

▲**23075**   Excision, tumor, soft tissue of shoulder area, subcutaneous; less than 3 cm

#●**23071**   3 cm or greater

⊘=Modifier 51 Exempt   ⊙=Moderate Sedation   ✚=Add-on Code   ✗=FDA approval pending

▲**23076**   Excision, tumor, soft tissue of shoulder area, subfascial (eg, intramuscular); less than 5 cm

#●**23073**   5 cm or greater

▲**23077**   Radical resection of tumor (eg, malignant neoplasm), soft tissue of shoulder area; less than 5 cm

●**23078**   5 cm or greater

▲**23200**   Radical resection of tumor; clavicle

▲**23210**   scapula

▲**23220**   Radical resection of tumor, proximal humerus

    ▶(23221, 23222 have been deleted)◀

 Rationale

In the Shoulder section, two reference notes have been added to direct the user to the appropriate code range (23065-23220) for placement of out-of-sequence codes 23071 and 23073. Codes 23071 and 23073 appear with a number symbol (#) to indicate that these codes appear out of numerical sequence. Code 23071 has been established to report excision of a subcutaneous soft tissue tumor of the shoulder area, 3 cm or greater. Code 23075 has been revised for standardization of the nomenclature to describe excision of a subcutaneous soft tissue tumor of the shoulder area, less than 3 cm. Code 23073 has been established to report excision of a subfascial soft tissue tumor of the shoulder area, greater than 5 cm. Code 23076 has been revised for standardization of the nomenclature to describe excision of a subfascial soft tissue tumor of the shoulder area, less than 5 cm.

Code 23078 has been established to report radical resection of a soft tissue tumor of the shoulder area, greater than 5 cm. Code 23077 has been revised for standardization of the nomenclature to describe radical resection of a soft tissue tumor of the shoulder area, less than 5 cm.

In support of the changes to the Shoulder section, codes 23200, 23210, and 23220 have been editorially revised, and codes 23221 and 23222 have been deleted. A parenthetical note has been added following code 23220 to reflect that these codes have been deleted.

 Clinical Example (23071)

A 43-year-old female undergoes excision of a 3.5-cm tumor overlying her scapula.

Description of Procedure (23071)

Under anesthesia, a 6-cm incision is made in the skin and subcutaneous tissue over the shoulder. Medial and lateral flaps are made. Careful dissection is carried around the tumor. The tumor is excised and sent to pathology. Hemostasis is obtained. The wound is inspected and irrigated. The wound is closed in layers with interrupted sutures.

 Clinical Example (23073)

A 47-year-old female undergoes excision of a 7.5-cm lipoma deep within the subscapularis muscle.

Description of Procedure (23073)

An incision is made over the anterior shoulder following the delto-pectoral groove. The subcutaneous tissue is incised, and the cephalic vein is identified and dissected up to the coracoid process. The pectoralis major tendon inserting in the humerus is retracted. A retractor is placed under the deltoid to expose the proximal humerus. The pectoral fascia is incised and retracted medially and laterally. The shoulder is then externally rotated, and dissection is performed on the inferior medial portion of the subscapularis muscle. (A retractor could be gently inserted to protect the axillary nerve where it comes across the inferior portion of the wound.) The shoulder is externally rotated, the subscapularis insertion on the anterior shoulder is identified, and a retractor is used to retract the conjoined tendon medially. The mass is able to be palpated just under the conjoined tendon both medial to it and lateral to it. With retractors medially holding the conjoined tendon, a horizontal split is made in the subscapularis muscle. This dissection is carried down until the tumor is encountered. The conjoined tendon is protected. Dissection is performed on both sides of the tendon. The musculocutaneus nerve is identified and protected. With the split in the subscapularis muscle accomplished, the lipoma is dissected out in one piece and handed out of the operative field. Retractors are used within the subscapularis to hold both the superior and inferior portions of it in place. The thoracoacromial arch is avoided during the surgery to minimize bleeding in the superior portion of the wound. The wound is irrigated. Instruments and gloves are then changed. The cavity in the subscapularis is carefully inspected, and there is found to be no residual tumor. A deep drain is placed within the subscapularis and brought out the anterior skin flap. The defect in the subscapularis is closed with an interrupted suture. The conjoined tendon is left in place. The musculocutaneus nerve entering the medial side of the biceps is inspected and found to be intact. The retractors protecting the inferior portion of the subscapularis are removed. The retractor holding back the cephalic vein is also removed. The wound is closed in layers.

 Clinical Example (23075)

A 56-year-old male undergoes excision of a 1.5-cm tumor overlying his deltoid muscle.

Description of Procedure (23075)

Under anesthesia, a 4-cm incision is made in the skin and subcutaneous tissue over the shoulder. Medial and lateral flaps are made. Careful dissection is carried around the tumor. The tumor is excised and sent to pathology. Hemostasis is obtained. The wound is inspected and irrigated. The wound is closed in layers with interrupted sutures.

 Clinical Example (23076)

A 47-year-old female undergoes excision of a 3.5-cm lipoma deep within the subscapularis muscle.

⃠=Modifier 51 Exempt   ⊙=Moderate Sedation   ✦=Add-on Code   ⅄=FDA approval pending

Description of Procedure (23076)

An incision is made over the anterior shoulder following the delto-pectoral groove. The subcutaneous tissue is incised, and the cephalic vein is identified and dissected up to the coracoid process. The pectoralis major tendon inserting in the humerus is retracted. A retractor is placed under the deltoid to expose the proximal humerus. The pectoral fascia is incised and retracted medially and laterally. The shoulder is then externally rotated, and dissection is performed on the inferior medial portion of the subscapularis muscle so a retractor could be gently inserted to protect the axillary nerve where it comes across the inferior portion of the wound. The shoulder is externally rotated, the subscapularis insertion on the anterior shoulder is identified, and a retractor is used to retract the conjoined tendon medially. The mass is able to be palpated just under the conjoined tendon both medial to it and lateral to it. With retractors medially holding the conjoined tendon, a horizontal split is made in the subscapularis muscle. This dissection is carried down until the tumor is encountered. The conjoined tendon is protected. Dissection is performed on both sides of the tendon. The musculocutaneus nerve is identified and protected. With the split in the subscapularis muscle accomplished, the lipoma is dissected out in one piece and handed out of the operative field. Retractors are used within the subscapularis to hold both the superior and inferior portions of it in place. The thoracoacromial arch is avoided during the surgery to minimize bleeding in the superior portion of the wound. The wound is irrigated. Instruments and gloves are then changed. The cavity in the subscapularis is carefully inspected, and no residual tumor is found. A deep drain is placed within the subscapularis and brought out the anterior skin flap. The defect in the subscapularis is closed with an interrupted suture. The conjoined tendon is left in place. The musculocutaneus nerve entering the medial side of the biceps is inspected and found to be intact. The retractors protecting the inferior portion of the subscapularis are removed. The retractor holding back the cephalic vein is also removed. The wound is closed in layers.

Clinical Example (23077)

A 40-year-old male presents with a 3-cm malignant fibrous histiocytoma in the right posterior deltoid muscle. At operation, the tumor and adjacent soft tissue are resected.

Description of Procedure (23077)

Under anesthesia, a 7-cm incision is made over the posterior deltoid tumor, excising the old biopsy tract. Medial and lateral subcutaneous flaps are raised. The innervation of the deltoid is protected. Careful dissection is carried into the deltoid muscle taking care to stay in normal muscle. A radical excision of the posterior deltoid is made. The tumor is removed en bloc, including necessary surrounding structures; preserving the axillary nerve. Frozen sections are taken from the surrounding tissue. The margins and tumor are sent to pathology. The pathology report is received and additional excision is carried out as necessary to obtain a clear margin. The wound is inspected and irrigated. Hemostasis is obtained. A deep drain is placed. The deep tissue is closed. The wound is closed in layers with interrupted sutures.

Clinical Example (23078)

A 40-year-old male presents with a 10-cm malignant fibrous histiocytoma in the right posterior deltoid muscle. At operation, a radical resection of the shoulder with adjacent soft tissue is performed.

Description of Procedure (23078)

Under anesthesia, a 14-cm incision is made over the posterior deltoid tumor, excising the old biopsy tract. Medial and lateral subcutaneous flaps are raised. The innervation of the deltoid is protected. The parascapular muscles are identified and protected. Careful dissection is carried into the deltoid muscle staying in normal muscle. A radical excision of the posterior deltoid is made. Subperiosteal dissection of the tumor off of the scapula is carried out. The tumor is removed en bloc, including necessary surrounding structures; preserving the axillary nerve. Frozen sections are taken from the surrounding tissue. The margins and tumor are sent to pathology. The pathology report is received, and additional excision is carried out as necessary to obtain a clear margin. The wound is inspected and irrigated. Hemostasis is obtained. A deep drain is placed. The deep tissue is closed with interrupted sutures. The wound is closed in layers with interrupted sutures.

 Clinical Example (23200)

A 40-year-old male presents with an osteosarcoma of the clavicle with its pushing border displacing the subclavian vessels inferiorly. At operation, a radical resection of the clavicle with adjacent soft tissue is performed.

Description of Procedure (23200)

A long incision is made paralleling the clavicle from the midline to the shoulder. The prior biopsy site is ellipsed with the biopsy area staying with the resected specimen. Skin and subcutaneous flaps are developed, avoiding entering the tissue plain of the prior biopsy. Deep fascial planes are opened. The brachial plexus is carefully dissected and exposed. The subclavian vein and artery are exposed and dissected away from the tumor. The subclavius muscle stays with the tumor mass about the clavicle. The sternoclavicular joint is opened and incised. The acromio-clavicular joint is opened and incised. The coracoclavicular ligaments are divided. The strap neck muscles and sternocleidomastoid musculature is divided above the clavicle. The deltoid and pectoralis inferior attachments are divided. The anterior and superior portion first rib region is sacrificed with the adjacent tissue and bony surface going with the tumor specimen to maintain an en bloc tumor resection. During the procedure, preoperative image studies are reviewed to verify intended planes of dissection and proximity of neurovascular bundles. The specimen is then removed from the field and marked for anatomic orientation. (This is documented on the pathology request form along with appropriate history and needed information.) The surgeon then breaks scrub and carries the specimen to the pathology department while the anesthesiologist and other operative personnel remain with the patient. Prior to this, the surgeon assesses the stability of the operative field and discusses with the anesthesiologist the stability of the patient. In the pathology department, the surgeon examines the resected specimen with the attending pathologist and orients the pathologist to the specimen anatomy. The specimen is then inked for margins, and any areas that are questionable are inspected by frozen section. If all margins appear satisfactory, the surgeon returns to the operating room, repeats preoperative scrub, and returns to the surgical field. Careful homeostasis is obtained, and drains are appropriately placed deep in the wound to protect the flaps. A meticulous multilayered wound closure is accomplished.

 Clinical Example (23210)

A 50-year-old male presents with a chondrosarcoma with its pushing border displacing the scapula outward from the chest wall but not extending into the glenohumeral joint. At operation, a radical resection of the scapula with adjacent soft tissue is performed.

Description of Procedure (23210)

A longitudinal slightly oblique incision is made vertically down and past the distal tip of the scapula. The prior biopsy site is ellipsed with the biopsy area staying with the resected specimen. Skin and subcutaneous flaps are developed avoiding entering the tissue plain of the prior biopsy. Deep fascial planes are opened. The trapezius and levator superiorly and the rhomboids medially are divided. The teres major and minor are divided laterally. The rotator cuff near the proximal humerus is divided after the deltoid is taken off of the acromion. The suprascapular neurovascular bundle is identified and divided. The glenohumeral joint is disarticulated. The serratus anterior is divided with the adjacent tissue going with the tumor specimen to effect an en bloc tumor resection. During the procedure, preoperative image studies are reviewed to verify intended planes of dissection and the proximity of neurovascular bundles. The specimen is then removed from the field and marked for anatomic orientation. (This is documented on the pathology request form along with appropriate history and needed information.) The surgeon then breaks scrub and carries the specimen to the pathology department while the anesthesiologist and other operative personnel remain with the patient. Prior to this, the surgeon assesses the stability of the operative field and discusses with the anesthesiologist the stability of the patient. In the pathology department, the surgeon examines the resected specimen with the attending pathologist and orients the pathologist to the specimen anatomy. The specimen is inked for margins, and any areas that are questionable are inspected by frozen section. If all margins appear satisfactory, the surgeon returns to the operating room, repeats preoperative scrub, and returns to the surgical field. Careful homeostasis is obtained, and drains are appropriately placed deep in the wound to protect the flaps. A meticulous multilayered wound closure is accomplished.

 Clinical Example (23220)

A 20-year-old male presents with an osteosarcoma of the proximal humerus with its pushing border displacing the axillary artery and lower brachial plexus and brachial nerves medially. The axillary nerve is intimately involved with the tumor. At operation, a radical resection of the proximal humerus with adjacent soft tissue including the deltoid muscle and axillary nerve is performed.

Description of Procedure (23220)

A longitudinal incision is made from the clavicle over the shoulder down to the two-thirds junction of the distal humerus. The prior biopsy site is ellipsed with the biopsy area staying with the resected specimen. Skin and subcutaneous flaps are developed, avoiding entering the tissue plain of the prior biopsy. Deep fascial planes are opened. The brachial plexus is exposed. The subclavian vein and artery are exposed and followed to the axillary region (axillary vein and artery) and are dissected away from the tumor. The deltoid attachments are divided proximally off of the clavicle and acromion or with these bone structures included in the tumor resection. The attachment of the respective muscle groups that make up the rotator cuff (eg, supraspinatus, infraspinatus, subscapular, teres), latissimus dorsi, and pectoralis major/minor are divided proximal to the insertion on the humerus away from the tumor mass. The axillary nerve is identified near the plexus and divided. The shoulder joint capsule is divided away from the proximal humerus. At the mid–humeral bony junction, exposure is accomplished without injuring radial, ulnar, median, or musculocutaneous nerves. The humerus is divided in the mid-shaft area. During the procedure, preoperative image studies are reviewed to verify intended planes of dissection and the proximity of neurovascular bundles. The specimen is then removed from the field and marked for anatomic orientation. (This is documented on the pathology request form along with appropriate history and needed information.) The surgeon then breaks scrub and carries the specimen to the pathology department while the anesthesiologist and other operative personnel remain with the patient. Prior to this, the surgeon assesses the stability of the operative field and discusses with the anesthesiologist the stability of the patient. In the pathology department, the surgeon examines the resected specimen with the attending pathologist and orients the pathologist to the specimen anatomy. The specimen is inked for margins, and any areas that are questionable are inspected by frozen section. Careful homeostasis is obtained, and drains are appropriately placed deep in the wound to protect the flaps. A meticulous multi-layered wound closure is accomplished.

Humerus (Upper Arm) and Elbow

EXCISION

24065   Biopsy, soft tissue of upper arm or elbow area; superficial

24066   deep (subfascial or intramuscular)

(For needle biopsy of soft tissue, use 20206)

24071   ▶Code is out of numerical sequence. See 24065-24155◀

24073   ▶Code is out of numerical sequence. See 24065-24155◀

▲24075   Excision, tumor, soft tissue of upper arm or elbow area, subcutaneous; less than 3 cm

#●24071   3 cm or greater

▲24076   Excision, tumor, soft tissue of upper arm or elbow area, subfascial (eg, intramuscular); less than 5 cm

#●24073   5 cm or greater

▲**24077** Radical resection of tumor (eg, malignant neoplasm), soft tissue of upper arm or elbow area; less than 5 cm

●**24079**   5 cm or greater

▲**24150** Radical resection of tumor, shaft or distal humerus

▶(24151 has been deleted)◀

▲**24152** Radical resection of tumor, radial head or neck

▶(24153 has been deleted)◀

Rationale

In the Humerus (Upper Arm) and Elbow section, two reference notes have been added to direct the user to the appropriate code range (24065-24155) for placement of out-of-sequence codes 24071 and 24073. Codes 24071 and 24073 appear with a number symbol (#) to indicate that these codes appear out of numerical sequence. Code 24071 has been established to report excision of a subcutaneous soft tissue of the upper arm or elbow area, 3 cm or greater. Code 24075 has been revised for standardization of the nomenclature to describe excision of a subcutaneous soft tissue of the upper arm or elbow, less than 3 cm.

Code 24073 has been established to report excision of a subfascial soft tissue of the upper arm or elbow area, 5 cm or greater. Code 24076 has been revised for standardization of the nomenclature to describe excision of a subfascial soft tissue tumor of the upper arm or elbow, less than 5 cm. Code 24079 has been established to report radical resection of a soft tissue tumor of the upper arm or elbow area, 5 cm or greater. Code 24077 has been revised for standardization of the nomenclature to describe radical resection of a soft tissue tumor of the upper arm or elbow area, less than 5 cm.

In support of the changes to the Humerus section, codes 24150 and 24152 have been editorially revised, and codes 24151 and 24153 have been deleted. Parenthetical notes have been following codes 24150 and 24152 to indicate these deletions.

Clinical Example (24071)

A 50-year-old female undergoes excision of a 4-cm tumor from the anterior aspect of the distal right arm.

Description of Procedure (24071)

Under anesthesia, a 7-cm incision is made in the skin and subcutaneous tissue over the tumor. Careful dissection is carried around the tumor. The tumor is excised and sent to pathology. The tourniquet is deflated, and any bleeders are cauterized. The wound is inspected and irrigated. The wound is closed in two layers with interrupted sutures.

Clinical Example (24073)

A 57-year-old male undergoes excision of a 6-cm myxoma from between the humerus and triceps.

Description of Procedure (24073)

A posterior incision is made over the arm. The subcutaneous tissue is split and the fascia over the triceps muscle is split. Because it is a myxoma, the triceps are retracted to one side and dissected off the posterior portion of the ulnar nerve traveling down the medial portion of the incision. The radial nerve, which is crossing distally in the wound from medial to lateral, is protected. The vessels traveling with the radial nerve are protected. Several perforators off the profunda brachial artery are ligated and incised. Once this interval is freed up, deeper dissection is carried down into the deep triceps and exposure is made over the mass overlying the humerus. The mass is homogenous in consistency, and dissection is accomplished by retracting the triceps up off the humerus and taking the mass off of the posterior aspect of the humerus. Superiorly in the wound, some of the vessels and part of the axillary nerve innervating the inferior deltoid are retracted to gain exposure to that portion of the wound. The mass is taken out in one piece. It is inspected intraoperatively and found to be consistent with a myxoma. It is handed off the operative field. The wound is then copiously irrigated. Retractors are removed, protecting both the ulnar nerve medially and the radial nerve inferiorly in the wound. The tourniquet is let down. Hemostasis is obtained and a drain is placed. A multilayered closure is performed.

 Clinical Example (24075)

A 50-year-old female undergoes excision of a 2-cm tumor from the anterior aspect of the distal right arm.

Description of Procedure (24075)

Under anesthesia, a 4-cm incision is made in the skin and subcutaneous tissue over the tumor. Careful dissection is carried around the tumor. The tumor is excised and sent to pathology. The tourniquet is deflated, and any bleeders are cauterized. The wound is inspected and irrigated. The wound is closed in two layers with interrupted sutures.

 Clinical Example (24076)

A 57-year-old male undergoes excision of a 3-cm myxoma from between the humerus and triceps.

Description of Procedure (24076)

A posterior incision is made over the arm. The subcutaneous tissue is split, and the fascia over the triceps muscle is split. Because it is a myxoma, the triceps are retracted to one side and dissected off the posterior portion of the ulnar nerve traveling down the medial portion of the incision. The radial nerve, which is crossing distally in the wound from medial to lateral, is protected. The vessels traveling with the radial nerve are also protected. Several perforators off the profunda brachial artery are ligated and incised. Once this interval is freed up, deeper dissection is carried down into the deep triceps, and exposure is made over the mass overlying the humerus. The mass is homogenous in consistency, and dissection is accomplished by retracting the triceps up off the humerus and taking the mass off of the posterior aspect of the humerus. Superiorly in the wound, some of the vessels and part of the axillary nerve innervating the inferior deltoid are retracted to gain exposure to that portion of the wound. The mass is taken out in one piece. It is inspected intraoperatively and found to be consistent with a myxoma. It is handed off the operative field. The wound is then copiously irrigated. Retractors are removed, protecting both the ulnar nerve medially and the radial nerve inferiorly in the wound. The tourniquet is let down. Hemostasis is obtained, and a drain is placed. A multilayered closure is performed.

 ## Clinical Example (24077)

A 50-year-old male undergoes radical resection of a 3-cm liposarcoma of the medial triceps muscles of the arm.

Description of Procedure (24077)

A volar longitudinal incision is made beginning at the elbow crease including an elliptical incision around the previous biopsy track to keep this en bloc with the specimen. Dissection is then carried through the skin and subcutaneous tissues angling away from the biopsy track to avoid entering tissues contaminated by the initial biopsy. The deep fascia is incised longitudinally and again includes an ellipse around the biopsy track. Dissection proceeds in medial and lateral directions to form appropriate flaps and facilitate deep dissection. Perforating vessels are encountered and are ligated and incised. Proximally, the radial and ulnar arteries as well as the median and ulnar nerves are identified, and dissection is carried adjacent to these structures to establish a plane of dissection that preserves them but remains in normal tissues outside of the tumor. Several perforating vessels leading to the tumor are ligated and incised. In the proximal portion of the surgical field, the involved flexor muscles are exposed above the proximal extent of the tumor. These structures are then incised to establish a proximal margin well beyond tumor extension.

At this point the neurovascular structures are again identified. They are carefully dissected and separated from the adjacent tumor and intended plane of dissection. Several motor branches are seen to run into the tumor and cannot be preserved so these branches are individually ligated and incised. Other motor branches are noted to bypass the tissues involved in the tumor, and these are protected and preserved. Dissection is then carried out along the medial and lateral aspects of the tumor keeping normal tissue between the tumor and the plane of dissection. Several perforating vessels are again encountered, and these are ligated and incised. Preoperative imaging studies are reviewed during the procedure to verify intended planes of dissection and proximity to neurovascular structures. Once the tumor has been dissected laterally, medial dissection is started, and the tumor and surrounding tissues are gently lifted from the wound from proximal to distal. Further perforating vessels are encountered and are ligated and incised. Further dissection is carried distally until the circumferential dissection is beyond the distal extent of the tumor. At this point, the involved flexor muscles are transected 2 cm from the farthest extent of the tumor as determined by imaging studies and clinical impression. The specimen is then removed from the field and marked for anatomic orientation. (This is documented on the pathology request form along with appropriate history and needed information.) The surgeon then breaks scrub and carries the specimen to the pathology department while the anesthesiologist and other operative personnel remain with the patient. Prior to this, the surgeon assesses the stability of the operative field and discusses with the anesthesiologist the stability of the patient. In the pathology department, the surgeon examines the resected specimen with the attending pathologist and orients the pathologist to the specimen anatomy. The specimen is inked for margins, and any areas that are questionable are inspected by frozen section. If all margins appear satisfactory, the surgeon returns to the operating room, repeats preoperative scrub, and returns to the surgical field. The tourniquet is let down. Hemostasis is obtained and drains are left deep in the wound. A multilayered closure is performed.

Clinical Example (24079)

A 50-year-old male undergoes radical resection of a 6-cm liposarcoma of the medial triceps muscles of the arm.

Description of Procedure (24079)

A volar longitudinal incision is made from the elbow crease to about 10 cm above the wrist including an elliptical incision around the previous biopsy track to keep this en bloc with the specimen. Dissection is then carried through the skin and subcutaneous tissues angling away from the biopsy track to avoid entering tissues contaminated by the initial biopsy. The deep fascia is incised longitudinally and again includes an ellipse around the biopsy track. Dissection proceeds in medial and lateral directions to form appropriate flaps and facilitate deep dissection. Perforating vessels are encountered and are ligated and incised. Proximally, the radial and ulnar arteries as well as the median and ulnar nerves are identified, and dissection is carried adjacent to these structures to establish a plane of dissection that preserves them but remains in normal tissues outside of the tumor. Several perforating vessels leading to the tumor are ligated and incised. In the proximal portion of the surgical field, the involved flexor muscles are exposed above the proximal extent of the tumor. These structures are then incised to establish a proximal margin well beyond tumor extension.

At this point the neurovascular structures are again identified. They are carefully dissected and separated from the adjacent tumor and intended plane of dissection. Several motor branches are seen to run into the tumor and cannot be preserved so these branches are individually ligated and incised. Other motor branches are noted to bypass the tissues involved in the tumor, and these are protected and preserved. Dissection is then carried along the medial and lateral aspects of the tumor keeping normal tissue between the tumor and the plane of dissection. Several perforating vessels are again encountered, and these are ligated and incised. Preoperative imaging studies are reviewed during the procedure to verify intended planes of dissection and proximity to neurovascular structures. Once the tumor has been dissected laterally, medial dissection is started, and the tumor and surrounding tissues are gently lifted from the wound from proximal to distal. Further perforating vessels are encountered and are ligated and incised. Further dissection is carried distally until the circumferential dissection is beyond the distal extent of the tumor. At this point, the involved flexor muscles are transected 2 cm from the farthest extent of the tumor as determined by imaging studies and clinical impression. The specimen is then removed from the field and marked for anatomic orientation. (This is documented on the pathology request form along with appropriate history and needed information.) The surgeon then breaks scrub and carries the specimen to the pathology department while the anesthesiologist and other operative personnel remain with the patient. Prior to this, the surgeon assesses the stability of the operative field and discusses with the anesthesiologist the stability of the patient. In the pathology department, the surgeon examines the resected specimen with the attending pathologist and orients the pathologist to the specimen anatomy. The specimen is inked for margins, and any areas that are questionable are inspected by frozen section. If all margins appear satisfactory, the surgeon returns to the operating room, repeats preoperative scrub, and returns to the surgical field. The tourniquet is let down. Hemostasis is obtained, and drains are left deep in the wound. A multilayered closure is performed.

Clinical Example (24150)

A 20-year-old male presents with an osteosarcoma in the distal one-third of the humerus with its pushing border displacing the brachial artery and arterial bifurcation anteriorly. At operation, a radical resection of the distal one-third humeral shaft and joint with adjacent soft tissue is performed.

Description of Procedure (24150)

A longitudinal incision is made paralleling the length of the arm from the proximal one-third to across the antecubital area down into the forearm. The prior biopsy site is ellipsed with the biopsy area staying with the resected specimen. Skin and subcutaneous flaps are developed avoiding entering the tissue plane of the prior biopsy. Deep fascial planes are opened. Median, ulnar, and radial nerves are identified proximally and distally and followed and dissected away from the tumor mass. The brachial vein and artery are exposed and dissected away from the tumor. The elbow joint is opened, and the capsule is exposed. The midshaft humerus is exposed. Involved muscle groups (eg, biceps, triceps brachialis) are divided proximally and distally to the tumor. Numerous perforating and named vessels are identified and ligated and incised. The shaft of the humerus is osteotomized. During the procedure, preoperative image studies are reviewed to verify intended planes of dissection and proximity of neurovascular bundles. The specimen is then removed from the field and marked for anatomic orientation. (This is documented on the pathology request form along with appropriate history and needed information.) The surgeon then breaks scrub and carries the specimen to the pathology department while the anesthesiologist and other operative personnel remain with the patient. Prior to this, the surgeon assesses the stability of the operative field and discusses with the anesthesiologist the stability of the patient. In the pathology department, the surgeon examines the resected specimen with the attending pathologist and orients the pathologist to the specimen anatomy. The specimen is inked for margins, and any areas that are questionable are inspected by frozen section. Careful homeostasis is obtained, and drains are appropriately placed deep in the wound to protect the flaps. A meticulous multilayered wound closure is accomplished.

Clinical Example (24152)

A 50-year-old male presents with a chondrosarcoma of the proximal radial head and neck with its pushing border displacing the radial nerve and the posterior interosseous nerve. At operation, a radical resection of the proximal radius with adjacent soft tissue is performed.

Description of Procedure (24152)

A longitudinal incision is made utilizing an approach extending from above the elbow anteriorly and paralleling the proximal radius anterolaterally. The prior biopsy site is ellipsed with the biopsy area staying with the resected specimen. Skin and subcutaneous flaps are developed, avoiding entering the tissue plain of the prior biopsy. Deep fascial planes are opened. The radial nerve is followed proximally down toward the radial head. The supinator is identified. The posterior interosseous nerve is identified. The brachial artery and vein are identified. The elbow joint is opened and incised. The tissues about the midshaft of the radius are opened and incised. The radial collateral ligament is identified and divided extraperiosteally off of the humeral condylar region. The midshaft interval is identified, and the radius is divided. During the procedure, preoperative image studies are reviewed to verify intended planes of dissection and proximity of neurovascular bundles. The specimen is then removed from the field and marked for anatomic orientation. (This is documented on the pathology request form along with appropriate history and needed information.) The surgeon then breaks scrub and carries the specimen to the pathology department while the anesthesiologist and other operative personnel remain with the patient. Prior to this, the surgeon assesses the stability of the operative field and discusses with the anesthesiologist the stability of the patient. In the pathology department, the surgeon examines the resected specimen with the attending pathologist and orients the pathologist to the specimen anatomy. The specimen is inked for margins, and any areas that are questionable are inspected by frozen section. Careful homeostasis is obtained, and drains are appropriately placed deep in the wound to protect the flaps. A meticulous multilayered wound closure is accomplished.

Forearm and Wrist

EXCISION

25065   Biopsy, soft tissue of forearm and/or wrist; superficial

25066   deep (subfascial or intramuscular)

(For needle biopsy of soft tissue, use 20206)

25071   ▶Code is out of numerical sequence. See 25065-25240◀

25073   ▶Code is out of numerical sequence. See 25065-25240◀

▲**25075**   Excision, tumor, soft tissue of forearm and/or wrist area, subcutaneous; less than 3 cm

#●**25071**   3 cm or greater

⊘=Modifier 51 Exempt   ⊙=Moderate Sedation   ✚=Add-on Code   ✗=FDA approval pending

▲25076	Excision, tumor, soft tissue of forearm and/or wrist area, subfascial (eg, intramuscular); less than 3 cm
#●25073	3 cm or greater
▲25077	Radical resection of tumor (eg, malignant neoplasm), soft tissue of forearm and/or wrist area; less than 3 cm
●25078	3 cm or greater
25085	Capsulotomy, wrist (eg, contracture)
▲25170	Radical resection of tumor, radius or ulna

🖎 Rationale

In the Forearm and Wrist section, two reference notes have been added to direct the user to the appropriate code range (25065-25240) for placement of out-of-sequence codes 25071 and 25073. Codes 25071 and 25073 appear with a number symbol (#) to indicate that these codes appear out of numerical sequence. Code 25071 has been established to report excision of a subcutaneous soft tissue of the forearm and/or wrist area, 3 cm or greater. Code 25075 has been revised for standardization of the nomenclature to describe excision of a subcutaneous soft tissue of the forearm and/or wrist area, less than 3 cm.

Code 25073 has been established to report excision of a subfascial soft tissue of the forearm and/or wrist areas, 3 cm or greater. Code 25076 has been revised for standardization of the nomenclature to describe excision of a subfascial soft tissue of the forearm and/or wrist area, less than 3 cm. Code 25078 has been established to report radical resection of a soft tissue tumor of the forearm and/or wrist area, 3 cm or greater. Code 25077 has been revised for standardization of the nomenclature to describe radical resection of a soft tissue tumor of the forearm and/or wrist area, less than 3 cm.

In support of the changes to the Forearm and Wrist, code 25170 has been editorially revised.

🩺 Clinical Example (25071)

A 50-year-old female undergoes excision of a 4-cm tumor from the anterior aspect of the forearm.

Description of Procedure (25071)

An incision is made over the tumor. Careful dissection is carried down to the tumor, taking care to protect any neurovascular structures. The tumor is dissected away from the adjacent tissues and removed. Cultures are taken. The wound is irrigated. The tourniquet is released and meticulous hemostasis is achieved. The wound is again irrigated. The wound is closed in layers.

🩺 Clinical Example (25073)

A 43-year-old male undergoes excision of a 6-cm lipoma from the volar compartment of the forearm.

Description of Procedure (25073)

An incision is made distal to the flexor crease of the elbow down the volar aspect of the forearm. The subcutaneous tissue is incised, and the fascia is split. Care is taken to avoid any of the antebrachial cutaneus nerves of the forearm. The interval between the brachial radialis muscle and the flexor carpi radialis muscle is split. The radial artery on the lateral side of the incision along with the radial sensory nerve are dissected free and retracted laterally. The flexor digitorum sublimis muscle is identified, and several perforating vessels off the radial artery are ligated and tied. The lateral aspect of the flexor digitorum sublimis is released, and a portion of the distal pronator teres muscle incised and retracted proximally. Next, the flexor digitorum superficialis is retracted toward the ulnar side of the arm. The median nerve and the anterior interosseous nerve and artery are exposed. The anterior interosseous innervation to the flexor digitorum profundus and flexor pollicis longus are identified and protected. A portion of the profundus is longitudinally split to expose the lipoma. The lipoma is deep and just sitting on the ulna and interosseous membrane. The median nerve is carefully protected along with the ulnar artery while splitting the flexor digitorum profundus. Very careful dissection is necessary to remove this deep lipoma. It is removed off the interosseous membrane as well as off the ulna. The tumor is removed in one piece. The flexor digitorum profundus is then loosely closed with interrupted sutures. The anterior interosseous and medial nerves are carefully inspected. The tourniquet is let down, and bleeders are ligated. The flexor digitorum is allowed to gently be put back into place laterally and held with interrupted reabsorbable sutures. A portion of a pronator teres tendon that had been released is repaired with a non-absorbable suture. A drain is placed in this layer and brought out through the skin. The retractors are all removed, and the brachial radialis and flexor carpi radialis are allowed to fall back into place. The fascia is left open. The wound is closed in layers.

 Clinical Example (25075)

A 50-year-old female undergoes excision of a 2-cm tumor from the anterior aspect of the forearm.

Description of Procedure (25075)

An incision is made over the tumor. Careful dissection is carried down to the tumor taking care to protect any neurovascular structures. The tumor is dissected away from the adjacent tissues and removed. The wound is irrigated. The tourniquet is released, and meticulous hemostasis is achieved. The wound is again irrigated. The wound is closed in layers.

 Clinical Example (25076)

A 43-year-old male undergoes excision of a 2-cm lipoma from the volar compartment of the forearm.

Description of Procedure (25076)

An incision is made over the tumor. Careful dissection is carried through the subcutaneous tissue and fascia to the tumor taking care to protect any neurovascular structures. The tumor is dissected away from the adjacent tissues and removed.

⃠=Modifier 51 Exempt ⊙=Moderate Sedation ✚=Add-on Code ☇=FDA approval pending

The wound is irrigated. The tourniquet is released, and meticulous hemostasis is achieved. The wound is again irrigated. The wound is closed in layers.

 Clinical Example (25077)

A 30-year-old male presents with a 3-cm malignant fibrous histiocytoma of the flexor carpi radialis. At operation, the tumor and adjacent soft tissue are resected.

Description of Procedure (25077)

A volar longitudinal incision is made from the elbow crease to about 5 cm above the wrist including an elliptical incision around the previous biopsy track to keep this en bloc with the specimen. Dissection is then carried out through the skin and subcutaneous tissues angling away from the biopsy track to avoid entering tissues contaminated by the initial biopsy. The deep fascia is then incised longitudinally and again includes an ellipse around the biopsy track. Dissection is then carried in medial and lateral directions to form appropriate flaps and facilitate deep dissection. Perforating vessels are encountered and are ligated and incised. Proximally, the radial and ulnar arteries as well as the median and ulnar nerves are identified, and dissection is carried adjacent to these structures to establish a plane of dissection that preserves them but remains in normal tissues outside of the tumor. Several perforating vessels leading to the tumor are ligated and incised. In the proximal portion of the surgical field, the involved flexor muscles are exposed above the proximal extent of the tumor. These structures are then incised to establish a proximal margin well beyond tumor extension.

At this point the neurovascular structures are again identified. They are carefully dissected and separated from the adjacent tumor and intended plane of dissection. Several motor branches are seen to run into the tumor and cannot be preserved so these branches are individually ligated and incised. Other motor branches are noted to bypass the tissues involved in the tumor, and these are protected and preserved. Dissection is then carried out along the medial and lateral aspects of the tumor keeping normal tissue between the tumor and the plane of dissection. Several perforating vessels are again encountered, and these are ligated and incised. Preoperative imaging studies are reviewed during the procedure to verify intended planes of dissection and proximity to neurovascular structures. Once the tumor has been dissected laterally, medial dissection is started, and the tumor and surrounding tissues are gently lifted from the wound from proximal to distal. Further perforating vessels are encountered and are ligated and incised. Further dissection is carried distally until the circumferential dissection is beyond the distal extent of the tumor. At this point, the involved flexor muscles are transected 2 cm from the farthest extent of the tumor as determined by imaging studies and clinical impression. Cultures are taken. The specimen is then removed from the field and marked for anatomic orientation. (This is documented on the pathology request form along with appropriate history and needed information.) The surgeon breaks scrub and carries the specimen to the pathology department while the anesthesiologist and other operative personnel remain with the patient. Prior to this, the surgeon assesses the stability of the operative field and discusses with the anesthesiologist the stability of the patient. In the pathology department, the surgeon examines the resected specimen with the attending pathologist and orients the pathologist to the specimen anatomy. The specimen is inked for margins, and any areas that are questionable are inspected by frozen section. If all margins appear satisfactory, the surgeon returns to the operating room, repeats preoperative scrub, and returns to the surgical field. The tourniquet is let down, and hemostasis is obtained and drains are left deep in the wound. A multilayered closure is then performed.

 Clinical Example (25078)
A 30-year-old male presents with a 7-cm malignant fibrous histiocytoma of the flexor muscles of the mid-forearm. At operation, the tumor and adjacent soft tissue are resected.

Description of Procedure (25078)
A volar longitudinal incision is made from the elbow crease to about 10 cm above the wrist including an elliptical incision around the previous biopsy track to keep this en bloc with the specimen. Dissection is then carried out through the skin and subcutaneous tissues angling away from the biopsy track to avoid entering tissues contaminated by the initial biopsy. The deep fascia is then incised longitudinally and again includes an ellipse around the biopsy track. Dissection is then carried in medial and lateral directions to form appropriate flaps and facilitate deep dissection. Perforating vessels are encountered and are ligated and incised. Proximally, the radial and ulnar arteries as well as the median and ulnar nerves are identified, and dissection is carried adjacent to these structures to establish a plane of dissection that preserves them but remains in normal tissues outside of the tumor. Several perforating vessels leading to the tumor are ligated and incised. In the proximal portion of the surgical field, the involved flexor muscles are exposed above the proximal extent of the tumor. These structures are then incised to establish a proximal margin well beyond tumor extension.

At this point the neurovascular structures are again identified. They are carefully dissected and separated from the adjacent tumor and intended plane of dissection. Several motor branches are seen to run into the tumor and cannot be preserved, so these branches are individually ligated and incised. Other motor branches are noted to bypass the tissues involved in the tumor and these are protected and preserved. Dissection is then carried out along the medial and lateral aspects of the tumor keeping normal tissue between the tumor and the plane of dissection. Several perforating vessels are again encountered, and these are ligated and incised. Preoperative imaging studies are reviewed during the procedure to verify intended planes of dissection and proximity to neurovascular structures. Once the tumor has been dissected laterally, medial dissection is started and the tumor and surrounding tissues are gently lifted from the wound from proximal to distal. Further perforating vessels encountered are ligated and incised. Further dissection is carried distally until the circumferential dissection is beyond the distal extent of the tumor. At this point, the involved flexor muscles are transected 2 cm from the farthest extent of the tumor as determined by imaging studies and clinical impression. The specimen is then removed from the field and marked for anatomic orientation. (This is documented on the pathology request form along with appropriate history and needed information.) The surgeon assesses the stability of the

⊘=Modifier 51 Exempt   ⊙=Moderate Sedation   ✛=Add-on Code   ⊬=FDA approval pending

operative field and discusses with the anesthesiologist the stability of the patient. The surgeon then breaks scrub and carries the specimen to the pathology department while the anesthesiologist and other operative personnel remain with the patient. In the pathology department, the surgeon examines the resected specimen with the attending pathologist and orients the pathologist to the specimen anatomy. The specimen is inked for margins, and any areas that are questionable are inspected by frozen section. If all margins appear satisfactory, the surgeon returns to the operating room, repeats preoperative scrub, and returns to the surgical field. The tourniquet is let down. Hemostasis is obtained, and drains are left deep in the wound. A multilayered closure is then performed.

Clinical Example (25170)

A 54-year-old male presents with an osteosarcoma of the radius with extension through the interosseous membrane, abutting the ulna, with an associated soft tissue mass extending from the bone. At operation, a radical resection of the radius with adjacent soft tissue is performed.

Description of Procedure (25170)

An incision is made in a longitudinal orientation, ellipsing the biopsy tract in a wide en bloc fashion from the elbow, incorporating the biopsy tract, extending the incision to the wrist. The dissection is carried down through the subcutaneous fat maintaining a cuff of tissue surrounding the biopsy tract and tumor. The incision is carried down through the limiting fascia of the forearm, extending down to the wrist. The tumor originates in the bone but is associated with a large soft tissue mass that involves the surrounding musculature. The dissection therefore proceeds through the volar musculature, once again maintaining a cuff of normal, non-tumor involved muscle on the tumor to maintain a wide margin around the tumor. The flexor carpi radialis and flexor carpi ulnaris, along with the flexor digitorum sublimis and profundus muscles, are dissected from the underlying soft tissue component of the bony tumor. The neurovascular bundle, associated with the tumor, is meticulously dissected free from the overlying tumor. The artery, vein, and nerves are sharply dissected from their sheath maintaining the sheath as a margin on the tumor. The interosseous membrane is approached and identified and then carefully divided in order to mobilize the radius.

At this point the dissection is carried over to the dorsal side of the forearm. The same approach is utilized here, dissecting the overlying extensor muscles from the underlying tumor, maintaining a cuff of normal tissue in a wide en bloc fashion. The neurovascular structures here are dissected free from the tumor and maintained to allow functional restoration of the limb. The dissection is carried further distal to the wrist joint. Proximally, the dissection is carried toward the elbow where the joint capsules of both the wrist and elbow are exposed. The remaining capsular structures are then transected, with care taken to protect the neurovascular structures (eg, artery, vein, and nerves, both radial and ulna), which lie intimately in contact with the capsular structures. The radius is then elevated forward to allow for exposure of the forearm. Care is taken to ligate each feeding vessel into the tumor. The dissection is carried proximally in this fashion until the level of the proposed osteotomy dictated by the preoperative planning is reached. At this point (typically 12 cm above the wrist), the dissection is carried circumferentially around the entire bone. The bone is then cut with a saw and the remaining soft tissues are dissected free from the specimen. The specimen consists of the skin of the biopsy tract, the underlying subcutaneous fat, fascia, muscle, tumor, bone, ligaments, tendons, and capsular structures, all in one piece, without any contamination of either tumor or prior surgery. The specimen is then removed from the field and marked for anatomic orientation. (This is documented on the pathology request form along with appropriate history and needed information.) The surgeon assesses the stability of the operative field and discusses with the anesthesiologist the stability of the patient. The surgeon then breaks scrub and carries the specimen to the pathology department while the anesthesiologist and other operative personnel remain with the patient. In the pathology department, the surgeon examines the resected specimen with the attending pathologist and orients the pathologist to the specimen anatomy. The specimen is inked for margins, and any areas that are questionable are inspected by frozen section. If positive margins are found, additional resection is required. The wound bed is inspected, bleeding vessels are ligated, and the neurovascular structures are reevaluated to ensure they are intact. During the remainder of the procedure, these structures must be protected from stretch, twisting, and retraction, as there is now no bone to provide structure of this limb. The soft tissue reconstruction can be begun once all frozen sections reveal clear margins. Gloves and instruments are changed to prevent any contamination. The muscles are mobilized in order to provide coverage over the remaining bone. The dissection is carried more proximally until the muscles can be rotated to fill in the void left by the tumor. Muscle bellies are repaired to themselves, as are the fascia. The fascial layers are closed in a watertight fashion over a drain, followed by closure of the subcutaneous tissues and skin.

Hand and Fingers

EXCISION

26100	Arthrotomy with biopsy; carpometacarpal joint, each
26105	metacarpophalangeal joint, each
26110	interphalangeal joint, each
26111	▶Code is out of numerical sequence. See 26100-26262◀
26113	▶Code is out of numerical sequence. See 26100-26262◀
▲**26115**	Excision, tumor or vascular malformation, soft tissue of hand or finger, subcutaneous; less than 1.5 cm
#●**26111**	1.5 cm or greater
▲**26116**	Excision, tumor, soft tissue, or vascular malformation, of hand or finger, subfascial (eg, intramuscular); less than 1.5 cm
#●**26113**	1.5 cm or greater

⊘=Modifier 51 Exempt   ⊙=Moderate Sedation   ✚=Add-on Code   ✗=FDA approval pending

▲**26117**   Radical resection of tumor (eg, malignant neoplasm), soft tissue of hand or finger; less than 3 cm

●**26118**   3 cm or greater

  26121   Fasciectomy, palm only, with or without Z-plasty, other local tissue rearrangement, or skin grafting (includes obtaining graft)

▲**26250**   Radical resection of tumor, metacarpal

    ▶(26255 has been deleted)◀

▲**26260**   Radical resection of tumor, proximal or middle phalanx of finger

    ▶(26261 has been deleted)◀

▲**26262**   Radical resection of tumor, distal phalanx of finger (eg, tumor)

✍ Rationale

In the Hand and Fingers section, two reference notes have been added to direct the user to the appropriate code range (26100-26262) for placement of out-of-sequence codes 26111 and 26113. Codes 26111 and 26113 appear with a number symbol (#) to indicate that these codes appear out of numerical sequence. Code 26111 has been established to report excision of a subcutaneous soft tissue tumor or vascular malformation of the hand or finger, 1.5 cm or greater. Code 26115 has been revised for standardization of the nomenclature to describe excision of a subcutaneous soft tissue tumor or vascular malformation of the hand or finger, less than 1.5 cm.

Code 26113 has been established to report excision of a subfascial soft tissue tumor or vascular malformation of the hand or finger, 1.5 cm or greater. Code 26116 has been revised for standardization of the nomenclature to describe excision of a subfascial soft tissue tumor or vascular malformation of the hand or finger, less than 1.5 cm.

Code 26118 has been established to report radical resection of a soft tissue tumor of the hand or finger, 3 cm or greater. Code 26117 has been revised for standardization of the nomenclature to describe radical resection of a soft tissue tumor of the hand or finger, less than 3 cm.

In support of the changes to the Hand and Fingers section, codes 26250, 26260, and 26262 have been editorially revised, and codes 26255 and 26261 have been deleted. Parenthetical notes have been added to indicate this change.

🩺 Clinical Example (26111)

A 45-year-old male undergoes excision of a 2-cm tumor from the palmar aspect of the index finger.

Description of Procedure (26111)

An incision is made over the tumor. Careful dissection of the tumor is carried out. The digital arteries and nerves are identified and carefully protected. The flexor tendon sheath is identified and protected. The tumor is meticulously dissected from the adjacent tissues. The wound is inspected for any residual tumor.

The wound is irrigated. The tourniquet is released, and meticulous hemostasis is achieved using a bipolar electrocautery. The skin is closed.

Clinical Example (26113)

A 35-year-old male presents with a 3.5-cm tumor in the thenar muscles of the left hand. At operation, the tumor and adjacent soft tissue are excised.

Description of Procedure (26113)

An incision is made over the thenar eminence. The subcutaneous tissue is dissected. The thenar fascia is opened. The flexor pollicis brevis muscle fibers are split to expose the tumor. Care is taken to avoid injury to the motor branch of the median nerve. The tumor and its capsule are excised. The tourniquet is released, and meticulous hemostasis is achieved using a bipolar electrocautery. The wound is inspected and irrigated. The wound is closed.

Clinical Example (26115)

A 45-year-old male undergoes excision of a 1-cm tumor from the palmar aspect of the index finger.

Description of Procedure (26115)

An incision is made over the tumor. Careful dissection of the tumor is carried out. The digital arteries and nerves are identified and carefully protected. The flexor tendon sheath is identified and protected. The tumor is meticulously dissected from the adjacent tissues. The wound is inspected for any residual tumor. The wound is irrigated. The tourniquet is released, and meticulous hemostasis is achieved using a bipolar electrocautery. The skin is then closed.

Clinical Example (26116)

A 35-year-old male undergoes excision of a 1.2-cm tumor of the thenar muscles of the right hand.

Description of Procedure (26116)

An incision is made over the thenar eminence. The subcutaneous tissue is dissected. The thenar fascia is opened. The flexor pollicis brevis muscle fibers are split to expose the tumor. Care is taken to avoid injury to the motor branch of the median nerve. The tumor and its capsule are excised. The tourniquet is released, and meticulous hemostasis is achieved using a bipolar electrocautery. The wound is inspected and irrigated. The wound is closed.

Clinical Example (26117)

A 20-year-old male presents with a 2-cm epithelioid sarcoma in the abductor pollicis brevis. At operation, the tumor and adjacent soft tissue are excised.

Description of Procedure (26117)

An incision is made excising the old biopsy tract. Medial and lateral skin flaps are raised. The tumor is removed en bloc, including necessary surrounding structures. Frozen sections are taken from the surrounding tissue. The margins and tumor are sent to pathology. Additional excision is carried out as necessary to obtain a clear margin. The tourniquet is released, and meticulous hemostasis is achieved using a bipolar electrocautery. The wound is inspected and irrigated. The wound is closed.

 Clinical Example (26118)

A 20-year-old male presents with a 4-cm epithelioid sarcoma in the abductor pollicis brevis and flexor pollicis brevis. At operation, the tumor and adjacent soft tissue are excised.

Description of Procedure (26118)

An incision is made excising the old biopsy tract. Medial and lateral skin flaps are raised. The tumor is removed en bloc, including necessary surrounding structures. Frozen sections are taken from the surrounding tissue. The margins and tumor are sent to pathology. Additional excision is carried out as necessary to obtain a clear margin. The tourniquet is released, and meticulous hemostasis is achieved using a bipolar electrocautery. The wound is inspected and irrigated. The wound is closed.

 Clinical Example (26250)

A 50-year-old male presents with a chondrosarcoma of the first metacarpal of the thumb with a small soft tissue mass. A radical resection of the first metacarpal is performed with preservation of the thumb.

Description of Procedure (26250)

An incision is made over the dorsal aspect of the first metacarpal. The neuro-vascular structures are carefully retracted. The extensor mechanism is retracted. Extraperiosteal dissection is carried out around the metacarpal. The metacarpal-phalangeal joint is identified, and the capsule is incised. The flexor tendon sheath is opened, and the flexor pollicis longus is retracted. The first metacarpal is carefully dissected away from the flexor pollicis longus and thenar muscles. The digital nerves and arteries are protected. The carpometacarpal joint is identified, and its capsule incised. The metacarpal, the attached soft tissue tumor extension, and the involved muscle are removed. The tourniquet is released, and meticulous hemostasis achieved. The wound is irrigated. A drain is placed in the wound. The wound is closed in layers.

Clinical Example (26260)

A 40-year-old female presents with a chondrosarcoma of the proximal phalanx of the thumb in her dominant hand. A radical resection of the tumor is performed with preservation of the thumb.

Description of Procedure (26260)

An incision is made over the dorsal aspect of the proximal phalanx. The neuro-vascular structures are carefully retracted. The extensor mechanism is retracted. Extraperiosteal dissection is carried out around the phalanx. The interphalangeal joint is identified, and the capsule is incised. The flexor tendon sheath is opened, and the flexor pollicis longus is retracted. The proximal phalanx is carefully dissected away from the flexor pollicis longus. The digital nerves and arteries are protected. The metacarpalphalangeal joint is identified, and its capsule incised. The phalanx is excised. The tourniquet is released, and meticulous hemostasis achieved. The wound is irrigated. A drain is placed in the wound. The wound is closed.

 Clinical Example (26262)

A 35-year-old female presents with chondrosarcoma of the distal phalanx of the thumb. A radical resection of the tumor is performed with preservation of the thumb.

Description of Procedure (26262)

An incision is made over the radial aspect of the distal phalanx. The neurovascular structures are carefully retracted. The extensor mechanism is retracted. Extraperiosteal dissection is carried out around the phalanx. The interphalangeal joint is identified, and the capsule is incised. The flexor tendon sheath is opened, and the flexor pollicis longus is retracted. The distal phalanx is carefully dissected away from the flexor pollicis longus, extensor policis longus, and nail organ. The digital nerves and arteries are protected. The phalanx is excised. The tourniquet is released, and meticulous hemostasis achieved. The wound is irrigated. A drain is placed in the wound. The wound is closed.

Pelvis and Hip Joint

EXCISION

27040	Biopsy, soft tissue of pelvis and hip area; superficial
27041	deep, subfascial or intramuscular
	(For needle biopsy of soft tissue, use 20206)
27043	▶Code is out of numerical sequence. See 27040-27080◀
27045	▶Code is out of numerical sequence. See 27040-27080◀
▲**27047**	Excision, tumor, soft tissue of pelvis and hip area, subcutaneous; less than 3 cm
#●**27043**	3 cm or greater
▲**27048**	Excision, tumor, soft tissue of pelvis and hip area, subfascial (eg, intramuscular); less than 5 cm
#●**27045**	5 cm or greater
▲**27049**	Radical resection of tumor (eg, malignant neoplasm), soft tissue of pelvis and hip area; less than 5 cm
#●**27059**	5 cm or greater
27050	Arthrotomy, with biopsy; sacroiliac joint
27059	▶Code is out of numerical sequence. See 27040-27080◀
▲**27075**	Radical resection of tumor; wing of ilium, 1 pubic or ischial ramus or symphysis pubis
▲**27076**	ilium, including acetabulum, both pubic rami, or ischium and acetabulum
▲**27077**	innominate bone, total

⊘=Modifier 51 Exempt   ⊙=Moderate Sedation   ✚=Add-on Code   ⊮=FDA approval pending

▲**27078**   ischial tuberosity and greater trochanter of femur

▶(27079 has been deleted)◀

 Rationale

In the Pelvis and Hip Joint section, three reference notes have been added to direct the user to the appropriate code range (27040-27080) for placement of out-of-sequence codes 27043, 27045, and 27059. Codes 27043, 27045, and 27059 appear with a number symbol (#) to indicate that these codes appear out of numerical sequence. Code 27043 has been established to report excision of a subcutaneous soft tissue tumor of the pelvis and hip area, 3 cm or greater. Code 27047 has been revised for standardization of the nomenclature to describe excision of a subcutaneous soft tissue tumor of the pelvis and hip area, less than 3 cm.

Code 27045 has been established to report excision of a subfascial soft tissue tumor of the pelvis and hip area, 5 cm or greater. Code 27048 has been revised for standardization of the nomenclature to describe excision of a subfascial soft tissue tumor of the pelvis and hip area, less than 5 cm.

Code 27059 has been established to report radical resection of a soft tissue tumor of the pelvis and hip area, 5 cm or greater. Code 27049 has been revised for standardization of the nomenclature to describe radical resection of a soft tissue tumor of the pelvis and hip area, less than 5 cm.

In support of the changes to the Pelvis and Hip Joint section, codes 27075, 27076, 27077, and 27078 have been editorially revised, and code 27079 has been deleted. A parenthetical note has been added to indicate code 27079 has been deleted.

 Clinical Example (27043)

A 42-year-old female undergoes excision of a 5-cm tumor in her lateral buttock.

Description of Procedure (27043)

An incision is made through the skin and subcutaneous tissue over the lesion. Subcutaneous flaps are raised with electrocautery to expose the lesion, and hemostasis is controlled. The tumor is excised along with proper margin of tissue. As the tumor is lifted out of the wound, small lymphatics and feeding blood vessels are ligated. Hemostasis is secured with electrocautery and sutures where needed. The wound is inspected and irrigated. The wound is closed in layers with interrupted sutures.

 Clinical Example (27045)

A 68-year-old female undergoes excision of an 8-cm lipoma deep in the gluteus maximus.

Description of Procedure (27045)

An incision is made from the greater trochanter up toward the posterior superior iliac spine. The subcutaneous tissue is split, and the fascia of the iliac tibial band and the gluteus maximus is identified and split. The gluteus maximus muscle is carefully split proximally, and several perforating vessels off the inferior gluteal artery are ligated and tied. Once that is done, self-retaining retractors are put into the gluteus maximus muscle, and a portion of the mass is seen. The greater trochanter is exposed in the distal portion of the wound, and the lipoma is released very carefully over the greater trochanter. Dissection of the lipoma off the posterior aspect of the gluteus medius is then performed. Distally in the wound the sciatic nerve is identified underneath the lipoma. Careful dissection is performed to remove the lipoma from on top of the sciatic nerve. The inferior gluteal nerve, artery, and vein are perforating the gluteus maximus in the distal portion of the wound. They are also identified, dissected out, and protected. Several branches off the inferior gluteal vessels are ligated and incised. The remainder of the lipoma is released off the deep surface of the gluteus maximus up toward the sciatic notch. Anteriorly, the remainder of the lipoma is removed off the back of the gluteus medius. Now the lipoma is attached only near the sciatic notch. The superior gluteal artery and vein are coming around the superior corner of the sciatic notch. Several vessels perforating the lipoma coming off the superior gluteal vessels are ligated and tied. Once that is done, dissection can be done to release the lipoma off the gluteal vessels. The remainder of the lipoma near the sciatic notch is very slowly released. The inferior gluteal vessels can be seen by the sciatic notch and are carefully protected. The sciatic nerve has been carefully protected along with the piriformis tendon coming through the notch. The mass is then removed in one piece. The wound is copiously irrigated, and the area is inspected to be certain there is no residual tumor. The specimen is handed off the field. A deep drain is placed and brought out through the gluteus maximus. The wound is closed in layers with interrupted sutures.

 ### Clinical Example (27047)

A 35-year-old male undergoes excision of a 2-cm tumor in his left buttock.

Description of Procedure (27047)

An incision is made through the skin and subcutaneous tissue over the lesion. Subcutaneous flaps are raised with electrocautery and hemostasis is controlled. The tumor is excised along with proper margin of tissue. Hemostasis is secured with electrocautery and sutures where needed. Small lymphatic channels are ligated. The wound is inspected and irrigated. The wound is closed in layers with interrupted sutures.

 ### Clinical Example (27048)

A 68-year-old female undergoes excision of a 4-cm lipoma deep in the gluteus maximus.

Description of Procedure (27048)

An incision is made through the skin and subcutaneous tissue over the lesion. Subcutaneous flaps are raised with electrocautery. The gluteus maximus muscle is exposed around the tumor. The tumor is excised along with surrounding muscle using electrocautery and dissection. As the tumor is lifted out of the wound, small lymphatics and feeding blood vessels are ligated. Hemostasis is secured with electrocautery and sutures where needed. The wound is inspected and irrigated. The devitalized muscle is debrided. Where possible, the muscle fascial defect is approximated. A drain is placed in the cavitary defect. The wound is closed in layers with interrupted sutures.

 Clinical Example (27049)

A 65-year-old woman presents with a deep, 4-cm malignant fibrous histiocytoma of the adductor muscles of the proximal thigh. At operation, the tumor and adjacent soft tissue are resected.

Description of Procedure (27049)

An incision is made over the trapezius. Medial and lateral subcutaneous flaps are raised. The overlying skin from the biopsy is excised with the tumor. The musculature is exposed around the tumor. The fascia is incised, and part of it is included with the specimen in the dissection for proper margins. A radical excision of the adductor longus and superficial adductor brevis is performed. The tumor is removed en bloc, including necessary surrounding structures. As the tumor is lifted out of the wound, small lymphatics and feeding blood vessels are ligated. The deep fascia is inspected for involvement by the tumor, as are the ribs and intercostal muscles. If deep margins are involved, then resection to the periosteum of the ribs and/or peritoneum is carried out. The surgeon then breaks scrub and carries the specimen to the pathology department while the anesthesiologist and other operative personnel remain with the patient. Prior to this, the surgeon assesses the stability of the operative field and discusses with the anesthesiologist the stability of the patient. In the pathology department, the surgeon then examines the resected specimen with the attending pathologist and orients the pathologist to the specimen anatomy. The specimen is then inked for margins, and any areas that are questionable are inspected by frozen section. If all margins appear satisfactory, then the surgeon returns to the operating room, repeats preoperative scrub, and returns to the surgical field. Additional excision is carried out as necessary to obtain a clear margin. Metallic clips are placed to mark the margins for possible postoperative radiotherapy guidance. The wound is inspected and irrigated. Devitalized muscle is debrided. A deep drain is placed. The wound is closed in layers with interrupted sutures.

Clinical Example (27059)

A 65-year-old female presents with a deep, 9-cm malignant fibrous histiocytoma of the adductor muscles of the proximal thigh. At operation, the tumor and adjacent soft tissue are resected.

Description of Procedure (27059)

Under anesthesia, an incision is made over the trapezius. Medial and lateral subcutaneous flaps are raised. The overlying skin from the biopsy is excised with the tumor. The musculature is exposed around the tumor. The fascia is incised, and part of it is included with the specimen in the dissection for proper margins. A radical excision of the adductor longus adductor brevis and a portion of the adductor magnus is performed. The tumor is removed en bloc, including necessary surrounding structures. As the tumor is lifted out of the wound, small lymphatics and feeding blood vessels are ligated. Frozen sections are taken from the surrounding tissue. The deep fascia is inspected for involvement by the tumor, as are the ribs and intercostal muscles. If deep margins are involved, then resection to the periosteum of the ribs and/or peritoneum is carried out. The surgeon then breaks scrub and carries the specimen to the pathology department while the anesthesiologist and other operative personnel remain with the patient. Prior to this, the surgeon assesses the stability of the operative field and discusses with the anesthesiologist the stability of the patient. In the pathology department, the surgeon examines the resected specimen with the attending pathologist and orients the pathologist to the specimen anatomy. The specimen is inked for margins, and any areas that are questionable are inspected by frozen section. If all margins appear satisfactory, the surgeon returns to the operating room, repeats preoperative scrub, and returns to the surgical field. Additional excision is carried out as necessary to obtain a clear margin. Metallic clips are placed to mark the margins for possible postoperative radiotherapy guidance. The wound is inspected and irrigated. The devitalized muscle is debrided. A deep drain is placed. The wound is closed in layers with interrupted sutures.

Clinical Example (27075)

A 40-year-old male presents with a chondrosarcoma of the left superior pubic ramus, involving the symphysis but sparing the acetabulum, and an associated soft tissue mass into the obturator foramen. At operation, a radical resection of the tumor is performed with the resection of the soft tissue mass and preservation of the limb.

Description of Procedure (27075)

A skin incision is made from the pubic symphysis over the inguinal ligament and over the superior bony rim of the pelvis going back posteriorly to the sacroiliac joint. A second incision is then made over the lateral aspect of the proximal femur extending proximally to the midlateral aspect of the first incision creating a large laterally based "T." This is carried down sharply through the skin and subcutaneous tissues, and hemostasis is obtained. The anterior portion of the incision is then taken down through the inguinal ligament from the pubic symphysis to the anterosuperior iliac spine. The femoral artery and vein are exposed and carefully dissected. Vessel loops are carefully placed around the femoral artery and vein in the pelvis so that proximal control can be maintained. The abdominal wall muscles are then dissected extraperiosteally from their insertion on the wing of the ileum. These muscles are retracted proximally. The lateral femoral cutaneous nerve is identified and protected. Dissection is then carried down over the iliacus muscle, which will be left with the resection specimen to form the medial wide margin. In the lower portion of the pelvis, the ureter is palpated, and this is facilitated by the previously placed ureteral stent. The ureter is carefully swept posteriorly, and the peritoneum in retracted away from the mass. Dissection is then carried through the iliacus muscle, but the psoas muscle is left intact. The femoral nerve is exposed within the anterior aspect of the psoas muscle and protected. Dissection is then carried posteriorly over the posterior aspect of the iliac wing back to the sacroiliac joint again staying extraperiosteal to keep away from the tumor. The tensor fascia lata, sartorius, and rectus femoris muscles originating from the anterior aspect of the pelvis are dissected. A lateral incision is made through the fascia lata and anterior and posterior flaps are fashioned. The gluteus maximus muscle is split in line with its fibers and the gluteus maximus is then separated from the underlying gluteus medius and minimus and is then retracted anteriorly and posteriorly. The gluteus medius is then separated from the underlying gluteus minimus, which is maintained with the specimen to serve as the lateral wide margin. This dissection is carried back to the sciatic notch, and the gluteal vessels and nerves to the medius and maximus are preserved while the branches to the minimus are sacrificed. The sciatic notch is then exposed from within the pelvis and from without. A large drain is then drawn through the sciatic notch to protect the underlying vessels and nerves. The sciatic nerve is then dissected inside and outside the pelvis so that it is visualized throughout this region. The posterior aspect of the ileum is then exposed followed by exposure of the sacral ala by dissection of the paraspinous muscles to expose the posterior aspect of the sacral ala. Final exposure of the planned areas for the bone cuts above the acetabulum and along the sacrum are performed. A pin is then placed through the supra-acetabular bone perpendicular to the long axis of the body with a second pin through the ala to outline the bone cuts and to make sure that the cuts will go through normal uninvolved bone to guarantee wide bone margins. With the portable X-ray obtained and showing the pins in good position, an oscillating saw is then used to make the bone cuts, which are completed with a curved periosteal elevator and a mallet so as not to damage the underlying nerves and vessels. Once these cuts are completed, the ileum can be mobilized by careful incision of the remaining soft tissue attachments. The specimen is then removed from the field and marked for anatomic orientation. (This is documented on the pathology request form along with appropriate history and needed information.) The surgeon then breaks scrub and carries the specimen to the pathology department while the anesthesiologist and other operative personnel remain with the patient. Prior to this, the surgeon assesses the stability of the operative field and discusses with the anesthesiologist the stability of the patient. In the pathology department, the surgeon examines the resected specimen with the attending pathologist and orients the pathologist to the specimen anatomy. The specimen is inked for margins, and any areas that are questionable are inspected by frozen section. If all margins appear satisfactory, the surgeon returns to the operating room, repeats preoperative scrub, and returns to the surgical field. Careful hemostasis is obtained. The wound is copiously irrigated. Two suction drains are left deep in the wound and brought out proximally. The gluteus medius and maximus are repaired to the abdominal wall muscles with nonabsorbable suture. The remaining soft tissue is repaired in layers with interrupted sutures and the skin with skin staples.

Clinical Example (27076)

A 60-year-old male presents with a malignant fibrous histiocytoma of the acetabulum and an associated soft tissue mass. At operation, a radical resection of the tumor with adjacent soft tissue is performed.

Description of Procedure (27076)

The incision starts at the medial aspect of the inguinal ligament and goes laterally over the proximal border of the pelvis and posteriorly to the sacroiliac joint, with a second arm of the incision coursing distally from the midlateral portion of the previous incision to a point 10 cm below the greater trochanter, ellipsing the biopsy tract in a wide en bloc fashion. The dissection is carried down through the subcutaneous fat maintaining a cuff of tissue surrounding the biopsy tract and tumor. The incision is carried down through the limiting fascia of the groin and pelvis to the fascia of the gluteus maximus and the inguinal ligament. The inguinal ligament is opened, and the femoral neurovascular bundle is exposed taking great care to protect these structures. The sartorius and tensor fascia lata muscles are incised extraperiosteally, and the anterior aspect of the pelvis is exposed keeping normal tissues between the tumor and the plane of dissection. The gluteus maximus muscle is then split along the lateral portion of the proximal thigh and this dissection is carried proximally so that this can be separated from the underlying gluteus medius. The gluteus maximus is then retracted posteriorly as its proximal origin is removed from the ileum. The gluteus medius and minimus are kept with the specimen to effect a wide margin laterally. The iliacus and psoas muscles are divided in the pelvis after first dissecting the femoral vessels in this region to effect a wide margin on the interior of the pelvis. Posteriorly, the sciatic nerve must be found and protected from undue tension or retractors. The abductor muscles are then divided from the greater trochanter, and the femur is internally rotated. The short external rotator muscles are then divided, and perforating vessels are ligated. The hip capsule is then dissected circumferentially and then incised keeping away from the pelvic origin, which is in close proximity to the tumor. The osteotomies of the posterior ileum, pubis, and ischium are carefully planned and scribed on the bony pelvis. The ligamentum teres is then incised. The osteotomies are then performed with an oscillating saw and completed with a cob and a mallet. Soft tissue attachments still connect the specimen to the underlying structures, and these are carefully divided. The hip is then dislocated, and the specimen is lifted gently out of the wound as the remaining soft tissue attachments are divided. The specimen is then removed from the field and marked for anatomic orientation. (This is documented on the pathology request form along with appropriate history and needed information.) The surgeon then breaks scrub and carries the specimen to the pathology department while the anesthesiologist and other operative personnel remain with the patient. Prior to this, the surgeon assesses the stability of the operative field and discusses with the anesthesiologist the stability of the patient. In the pathology department, the surgeon examines the resected specimen with the attending pathologist and orients the pathologist to the specimen anatomy. The specimen is inked for margins, and any areas that are questionable are inspected by frozen section. If all margins appear satisfactory, the surgeon returns to the operating room, repeats preoperative scrub, and returns to the surgical field. Hemostasis of the wound is secured. The remaining bone edges are rasped to a fine finish. Irrigation is performed. The gluteus maximus is repaired and reapproximated to itself. The fascia is closed over a drain. Subcutaneous tissues and skin are closed in the usual fashion.

Clinical Example (27077)

A 25-year-old women presents with an osteosarcoma of the acetabulum with extension to the ilium, ischium, and the superior pubic ramus to the symphysis. At operation, a radical resection of the entire hemipelvis is performed with preservation of the limb.

⊘=Modifier 51 Exempt   ⊙=Moderate Sedation   ✚=Add-on Code   ✗=FDA approval pending

Description of Procedure (27077)

A skin incision is made from the pubic symphysis over the inguinal ligament and over the superior bony rim of the pelvis going back posteriorly to the sacroiliac joint. A second incision is then made over the lateral aspect of the proximal femur extending proximally to the midlateral aspect of the first incision creating a large laterally based "T." This is carried down sharply through the skin and subcutaneous tissues, and hemostasis is obtained. The anterior portion of the incision is then taken down through the inguinal ligament from the pubic symphysis to the anterosuperior iliac spine. The femoral artery and vein are exposed and carefully dissected. Vessel loops are carefully placed around the femoral artery and vein in the pelvis so that proximal control can be maintained. The abdominal wall muscles are then dissected extraperiosteally from their insertion on the wing of the ileum. These muscles are retracted proximally. In the course of doing this, the lateral femoral cutaneous nerve is identified and protected. Dissection is then carried down over the iliacus muscle, which will be left with the resection specimen to form the medial wide margin. In the lower portion of the pelvis, the ureter is palpated, and this is facilitated by the previously placed ureteral stent. The ureter is carefully swept posteriorly, and the peritoneum in retracted away from the mass. Dissection is then carried through the iliacus and psoas muscles. The femoral nerve is exposed within the anterior aspect of the psoas muscle and protected. Dissection is then carried posteriorly over the posterior aspect of the iliac wing back to the sacroiliac joint. The muscles originating from the anterior aspect of the pelvis are then dissected extraperiosteally, and these include the tensor fascia lata, sartorius, and rectus femoris muscles. The lateral incision is then incised through the fascia lata, and anterior and posterior flaps are fashioned. The gluteus maximus muscle is split in line with its fibers, and the gluteus maximus is then separated from the underlying gluteus medius and minimus and is then retracted anteriorly and posteriorly. The gluteus medius is then separated from the underlying gluteus minimus, which is maintained with the specimen to serve as the lateral wide margin. This dissection is carried back to the sciatic notch, and the gluteal vessels and nerves to the medius and maximus are preserved while the branches to the minimus are sacrificed. The sciatic notch is then exposed from within the pelvis and from without. A large drain is then drawn through the sciatic notch to protect the underlying vessels and nerves. The sciatic nerve is then dissected inside and outside the pelvis so that it is visualized throughout this region. The posterior aspect of the ileum is then exposed followed by exposure of the sacral ala by dissection of the paraspinous muscles to expose the posterior aspect of the sacral ala. Dissection is then carried around the hip capsule circumferentially, and the anterior and posterior circumflex vessels are identified, ligated, and incised. The ligamentum teres is incised, and the hip joint is dislocated. The insertion of the iliopsoas muscle on the lesser is identified and incised. Dissection is then carried down the outside of the ischium detaching the origin of the hamstring muscles, being careful to remain in the extraperiosteal plane to keep away from the underlying tumor. Dissection is then carried over the pubis, and the femoral artery and vein are skeletonized in this area and carefully retracted anteriorly. The inner wall of the pubis is then dissected, and the pubis is separated from the bladder in the space of Retzius. The obturator vessels and nerves are visualized in the pelvis and ligated and incised. The origin of the adductor muscles is then dissected extraperiosteally, and the obturator vessels and nerves are identified, ligated, and incised in the adductor muscles outside the pelvis. A large drain is placed around the pubic symphysis to protect the bladder during subsequent bone cuts. Final exposure of the planned areas for the bone cuts, through the pubic symphysis and along the sacrum, is performed. An oscillating saw is then used to make the bone cuts, which are then completed with a curved periosteal elevator and a mallet so as not to damage the underlying nerves and vessels. Once these cuts are completed, the innominate bone can be mobilized by careful incision of the remaining soft tissue attachments. The specimen is then removed from the field and marked for anatomic orientation. (This is documented on the pathology request form along with appropriate history and needed information.) The surgeon then breaks scrub and carries the specimen to the pathology department while the anesthesiologist and other operative personnel remain with the patient. Prior to this, the surgeon assesses the stability of the operative field and discusses with the anesthesiologist the stability of the patient. In the pathology department, the surgeon examines the resected specimen with the attending pathologist and orients the pathologist to the specimen anatomy. The specimen is inked for margins, and any areas that are questionable are inspected by frozen section. If all margins appear satisfactory, the surgeon returns to the operating room, repeats preoperative scrub, and returns to the surgical field. Careful hemostasis is then obtained, and the wound is copiously irrigated. Two suction drains are then left deep in the wound and brought out proximally. The gluteus medius and maximus are repaired to the abdominal wall muscles with nonabsorbable suture. The remaining soft tissue is then repaired in layers with interrupted sutures and the skin with skin staples.

Clinical Example (27078)

A 52-year-old female presents with a malignant fibrous histiocytoma of the ischial tuberosity. At operation, a radical resection of the tumor with adjacent soft tissues is performed.

Description of Procedure (27078)

A longitudinal incision is made, ellipsing the biopsy tract in a wide en bloc fashion. The incision is made from the upper buttocks to the upper thigh, incorporating the biopsy tract. The dissection is carried down through the subcutaneous fat maintaining a cuff of tissue surrounding the biopsy tract and tumor. The incision is carried down through the limiting fascia of the buttocks to the fascia of the gluteus maximus. The fascia is opened, and the fibers of the muscles are split in order to gain exposure down to the ischium without having to transect the muscle bellies. Extreme care is required in order to prevent injury to the sciatic nerve. The sciatic nerve must be found and protected from undue tension or retractors. A tape is placed around the nerve, and it is gently reflected to one side. The hamstring origin is then approached and transected from the underlying bone. A portion of the muscle origin, however, must be maintained in continuity with the ischium in order to secure a clear margin around the tumor. An extraperiosteal dissection is then carried proximally along the ischium, toward the pubic rami, both superior and inferior to the edges of the tumor. Once the affected bone is completely dissected free from surrounding soft tissues, a

⊘=Modifier 51 Exempt   ⊙=Moderate Sedation   ✛=Add-on Code   ⊼ =FDA approval pending

subperiosteal dissection is performed circumferentially around either end of the bone beyond the area of the tumor involvement. A saw is then used to create the osteotomy at least 2 cm proximal to the tumor-laden ischium, and then another osteotomy is created distal to the tumor. Large amounts of remaining soft tissue are then dissected leaving normal tissue with the specimen. By completing the osteotomies, the specimen can be mobilized and ultimately freed from the surrounding tissues. The specimen is then removed from the field and marked for anatomic orientation. (This is documented on the pathology request form along with appropriate history and needed information.) The surgeon assesses the stability of the operative field and discusses with the anesthesiologist the stability of the patient. The surgeon then breaks scrub and carries the specimen to the pathology department while the anesthesiologist and other operative personnel remain with the patient. In the pathology department, the surgeon examines the resected specimen with the attending pathologist and orients the pathologist to the specimen anatomy. The specimen is inked for margins, and any areas that are questionable are inspected by frozen section. The remaining bone edges are rasped to a fine finish. Irrigation is performed. The gluteus maximus is repaired and reapproximated to itself. The fascia is closed over a drain. Subcutaneous tissues and skin are closed in the usual fashion.

Femur (Thigh Region) and Knee Joint

EXCISION

▲27327 Excision, tumor, soft tissue of thigh or knee area;, subcutaneous; less than 3 cm

#●27337 3 cm or greater

▲27328 Excision, tumor, soft tissue of thigh or knee area, subfascial (eg, intramuscular); less than 5 cm

#●27339 5 cm or greater

27329 ▶Code is out of numerical sequence. 27323-27365◀

27334 Arthrotomy, with synovectomy, knee; anterior OR posterior

27335 anterior AND posterior including popliteal area

27337 ▶Code is out of numerical sequence. 27323-27365◀

27339 ▶Code is out of numerical sequence. 27323-27365◀

27360 Partial excision (craterization, saucerization, or diaphysectomy) bone, femur, proximal tibia and/or fibula (eg, osteomyelitis or bone abscess)

#▲27329 Radical resection of tumor (eg, malignant neoplasm), soft tissue of thigh or knee area; less than 5 cm

●27364 5 cm or greater

▲27365 Radical resection of tumor, femur or knee

▶(For radical resection of tumor, soft tissue of thigh or knee area, see 27329, 27364)◀

✍️ Rationale

In the Femur (Thigh Region) and Knee Joint section, three reference notes have been added to direct the user to the appropriate code range (27323-27365) for placement of out-of-sequence codes 27337, 27339, and 27329. Codes 27337, 27339, and 27329 appear with a number symbol (#) to indicate that these codes appear out of numerical sequence. Code 27337 has been established to report excision of a subcutaneous soft tissue tumor of the thigh or knee area, 3 cm or greater. Code 27327 has been revised for standardization of the nomenclature to describe excision of a subcutaneous soft tissue tumor of the thigh or knee area, less than 3 cm.

Code 27339 has been established to report excision of a subfascial soft tissue tumor of the thigh or knee area, 5 cm or greater. Code 27328 has been revised for standardization of the nomenclature to describe excision of a subfascial soft tissue tumor of the thigh or knee area, less than 5 cm.

Code 27364 has been established to report radical resection of a soft tissue tumor of the thigh or knee area, 5 cm or greater. Code 27329 has been revised for standardization of the nomenclature to describe radical resection of a soft tissue tumor of the thigh and knee area, less than 5 cm.

In support of the changes to the Femur (Thigh Region) and Knee Joint section, code 27365 has been editorially revised. In addition, the parenthetical note following code 27365 has been revised to reflect the appropriate codes for radical resection of soft tissue tumor of the thigh or knee area, codes 27329 and 27364.

 Clinical Example (27327)

A 38-year-old woman undergoes excision of a 2-cm tumor in her lateral thigh.

Description of Procedure (27327)

Under anesthesia, a 4-cm incision is made in the skin and subcutaneous tissue over the tumor on the lateral thigh. Careful dissection is performed around the subcutaneous mass. The 2-cm mass is removed from the surrounding tissue. The tumor is handed off of the field. Hemostasis is obtained. The wound is inspected and irrigated. The wound is closed in layers with interrupted sutures.

 Clinical Example (27328)

A 39-year-old man undergoes excision of a 3.5-cm tumor posterior to the knee joint that is pigmented villonodular synovitis.

Description of Procedure (27328)

Under anesthesia, a 6-cm incision is made over the tumor on the posterior knee. The subcutaneous tissue is opened, and the fascia over the popliteal space is split. The tumor is identified between the semimembranosus and the medial head of the gastrocnemius muscles. The neurovascular bundle is retracted laterally. Dissection is carried around the mass, and the mass is released off of the muscles. The tumor is released from the posterior knee capsule. The tumor is handed off of the field. The wound is inspected and irrigated. The posterior capsule is repaired. A deep drain is placed. The fascia is carefully closed. The superficial wound is closed in layers with interrupted sutures.

Clinical Example (27329)

A 50-year-old male presents with a 3-cm deep malignant fibrous histiocytoma of the hamstring muscles of the midposterior thigh. At operation, the tumor and adjacent soft tissue are resected.

Description of Procedure (27329)

Under anesthesia, a 7-cm incision is made over the medial hamstrings. Medial and lateral subcutaneous flaps are made. Dissection is carried through the fascia into the semimembranosus muscle. The gracilis and semitendinosus are mobilized and retracted. The sciatic nerve is identified and protected. The semimembranosus muscle is dissected, and the tumor is removed en bloc, including necessary surrounding normal tissue. Frozen sections are taken from the surrounding tissue. The margins and tumor are sent to pathology. The pathology report is received, and additional excision is carried out as necessary to obtain a clear margin. Careful hemostasis is obtained. The wound is inspected and irrigated. The sciatic nerve is inspected. A deep drain is placed. The deep fascia is closed with interrupted sutures. The superficial wound is closed in layers with interrupted sutures.

Clinical Example (27337)

A 45-year-old female undergoes excision of a 5-cm tumor in her medial anterior thigh.

Description of Procedure (27337)

A sterile tourniquet is applied and inflated. Under anesthesia, a 7-cm incision is made in the skin and subcutaneous tissue over the anteromedial thigh. Medial and lateral flaps are raised, and careful dissection is performed around the 5-cm tumor. The tumor is removed. Hemostasis is obtained. The wound is inspected and irrigated. The wound is closed in layers with interrupted sutures.

Clinical Example (27339)

A 39-year-old male undergoes excision of a 10-cm tumor posterior to the knee joint that is pigmented villonodular synovitis.

Description of Procedure (27339)

A 13-cm incision curving across the posterior knee crease is performed. The subcutaneous flaps are raised, and the fascia is split. The cutaneous branches of the sural nerve in the midline of the calf are carefully protected. A large brownish mass is identified and dissected off the surrounding tissues. Because it is coming off the posterior knee joint, dissection is gradually carried down toward the knee. The semi-membranous tendon is retracted medially, and the mass indeed comes out lateral rather than medial to the medial head of the gastrocnemius muscle. The medial head of the gastrocnemius muscle is retracted, and then because the mass is lateral, care is taken to protect the innervation to the medial head of the gastrocnemius muscle as well as to the tibia nerve, popliteal artery, and popliteal vein. The mass is mobilized off the lateral head of the gastrocnemius muscle. It is also mobilized distally off the proximal end of the soleus. A small portion of proximal soleus is released to allow the tibia nerve and the popliteal vessels to be retracted. The popliteal vessels are retracted laterally along with the tibial nerve, exposing the posterior knee joint. The mass is taken down directly until it enters the posterior knee joint under the medial head of the gastrocnemius. The mass is removed. A deep drain is placed. The medial and lateral heads of the gastroc muscle along with the neurovascular bundle are allowed to fall back into place. Several small branches of the popliteal artery are ligated to expose this portion of the joint. The remainder of the fascia is left open to prevent compartment syndrome in the superficial posterior compartment. Absorbable sutures are used on the subcutaneous and interrupted nylons are used on the skin.

 ### Clinical Example (27364)
A 50-year-old male presents with an 8-cm deep malignant fibrous histiocytoma of the hamstring muscles of the midposterior thigh. At operation, the tumor and adjacent soft tissue are resected.

Description of Procedure (27364)
Under anesthesia, a 12-cm incision is made over the medial hamstrings. Medial and lateral subcutaneous flaps are made. Dissection is carried through the fascia into the semimembranosus muscle. The gracilis and semitendinosus are mobilized and retracted. The sciatic nerve is identified and protected. The semimembranosus muscle is dissected, and the large tumor is removed en bloc, including necessary surrounding normal tissue. Frozen sections are taken from the surrounding tissue. The margins and tumor are sent to pathology. The pathology report is received, and additional excision is carried out as necessary to obtain a clear margin. Careful hemostasis is obtained. The wound is inspected and irrigated. The sciatic nerve is inspected. A deep drain is placed. The deep fascia is closed with inter-rupted sutures. The superficial wound is closed in layers with interrupted sutures.

 ### Clinical Example (27365)
A 14-year-old female presents with an osteosarcoma of the distal femur. At opera-tion, a radical resection of the tumor with adjacent soft tissues is performed.

Description of Procedure (27365)
A longitudinal incision is made, ellipsing the biopsy tract in a wide en bloc fash-ion. The incision is made from the upper thigh, incorporating the biopsy tract, extending the incision to approximately 12 cm below the knee. The dissection is carried down through the subcutaneous fat maintaining a cuff of tissue surround-ing the biopsy tract and tumor. The incision is carried down through the limiting fascia of the thigh, extending down to the patella and along its side, then to the tibial tubercle. The tumor originated in the distal end of the femur but has an associated soft tissue mass that involves the quadriceps and hamstrings. The dis-section therefore proceeds through the quadriceps, once again maintaining a cuff of quadriceps muscle on the tumor to maintain a wide margin. The rectus femoris muscle is dissected from the underlying vastus intermedius followed by dissec-tion through a portion of the vastus lateralis and the vastus medialis. The vastus intermedius is maintained around the soft tissue component of the tumor. At the level of the knee, an arthrotomy is made, incising through the joint capsule at the level of the tibia to ensure a cuff of tissue being maintained around the tumor and distal femur. Dissection is carried farther toward the patellar tendon, along its length down to its insertion into the tibia. This allows for the mobilization of

⊘=Modifier 51 Exempt   ⊙=Moderate Sedation   ✚=Add-on Code   ✗=FDA approval pending

the patella. The patella is everted, thus exposing the joint. The anterior cruciate ligament is identified and divided. The posterior cruciate ligament is divided followed by subluxation of the knee forward in order to bring the menisci into view. Both the lateral collateral ligament and the medial collateral ligament are identified and divided, followed by total meniscectomy of both the medial and lateral menisci. The remaining capsular structures are then transected, being very careful of the neurovascular structures (eg, artery, vein, and both tibial and peroneal nerves), which lie intimately in contact with the back of the knee joint. The femur is elevated forward to allow for exposure of the back of the thigh. The neurovascular structures are identified and carefully dissected one by one off of the overlying femur. The sheath must be opened in order to be able to dissect the vein, nerve, and artery in a sub-adventitial fashion from the tumor. The hamstring muscles are carefully divided from the now-overlying soft tissue component of the tumor and femur. Each hamstring muscle is individually divided by dissection from the overlying mass. This allows for completion of the dissection of the artery, then vein, then both peroneal and tibial components of the sciatic nerve from the remaining muscles and tumor, is performed. Care is taken to ligate each feeding vessel into the tumor and femur as it is approached as the tumor does often have neovascularity. The dissection is carried proximally in this fashion until the level of the proposed osteotomy dictated by the preoperative planning. At this point (18 cm above the knee), the dissection is carried circumferentially around the entire femur. The periosteum is elevated from the femur 2 cm proximal to the proposed cut in the bone to allow for later overlap of the periosteum over the prosthesis. The bone is marked with a saw blade to demonstrate orientation once the prosthesis is inserted. The bone is then cut with a saw and the remaining soft tissues are dissected free from the specimen. The specimen consists of the skin of the biopsy tract, the underlying subcutaneous fat, fascia, muscle, tumor, bone, ligaments, tendons, and capsular structures, all in one piece. The specimen is then removed from the field and marked for anatomic orientation. (This is documented on the pathology request form along with appropriate history and needed information.) The surgeon then breaks scrub and carries the specimen to the pathology department while the anesthesiologist and other operative personnel remain with the patient. Prior to this, the surgeon assesses the stability of the operative field and discusses with the anesthesiologist the stability of the patient. In the pathology department, the surgeon examines the resected specimen with the attending pathologist and orients the pathologist to the specimen anatomy. The specimen is inked for margins, and any areas that are questionable are inspected by frozen section. If all margins appear satisfactory, the surgeon returns to the operating room, repeats preoperative scrub, and returns to the surgical field. The wound bed is inspected, bleeding vessels are taken care of, and the neurovascular structures are reevaluated to ensure they are intact. During the remainder of the procedure, these structures must be protected from stretch, twisting, and retraction, as there is now no bone to provide structure of this limb. The fascial layers are closed in a watertight fashion over a large bore drain, followed by closure of the subcutaneous tissues and skin.

Leg (Tibia and Fibula) and Ankle Joint

EXCISION

▲27615   Radical resection of tumor (eg, malignant neoplasm), soft tissue of leg or ankle area; less than 5 cm

●27616   5 cm or greater

▲27618   Excision, tumor, soft tissue of leg or ankle area, subcutaneous; less than 3 cm

#●27632   3 cm or greater

▲27619   Excision, tumor, soft tissue of leg or ankle area, subfascial (eg, intramuscular); less than 5 cm

#●27634   5 cm or greater

27632   ▶Code is out of numerical sequence. See 27613-27647◀

27634   ▶Code is out of numerical sequence. See 27613-27647◀

▲27640   Partial excision (craterization, saucerization, or diaphysectomy), bone (eg, osteomyelitis); tibia

        ▶(For exostosis excision, use 27635)◀

▲27641   fibula

        ▶(For exostosis excision, use 27635)◀

▲27645   Radical resection of tumor, tibia

▲27646   fibula

▲27647   talus or calcaneus

✍ Rationale

In the Leg (Tibia and Fibula) and Ankle Joint section, two reference notes have been added to direct the user to the appropriate code range (27613-27647) for placement of out-of-sequence codes 27632 and 27634. Codes 27632 and 27634 appear with a number symbol (#) to indicate that these codes appear out of numerical sequence. Code 27616 has been established to report radical resection of a soft tissue tumor of the leg or ankle area, 5 cm or greater. Code 27615 has been revised for standardization of the nomenclature to describe radical resection of a soft tissue tumor of a leg or ankle area, less than 5 cm.

Code 27632 has been established to report excision of a subcutaneous soft tissue tumor of the leg or ankle area, 3 cm or greater. Code 27618 has been revised for standardization of the nomenclature to describe excision of a subcutaneous soft tissue tumor of the leg or ankle area, less than 3 cm.

Code 27634 has been established to report excision of a subfascial soft tissue tumor of the leg or ankle area, 5 cm or greater. Code 27619 has been revised for standardization of the nomenclature to describe excision of a subfascial soft tissue tumor of the leg or ankle area, less than 5 cm.

In support of the changes to the Leg (Tibia and Fibula) and Ankle Joint section, codes 27640, 27641, 27645, 27646, and 27647 have been editorially revised. Codes

27640 and 27641 have been revised with the deletion of the verbiage "or exosto-sis," and codes 27645, 27646, and 27647 have been revised with the removal of the verbiage "bone." Two cross-references have been added following codes 27640 and 27641 to direct the user to code 27635 for exostosis excision services.

Clinical Example (27615)

A 45-year-old male presents with a 3.5-cm deep fibrosarcoma of the soleus muscle of the superficial posterior compartment of the calf. At operation, the tumor and adjacent soft tissue are excised.

Description of Procedure (27615)

Under anesthesia, an 8-cm posterior longitudinal incision is made around the previous biopsy track to keep this en bloc with the specimen. Dissection is then carried through the skin and subcutaneous tissues angling away from the biopsy track to avoid entering tissues contaminated by the initial biopsy. The deep fas-cia is then incised longitudinally and again includes an ellipse around the biopsy track. Dissection is then carried in medial and lateral directions to form appropri-ate flaps and facilitate deep dissection. Perforating vessels are encountered and are ligated and incised. Proximally, the femoral vessels are identified and dissection is carried adjacent to these structures to establish a plane of dissection. Several perforating branches leading to the tumor are ligated and incised. In the proxi-mal portion of the surgical field, the involved calf muscles are exposed above the proximal extent of the tumor. Incision is carried across these structures to estab-lish a proximal margin well beyond tumor extension. At this point the posterior tibial nerve and vascular bundle are identified. Several motor branches are seen to run into the tumor and cannot be preserved, so these branches are individually ligated and incised. Other motor branches are noted to bypass the tissues involved in the tumor, and these are protected and preserved. Dissection is then carried along the medial and lateral aspects of the tumor, keeping normal tissue between the tumor and the plane of dissection. Preoperative imaging studies are reviewed during the procedure to verify intended planes of dissection and proximity to neurovascular structures. Once the tumor has been dissected laterally, medial dis-section is started, and the tumor and surrounding tissues are gently lifted from the wound from proximal to distal. Further dissection is carried distally until the cir-cumferential dissection is beyond the distal extent of the tumor. At this point, the involved calf muscles are transected 2 cm from the farthest extent of the tumor as determined by imaging studies and clinical impression. The specimen is then removed from the field and marked for anatomic orientation. (This is documented on the pathology request form along with appropriate history and needed informa-tion.) The surgeon assesses the stability of the operative field and discusses with the anesthesiologist the stability of the patient. The surgeon then breaks scrub and carries the specimen to pathology while the anesthesiologist and other opera-tive personnel remain with the patient. In the pathology department, the surgeon examines the resected specimen with the attending pathologist and orients the pathologist to the specimen anatomy. The specimen is inked for margins, and any areas that are questionable are inspected by frozen section. If all margins appear satisfactory, the surgeon returns to the operating room, repeats preoperative scrub, and returns to the surgical field. The wound is inspected and irrigated. A deep drain is placed. The wound is closed in layers with interrupted sutures. Careful monitoring of blood loss during the procedure is necessary with appropriate blood and fluid replacement.

 Clinical Example (27616)

A 45-year-old male presents with a 7.5-cm fibrosarcoma of the muscles of the posterior compartment of the calf. At operation, the tumor and adjacent soft tissue are excised.

Description of Procedure (27616)

Under anesthesia, a posterior longitudinal incision is made from the popliteal crease to about 10 cm above the ankle including an elliptical incision around the previous biopsy track to keep this en bloc with the specimen. Dissection is then carried through the skin and subcutaneous tissues angling away from the biopsy track to avoid entering tissues contaminated by the initial biopsy. The deep fascia is then incised longitudinally and again includes an ellipse around the biopsy track. Dissection is then carried in medial and lateral directions to form appropriate flaps and facilitate deep dissection. Perforating vessels are encountered and are ligated and incised. Proximally, the femoral vessels are identified, and dissection is carried adjacent to these structures to establish a plane of dissection. Several perforating branches leading to the tumor are ligated and incised. In the proximal portion of the surgical field, the involved calf muscles are exposed above the proximal extent of the tumor. Incision is carried across these structures to establish a proximal margin well beyond tumor extension. At this point the posterior tibial nerve and vascular bundle are identified. Several motor branches are seen to run into the tumor and cannot be preserved so these branches are individually ligated and incised. Other motor branches are noted to bypass the tissues involved in the tumor, and these are protected and preserved. Dissection is then carried along the medial and lateral aspects of the tumor keeping normal tissue between the tumor and the plane of dissection. Preoperative imaging studies are reviewed during the procedure to verify intended planes of dissection and proximity to neurovascular structures. Once the tumor has been dissected laterally, medial dissection is started, and the tumor and surrounding tissues are gently lifted from the wound from proximal to distal. Dissection is carried distally until the circumferential dissection is beyond the distal extent of the tumor. At this point, the involved calf muscles are transected 2 cm from the farthest extent of the tumor as determined by imaging studies and clinical impression. The specimen is then removed from the field and marked for anatomic orientation. (This is documented on the pathology request form along with appropriate history and needed information.) The surgeon then breaks scrub and carries the specimen to the pathology department while the anesthesiologist and other operative personnel remain with the patient. Prior to this, the surgeon assesses the stability of the operative field and discusses with the anesthesiologist the stability of the patient. In the pathology department, the surgeon examines the resected specimen with the attending pathologist and orients the pathologist to the specimen anatomy. The specimen is inked for margins, and any areas that are questionable are inspected by frozen section. If all margins appear satisfactory, the surgeon returns to the operating room, repeats preoperative scrub, and returns to the surgical field. The wound is inspected and

⊘=Modifier 51 Exempt   ⊙=Moderate Sedation   ✚=Add-on Code   ✗=FDA approval pending

irrigated. A deep drain is placed. The wound is closed in layers with interrupted sutures. Careful monitoring of blood loss during the procedure is necessary with appropriate blood and fluid replacement.

 Clinical Example (27618)

A 36-year-old undergoes excision of 2-cm tumor in her left lateral lower leg.

Description of Procedure (27618)

Under anesthesia, a 4-cm incision is made in the skin and subcutaneous tissue over the tumor on the leg. Careful dissection around the tumor is performed. The tumor is excised en bloc. The wound is inspected and irrigated. The tourniquet is deflated and any bleeders are cauterized. The wound is closed in layers with interrupted sutures.

 Clinical Example (27619)

A 71-year-old female undergoes excision of a 3.5-cm lipoma on the interosseous membrane deep to the anterior and lateral compartments of the leg.

Description of Procedure (27619)

Under anesthesia, a 7-cm skin incision is made just anterior to the fibula. The subcutaneous tissue and the fascia are split. The muscles of the anterior compartment of the leg are identified and are retracted anteriorly off of the interosseus membrane. Any perforating vessels are ligated and tied. The tumor is carefully dissected off the interosseus membrane protecting the deep structures of the leg. The tumor is sent to pathology. The wound is irrigated and inspected. The fascia is left open to prevent compartment syndrome. A drain is placed. The tourniquet is deflated and any bleeders are cauterized. The wound is closed in layers with interrupted sutures.

 Clinical Example (27632)

A 40-year-old male undergoes excision of a 3.5-cm tumor in the medial calf.

Description of Procedure (27632)

Under anesthesia, a 6-cm incision is made in the skin and subcutaneous tissue over the tumor on the leg. Careful dissection around the tumor is performed. The tumor is excised en bloc. The wound is inspected and irrigated. The tourniquet is deflated and any bleeders are cauterized. The wound is closed in layers with interrupted sutures.

Clinical Example (27634)

A 71-year-old female undergoes excision of a 7.5-cm lipoma on the interosseous membrane deep to the anterior and lateral compartments of the leg.

Description of Procedure (27634)

Under anesthesia, a 10-cm skin incision is made just anterior to the fibula. The subcutaneous tissue is split, and the fascia is split. The muscles of the anterior compartment of the leg are identified and are retracted anteriorly off of the interosseus membrane. The tumor is carefully dissected off the interosseus membrane protecting the deep structures of the leg. Any perforating vessels are ligated and tied. The tumor is sent to pathology. The wound is irrigated and inspected. The fascia is left open to prevent compartment syndrome. A drain is placed. The tourniquet is deflated and any bleeders are cauterized. The wound is closed in layers with interrupted sutures.

Clinical Example (27645)

A 15-year-old female presents with a Ewing's sarcoma of the proximal tibia. At operation, a radical resection of the tumor with adjacent soft tissues is performed.

Description of Procedure (27645)

A longitudinal incision is made, ellipsing the biopsy tract in a wide en bloc fashion. The incision is made from the lower thigh, incorporating the biopsy tract, extending the incision to approximately 4 inches above the ankle. The dissection is carried down through the subcutaneous fat maintaining a cuff of tissue surrounding the biopsy tract and tumor. The incision is carried down through the limiting fascia of the leg, extending down to the patella and along its side, then toward the tibial tubercle. The dissection is then carried farther down the leg to nearly the ankle. The tumor originated in the proximal end of the tibia but has an associated soft tissue mass that involves the anterior and posterior musculature of the entire leg. The dissection therefore then proceeds through the tibialis anterior and the extensors of the foot and ankle, then laterally through the peroneal muscles, maintaining a cuff of normal tissue on the tumor to maintain wide margins around the tumor. The tibialis anterior, extensors, and peroneals are dissected from the underlying musculature overlying the bone itself. All neurovascular structures are meticulously dissected free from the overlying tumor. At the level of the knee, an arthrotomy is made, incising through the joint capsule at the level of the femur to ensure a cuff of tissue being maintained around the tumor and proximal tibia. Dissection is carried farther toward the patellar tendon, along its length up to its origin on the patella. (This allows for the mobilization of the patella.) The patella tendon is transected from the tibial tubercle. The patella is everted, thus exposing the joint. The anterior cruciate ligament is identified and divided. The posterior cruciate ligament is divided followed by subluxation of the knee forward in order to bring the menisci into view. Both the lateral collateral ligament is identified and divided as well as the medial collateral ligament followed by total meniscectomy of both the medial and lateral menisci. The remaining capsular structures are then transected, being careful of the neurovascular structures (eg, artery, vein, and both tibial and peroneal nerves) that lie intimately in contact with the back of the knee joint. The tibia is elevated forward to allow for exposure of the back of the leg. The gastrocnemius and soleus muscles are carefully divided from the now-overlying soft tissue component of the tumor and tibia. Dissection of first the artery, then vein, then both peroneal and tibial components of the sciatic nerve from the remaining muscles and tumor is performed. Care is taken to ligate each feeding vessel into the tumor and femur as it is approached as the tumor does often have neovascularity. The dissection is carried distally in this fashion until the level of the proposed osteotomy dictated by the preoperative planning. At this point (16 cm below the knee), the dissection is carried circumferentially around the entire tibia. The periosteum is elevated from the tibia 1 to 2 cm distal from the proposed cut in the bone to allow for later overlap of the periosteum over the prosthesis. The bone is marked with a saw blade to demonstrate orientation for later reconstruction. The bone is then cut with a saw, and the remaining soft tissues are dissected free from the specimen. The specimen consists of the skin of the biopsy tract, the underlying subcutaneous fat, fascia, muscle, tumor, bone, ligaments, tendons, and capsular structures, all in one piece, without any contamination of the tumor from prior surgery. The specimen is then removed from the field and marked for anatomic orientation. (This is documented on the pathology request form along with appropriate history and needed information.) The surgeon then breaks scrub and carries the specimen to the pathology department while the anesthesiologist and other operative personnel remain with the patient. Prior to this, the surgeon assesses the stability of the operative field and discusses with the anesthesiologist the stability of the patient. In the pathology department, the surgeon examines the resected specimen with the attending pathologist and orients the pathologist to the specimen anatomy. The specimen is inked for margins, and any areas that are questionable are inspected by frozen section. If all margins appear satisfactory, the surgeon returns to the operating room, repeats preoperative scrub, and returns to the surgical field. The wound bed is inspected, bleeding vessels are ligated, and the neurovascular structures are reevaluated to ensure they are intact. During the remainder of the procedure, these structures must be protected from stretch, twisting, and retraction, as there is now no bone to provide structure of this limb. Muscles are mobilized in order to provide coverage for the closure. The remaining gastrocnemius, tibials, and peroneals are mobilized by dissecting them free from their fascial boundaries and brought together to provide a good wound bed. Muscles are sutured to each other followed by closure of fascia over a drain, then skin closure.

Clinical Example (27646)

A 65-year-old female presents with a malignant fibrous histiocytoma of the fibula. At operation, a radical resection of the tumor with adjacent soft tissues is performed.

Description of Procedure (27646)

A longitudinal incision is made, ellipsing the biopsy tract in a wide en bloc fashion. The incision is made from the distal thigh, incorporating the biopsy tract, extending the incision to approximately 10 cm above the ankle. The dissection is carried down through the subcutaneous fat maintaining a cuff of tissue surrounding the biopsy tract and tumor. The incision is carried down through the limiting fascia of the leg, extending down from the lateral distal thigh to the ankle. The tumor is associated with a large soft tissue mass that involves the anterior and posterior musculature of the leg. The dissection therefore proceeds through the peroneal longus and brevis muscles, and the extensor muscles of the foot and ankle, maintaining a cuff of normal muscle on the tumor to affect a wide margin. The muscle bellies are dissected from the underlying musculature overlying the bone itself. All neurovascular structures are meticulously dissected free from the overlying tumor. At the level of the knee, an arthrotomy is made through the capsule of the tibio-fibular joint in order to mobilize the fibula. Care is necessary, as the anterior tibial vessels course directly in the path and must be dissected free and preserved. The lateral collateral ligament must be divided for resection of the fibula. The gastrocnemius and soleus muscles are carefully divided from the overlying soft tissue component of the tumor and tibia. Dissection of the popliteal artery and vein and tibial and peroneal nerves from the remaining muscles and tumor is performed. Care is taken to ligate each feeding vessel into the tumor. The dissection is carried distally in this fashion until the level of the proposed osteotomy dictated by the preoperative planning. At this point, 18 cm below the knee, the dissection is carried circumferentially around the entire fibula. The bone is then cut with a saw and the remaining soft tissues are dissected free from the specimen. The specimen, all in one piece, consists of the skin of the biopsy tract and the underlying subcutaneous fat, fascia, muscle, tumor, bone, ligaments, tendons, and capsular structures. The specimen is then removed from the field and marked for anatomic orientation. (This is documented on the pathology request form along with appropriate history and needed information.) The surgeon breaks scrub and carries the specimen to the pathology department while the anesthesiologist and other operative personnel remain with the patient. Prior to this, the surgeon assesses the stability of the operative field and discusses with the anesthesiologist the stability of the patient. In the pathology department, the surgeon examines the resected specimen with the attending pathologist and orients the pathologist to the specimen anatomy. The specimen is inked for margins, and any areas that are questionable are inspected by frozen section. If all margins appear satisfactory, the surgeon returns to the operating room, repeats preoperative scrub, and returns to the surgical field. The wound bed is inspected, bleeding vessels are taken care of, and the neurovascular structures are reevaluated to ensure they are intact. During the remainder of the procedure, these structures must be protected from stretch, twisting, and retraction, as there is now no bone to provide structure of this limb and the nerve could inadvertently be stretched. The fascial layers are closed in a watertight fashion over a drain, followed by closure of the subcutaneous tissues and skin.

Clinical Example (27647)

A 14-year-old female presents with a Ewing's sarcoma of the calcaneus. At operation, a radical resection of the calcaneus is performed.

Description of Procedure (27647)

A longitudinal incision is made, ellipsing the biopsy tract in a wide en bloc fashion. The incision is made from the distal leg, incorporating the biopsy tract, extending the incision to the midfoot in a hockey stick configuration. The dissection is carried down through the subcutaneous fat maintaining a cuff of tissue surrounding the biopsy tract and tumor. The incision is carried down through the limiting fascia of the foot and ankle, extending down from the distal leg to the midfoot. The tumor is associated with a soft tissue mass that involves the medial and lateral compartments at the ankle. The dissection proceeds, and flaps are created to allow for later reconstruction. Due to the soft tissue component of the tumor, this requires intraoperative modification of flaps in order to ensure that the wound will be able to be closed and that the skin flaps will survive. A cuff of normal muscle is maintained on the tumor to insure a wide margin. The muscle bellies are dissected from the underlying musculature. All neurovascular structures are meticulously dissected free from the overlying tumor. At the level of the articular surface, an arthrotomy is made through the capsule of the ankle joint in order to mobilize the calcaneus. (Care is necessary, as the dorsal vessels course directly in the path and must be dissected free and preserved.) The collateral ligament must be divided for resection of the bone. Care is taken to ligate each feeding vessel into the tumor. The dissection is carried distally in this fashion until the level of the proposed resection dictated by the preoperative planning. At this point, typically, the dissection is carried circumferentially around the entire bone. The remaining soft tissues are dissected free from the specimen. The specimen consists of the skin of the biopsy tract and the underlying subcutaneous fat, fascia, muscle, tumor, bone, ligaments, tendons, and capsular structures, all in one piece, without any contamination from tumor from prior surgery. The specimen is then removed from the field and marked for anatomic orientation. (This is documented on the pathology request form along with appropriate history and needed information.) The surgeon breaks scrub and carries the specimen to the pathology department while the anesthesiologist and other operative personnel remain with the patient. Prior to this, the surgeon assesses the stability of the operative field and discusses with the anesthesiologist the stability of the patient. In the pathology department, the surgeon examines the resected specimen with the attending pathologist and orients the pathologist to the specimen anatomy. The specimen is then inked for margins, and any areas that are questionable are inspected by frozen section. If all margins appear satisfactory, the surgeon returns to the operating room, repeats preoperative scrub, and returns to the surgical field. The wound bed is inspected, bleeding vessels are taken care of, and the neurovascular structures are reevaluated to ensure they are intact. During the remainder of the procedure, these structures must be protected from stretch, twisting, and retraction, as there is now no bone to provide structure of this limb and the nerve could inadvertently be stretched. The remaining muscles are rotated to fill in the void left by the resection. All muscle flaps are sutured in place to ensure that the prosthesis is completely covered. The fascial layers are closed in a watertight fashion followed by closure of the subcutaneous tissues and skin.

Foot and Toes

EXCISION

28039	▶Code is out of numerical sequence. See 28043-28175◀
28041	▶Code is out of numerical sequence. See 28043-28175◀
▲**28043**	Excision, tumor, soft tissue of foot or toe, subcutaneous tissue; less than 1.5 cm
#●**28039**	1.5 cm or greater
▲**28045**	Excision, tumor, soft tissue of foot or toe, subfascial (eg, intramuscular); less than 1.5 cm
#●**28041**	1.5 cm or greater
▲**28046**	Radical resection of tumor (eg, malignant neoplasm), soft tissue of foot or toe; less than 3 cm
●**28047**	3 cm or greater

▲**28171**   Radical resection of tumor; tarsal (except talus or calcaneus)

▲**28173**   metatarsal

▲**28175**   phalanx of toe

Rationale

In the Foot and Toes section, two reference notes have been added to direct the user to the appropriate code range (28043-28175) for placement of out-of-sequence codes 28039 and 28041. Codes 28039 and 28041 appear with a number symbol (#) to indicate that these codes appear out of numerical sequence. Code 28039 has been established to report excision of a subcutaneous soft tissue tumor of the foot or toe area, 1.5 cm or greater. Code 28043 has been revised for standardization of the nomenclature to describe excision of a subcutaneous soft tissue tumor of the foot or toe area, less than 1.5 cm.

Code 28041 has been established to report excision of a subfascial soft tissue tumor of the foot or toe area, 1.5 cm or greater. Code 28045 has been revised for standardization of the nomenclature to describe excision of a subfascial soft tissue tumor of the foot or toe area, less than 1.5 cm.

Code 28047 has been established to report radical resection of a soft tissue tumor of the foot or toes, 3 cm or greater. Code 28046 has been revised for standardization of the nomenclature to describe radical resection of a soft tissue tumor of the foot or toe area, less than 3 cm.

In support of the changes to the Foot and Toes section, codes 28171, 28173, and 28175 have been editorially revised.

Clinical Example (28039)

A 60-year-old female undergoes excision of a 2.0-cm fibrous tumor in the subcutaneous tissue of the right foot.

Description of Procedure (28039)

An incision is made on the plantar aspect of the first intermetatarsal space. Dissection is carried out to reveal a fibrous lesion. The lesion is dissected from surrounding tissue, and all bleeders are cauterized. The lesion is delivered from the wound. The wound site is irrigated and inspected. The wound is closed in layers with simple interrupted sutures, and the skin is coapted with a running mattress of nylon. The tourniquet is deflated, and normal capillary return is seen in the toes.

Clinical Example (28041)

A 62-year-old male undergoes excision of a 5-cm hemangioma in the deep plantar space of the foot.

Description of Procedure (28041)

A curvilinear incision is made on the sole of the foot. The subcutaneous tissue is incised, and the plantar fascia is split. The lateral plantar nerve and artery are identified in the wound as they come through the medial side of the foot. The aponeurosis of the plantar fascia is also identified and is split along the medial side to allow access to the sole of the foot. The flexor digitorum brevis muscle is

⊘=Modifier 51 Exempt   ⊙=Moderate Sedation   ✚=Add-on Code   ✔=FDA approval pending

retracted laterally, and a portion of it is released off the anterior calcaneus. (This allows clear exposure of the lateral plantar nerve and artery and the medial plantar nerve and artery.) The mass is just between the two nerves and is noted to be wrapping around the interval at the medial side of the quadratus plantae muscle. The flexor digitorum longus tendon is mobilized off the quadratus plantae and retracted medially. The quadratus plantae muscle is retracted laterally, and the mass is exposed. Careful resection is performed to remove the mass from the space in one piece. The flexor hallucis tendon is mobilized medially. The tumor is dissected off the abductor hallucis muscle. Once it is removed, the flexor digitorum and the quadratus plantae muscle are allowed to fall back into position. Both the medial plantar artery and nerve and the lateral plantar artery and nerve are inspected. The flexor digitorum brevis muscle is allowed to fall back into position, and several absorbable sutures are put into the base where it has been released partially off the calcaneus. The plantar aponeurosis is left to fall back into place. Any branches of the medial plantar artery that perforated the septum are ligated. The fascia is closed with interrupted suture. The subcutaneous wound is closed with absorbable suture. Nylon is used in the curvilinear incision on the sole of the foot.

Clinical Example (28043)

A 60-year-old female undergoes excision of a 1.2-cm fibrous tumor in the subcutaneous tissue of the right foot.

Description of Procedure (28043)

An incision is made on the plantar aspect of the first intermetatarsal space. Dissection is carried out to reveal the fibrous lesion. The tumor is dissected from surrounding tissue and all bleeders are cauterized. The lesion is delivered from the wound. The wound is irrigated, inspected, and closed in layers with interrupted sutures. The skin is coapted with a running mattress of nylon. The tourniquet is deflated, and normal capillary return is seen in the toes.

Clinical Example (28045)

A 62-year-old male undergoes excision of a 1.2-cm hemangioma in the deep plantar space of the foot.

Description of Procedure (28045)

An incision is made on the plantar aspect of the right arch. Dissection is carried out to reveal a 1.2-cm diameter purplish lesion. The tumor is dissected from the surrounding tissue, and all bleeders are cauterized. The lesion is delivered from the wound. The wound site is irrigated and inspected. The wound is closed in layers with simple interrupted sutures, and the skin is coapted with a running mattress of nylon. The tourniquet is deflated, and normal capillary return is seen in the toes.

Clinical Example (28046)

A 25-year-old male presents with a 2-cm fibrosarcoma growing in the deep plantar space. At operation, the tumor and adjacent soft tissue are resected.

Description of Procedure (28046)

An elliptical incision is made on the sole of the foot around the previous biopsy track to keep this en bloc with the specimen. Dissection is then carried through the skin and subcutaneous tissues, angling away from the biopsy track to avoid entering tissues contaminated by the initial biopsy. The deep fascia is then incised longitudinally and includes an ellipse around the biopsy track. Dissection is then carried in medial and lateral directions to form appropriate flaps and facilitate deep dissection. The lateral plantar nerve and artery are identified in the wound, as they come through the medial side of the foot. They are carefully dissected and separated from the adjacent tumor and intended plane of dissection. In the proximal portion of the surgical field, the involved muscles are exposed above the proximal extent of the tumor. Dissection is then carried along the medial and lateral aspects of the tumor, keeping normal tissue between the tumor and the plane of dissection. Preoperative imaging studies are reviewed during the procedure to verify intended planes of dissection and proximity to neurovascular structures. Once the tumor has been dissected laterally, medial dissection is started, and the tumor and surrounding tissues are gently lifted from the wound from proximal to distal. Further dissection is carried distally until the circumferential dissection is beyond the distal extent of the tumor. At this point, the involved intrinsic foot muscles are transected 2 cm from the farthest extent of the tumor as determined by imaging studies and clinical impression. The specimen is then removed from the field and marked for anatomic orientation. (This is documented on the pathology request form along with appropriate history and needed information.) The surgeon then breaks scrub and carries the specimen to the pathology department while the anesthesiologist and other operative personnel remain with the patient. Prior to this, the surgeon assesses the stability of the operative field and discusses with the anesthesiologist the stability of the patient. In the pathology department, the surgeon examines the resected specimen with the attending pathologist and orients the pathologist to the specimen anatomy. The specimen is inked for margins, and any areas that are questionable are inspected by frozen section. If all margins appear satisfactory, the surgeon returns to the operating room, repeats preoperative scrub, and returns to the surgical field. The wound is inspected and irrigated. A deep drain is placed. The wound is closed in layers with interrupted sutures.

 Clinical Example (28047)

A 25-year-old male presents with a 6-cm synovial sarcoma in the deep plantar space of the foot. At operation, the tumor and adjacent soft tissue are resected.

Description of Procedure (28047)

An elliptical incision is made on the sole of the foot around the previous biopsy track to keep this en bloc with the specimen. Dissection is then carried through the skin and subcutaneous tissues angling away from the biopsy track to avoid entering tissues contaminated by the initial biopsy. The deep fascia is then incised longitudinally and again includes an ellipse around the biopsy track. Dissection is then carried in medial and lateral directions to form appropriate flaps and facilitate deep dissection. The lateral plantar nerve and artery are identified in the wound, as they come through the medial side of the foot. They are carefully dissected and separated from the adjacent tumor and intended plane of dissection. In the proximal portion of the surgical field, the involved muscles are exposed above the proximal extent of the tumor. Dissection is then carried along the

⊘=Modifier 51 Exempt ⊙=Moderate Sedation ✚=Add-on Code ✗=FDA approval pending

medial and lateral aspects of the tumor, keeping normal tissue between the tumor and the plane of dissection. Preoperative imaging studies are reviewed during the procedure to verify intended planes of dissection and proximity to neurovascular structures. Once the tumor has been dissected laterally, medial dissection is started, and the tumor and surrounding tissues are gently lifted from the wound from proximal to distal. Further perforating vessels are ligated and incised. Further dissection is carried distally until the circumferential dissection is beyond the distal extent of the tumor. At this point, the involved intrinsic foot muscles are transected 6 cm from the farthest extent of the tumor as determined by imaging studies and clinical impression. The specimen is then removed from the field and marked for anatomic orientation. (This is documented on the pathology request form along with appropriate history and needed information.) The surgeon then breaks scrub and carries the specimen to the pathology department while the anesthesiologist and other operative personnel remain with the patient. Prior to this, the surgeon assesses the stability of the operative field and discusses with the anesthesiologist the stability of the patient. In the pathology department, the surgeon examines the resected specimen with the attending pathologist and orients the pathologist to the specimen anatomy. The specimen is inked for margins, and any areas that are questionable are inspected by frozen section. If all margins appear satisfactory, the surgeon returns to the operating room, repeats preoperative scrub, and returns to the surgical field. The wound is inspected and irrigated. A deep drain is placed. The wound is closed in layers with interrupted sutures.

Clinical Example (28171)

A 30-year-old male presents with a giant cell tumor with complete destruction of the cuboid bone and a soft tissue mass. A radical resection of the tumor is performed with excision of the cuboid and the soft tissue mass with preservation of the foot.

Description of Procedure (28171)

A 6-cm incision is made over the lateral aspect of the foot over the distal calcaneus and cuboid bones. Subcutaneous flaps are raised. The deep fascia is split, and the cuboid and its soft tissue mass are exposed. The calcaneocuboid joint is exposed. The cuboid-metatarsal joints are exposed. The peroneal tendons are retracted out of the way. The distal sural nerve is protected. Wide resection of the tumor is performed around the mass to the navicular bone medially. Surrounding tissue is sent to the pathology department for margins along with the tumor for frozen section. The pathology report is received, and additional tissue is removed as necessary. The wound is inspected and irrigated. The tourniquet is deflated, and hemostasis is obtained. A deep drain is placed. The deep tissue is closed with interrupted sutures. The superficial wound is closed in layers with interrupted sutures.

Clinical Example (28173)

A 45-year-old female presents with a chondrosarcoma of her first metatarsal with a small soft tissue mass. A radical resection of the first metatarsal and the mass is performed with preservation of the great toe.

Description of Procedure (28173)

A 7-cm incision is made excising the previous biopsy tract to keep it with the specimen. Subcutaneous flaps are raised. The sensory nerves are retracted carefully. The extensor tendons are retracted and carefully protected. The metatarsal-navicular joint is identified and isolated. The metatarsal-phalangeal joint is isolated and protected. A wide dissection is carried around the metatarsal with the chondrosarcoma. The plantar neurovascular bundles are identified and retracted. The plantar flexor tendons are retracted. The tumor is removed through the two joints including the joint capsules. Surrounding tissue is sent for frozen section along with the tumor to the pathology department. Any additional resection will be performed pending the report of the frozen section's results. The wound is then inspected and irrigated. A deep drain is placed. The tourniquet is let down and hemostasis is achieved. Deep closure is performed with interrupted sutures. Superficial closure is performed with interrupted sutures.

 Clinical Example (28175)

A 30-year-old female presents with a giant cell tumor of the proximal phalanx of the great toe with complete destruction of the phalanx and a small soft tissue mass. A radical resection of the tumor and soft tissue mass is performed with preservation of the great toe.

Description of Procedure (28175)

A 5-cm incision is made over the dorsomedial proximal phalanx of the great toe. Subcutaneous flaps are raised, and the deep tissue is exposed. The extensor tendons are retracted laterally. The metatarsal-phalangeal joint is exposed and protected. The interphalangeal joint is exposed and protected. The neurovascular bundle is identified and protected. The deep flexor tendons are mobilized and protected. Careful dissection is carried around the tumor, and it is removed en bloc. Frozen section margins are taken from the surrounding tissue. The pathology report is received, and any additional tissue is removed as necessary. Inspection and irrigation of the wound is performed. The tourniquet is let down, and hemostasis is obtained. Deep closure is performed with interrupted sutures. Superficial closure is performed with interrupted sutures.

Application of Casts and Strapping

BODY AND UPPER EXTREMITY

Strapping—Any Age

29200   Strapping; thorax

▶(29220 has been deleted)◀

▶(To report low back strapping, use 29799)◀

29240   shoulder (eg, Velpeau)

⊘=Modifier 51 Exempt   ⊙=Moderate Sedation   ✛=Add-on Code   ✗=FDA approval pending

🖎 Rationale

Code 29220 for low back strapping has been deleted as it is considered an obsolete procedure. A cross-reference to instruct the use of the unlisted procedure code 29799, instead of other strapping codes (29200 – thorax, 29240 – shoulder, 29260 – elbow or wrist, 29280 – hand or finger) has been added for the rare circumstance when this procedure is performed.

LOWER EXTREMITY

Strapping—Any Age

29520   Strapping; hip

29530   knee

29540   ankle and/or foot

▶(Do not report 29540 in conjunction with 29581)◀

29550   toes

29580   Unna boot

▶(Do not report 29580 in conjunction with 29581)◀

●**29581**   Application of multi-layer venous wound compression system, below knee

▶(Do not report 29581 in conjunction with 29540, 29580)◀

🖎 Rationale

Code 29581 has been established to report treatment of chronic venous insufficiency with multi-layer compression. Instructional notes have been added following codes 29540, 29580, and 29581 to indicate that these codes should not be reported with code 29581.

⚕ Clinical Example (29581)

A 50-year-old female returns to the office for treatment of a medial calf ulcer. It measures 3 x 3 cm and demonstrates no signs of infection. She has palpable pedal pulses. Pigmented skin changes in the gaiter distribution of both lower extremities are consistent with chronic venous insufficiency. The wound is examined, cleansed, and a multilayer venous ulcer compression dressing is applied.

Description of Procedure (29581)

The ulcer is cleansed and a primary wound dressing is then applied. With the foot in a dorsiflexed position, application of the compression bandage is initiated with a circular winding at the base of the toes. The second circular winding follows and covers the top of the foot and articulating aspect of the ankle joint. The next winding is applied and covers the back of the heel and the calf. Frequent checks are performed to ensure the foot is in a neutral position relative to the ankle. Each subsequent application is applied at the specific stretch needed for the desired compression.

Respiratory System

Nose

EXCISION

30140 Submucous resection inferior turbinate, partial or complete, any method

(Do not report 30130 or 30140 in conjunction with 30801, 30802, 30930)

(For submucous resection of superior or middle turbinate, use 30999)

(For endoscopic resection of concha bullosa of middle turbinate, use 31240)

(For submucous resection of nasal septum, use 30520)

30150 Rhinectomy; partial

30160 total

►(For closure and/or reconstruction, primary or delayed, see **Integumentary System**, 13150-13160, 14060-14302, 15120, 15121, 15260, 15261, 15760, 20900-20912)◄

Rationale

A potentially misleading parenthetical note that instructs users to use modifier 52 *Reduced Services* for reduction of turbinates has been deleted.

In support of the deletion of code 14300 and the establishment of code 14302, the cross-reference following code 30160 has been revised with the deletion of code 14300 and the addition of code 14302.

DESTRUCTION

▲30801 Ablation, soft tissue of inferior turbinates, unilateral or bilateral, any method (eg, electrocautery, radiofrequency ablation, or tissue volume reduction); superficial

►(For ablation of superior or middle turbinates, use 30999)◄

▲30802 intramural (ie, submucosal)

►(Do not report 30801 in conjunction with 30802)◄

(Do not report 30801, 30802, 30930 in conjunction with 30130 or 30140)

(For cautery performed for control of nasal hemorrhage, see 30901-30906)

Rationale

Codes 30801 and 30802 have been revised to clarify that radiofrequency ablation of the mucosa of the inferior turbinates are inherently included as part of the ablation service. These service codes are also intended to identify reduction of turbinates. In addition, these codes have been editorially revised to better describe what is being performed (tissue ablation) and to distinguish these codes (which are used for conditions such as airway obstruction) from other services (eg, epistaxis control). In addition, an exclusionary cross-reference has been included to note that codes 30801 and 30802 should not be used together. This is due to the fact that intramural ablation of the turbinates (30802) inherently includes superficial ablation procedure (30801).

Clinical Example (31627)

A 65-year-old smoker has a single 9.0 mm lung nodule on CT of the chest. The peripheral nodule is not amenable to biopsy by routine bronchoscopy. The patient is scheduled for navigational bronchoscopy.

Description of Procedure (31627)

Previously acquired CT scan of the lungs is imported into the planning laptop with special software for performing navigational bronchoscopy. A three-dimensional image of the patient's lungs is generated by the planning software. The physician marks the anatomical points and target lesion(s) on the virtual and CT images. The virtual and CT images are used to plan the path that the guide catheter (extended working channel) and the steerable navigation catheter (locatable guide) will follow in the bronchial tree. The patient's virtual plan is saved and exported to a flash drive. The patient's virtual plan is downloaded into the computer. Moderate sedation is administered. The guide catheter and steerable navigation catheter are inserted together (one inside the other) into the bronchoscope channel CT images and steering directions on the monitor are used by the physician to navigate the guide catheter and steerable navigation catheter in real-time to the target areas. The guide catheter is locked in place and the steerable navigation catheter is removed. Endobronchial tools inserted through the guide catheter are used to collect tissue samples, which are separately reported as a biopsy.

Trachea and Bronchi

ENDOSCOPY

⊙▲**31622** Bronchoscopy, rigid or flexible, including fluoroscopic guidance, when performed; diagnostic, with cell washing, when performed (separate procedure)

⊙**31623** with brushing or protected brushings

⊙**31624** with bronchial alveolar lavage

⊙**31625** with bronchial or endobronchial biopsy(s), single or multiple sites

⊙●**31626** with placement of fiducial markers, single or multiple

▶(Report supply of device separately)◀

✚⊙●**31627** with computer-assisted, image-guided navigation (List separately in addition to code for primary procedure[s])

▶(31627 includes 3D reconstruction. Do not report 31627 in conjunction with 76376, 76377)◀

▶(Use 31627 in conjunction with 31615, 31622-31631, 31635, 31636, 31638-31643)◀

⊙**31628** with transbronchial lung biopsy(s), single lobe

▲31641   destruction of tumor or relief of stenosis by any method other than excision (eg, laser therapy, cryotherapy)

(For bronchoscopic photodynamic therapy, report 31641 in addition to 96570, 96571 as appropriate)

▲31643   with placement of catheter(s) for intracavitary radioelement application

(For intracavitary radioelement application, see 77761-77763, 77785-77787)

⊙▲31645   with therapeutic aspiration of tracheobronchial tree, initial (eg, drainage of lung abscess)

⊙▲31646   with therapeutic aspiration of tracheobronchial tree, subsequent

(For catheter aspiration of tracheobronchial tree at bedside, use 31725)

⊙▲31656   with injection of contrast material for segmental bronchography (fiberscope only)

(For radiological supervision and interpretation, see 71040, 71060)

Rationale

Numerous changes have been made to the Trachea and Bronchi/Endoscopy section. Code 31622 has been editorially revised to clarify the descriptor by revising the "with or without" language to "when performed" regarding the fluoroscopic guidance and cell washing.

Code 31626 has been established to describe bronchoscopy with placement of fiducial markers. Bronchoscopic placement of fiducial markers is performed in conjunction with navigational bronchoscopic procedures. An instructional note has been added following code 31626 instructing users to report supply of the fiducial markers separately. Code 31626 has the conscious sedation symbol (⊙), as conscious sedation is inherent in the procedure and should not be reported separately.

Code 31627 has been established to describe bronchoscopy with computer-assisted, image-guided navigation, also referred to as *navigational bronchoscopy*. Bronchoscopic procedures, such as bronchial or endobronchial biopsy, are performed using navigational bronchoscopy when treating peripheral lesions that are difficult to access. Code 31627 is an add-on code for use in conjunction with bronchoscopic procedures. Three-dimensional reconstruction is included in code 31627. Instructional notes have been added following code 31627, instructing users that codes 76376 and 76377 should not be reported with 31627, and that code 31627 should be reported in conjunction with codes 31615, 31622-31631, 31635, 31636, and 31638-31643. Code 31627 has the conscious sedation symbol (⊙), as conscious sedation is inherent in the procedure and should not be reported separately.

Codes 31641-31656 have been revised for 2010. Code 31641 has been changed from a parent code to an indented code under code 31622. Because codes 31643-31656 have been indented codes following code 31641, they are now indented under 31622 as well. The family of codes now begins with 31622 and ends with 31656. This revision further clarifies that fluoroscopic guidance, when performed, is included in this entire family of codes.

⦸=Modifier 51 Exempt   ⊙=Moderate Sedation   ✚=Add-on Code   ✗=FDA approval pending

Clinical Example (31626)

A 65-year-old smoker has a single 9.0-mm lung nodule as indicated on a computed tomography (CT) scan of the chest. The peripheral nodule is not amenable to biopsy by routine bronchoscopy, so the patient is scheduled for navigational bronchoscopy.

Description of Procedure (31626)

The patient is placed on supplemental oxygen in the bronchoscopy suite, which has resuscitative equipment in place. An IV is started, and the physician supervises the nebulized administration of inhaled topical anesthesia. The physician next applies local topical anesthesia to the propharynx and nasopharanx. The physician then supervises administration of moderate sedation while a registered nurse or physician assistant properly monitors the pulse, blood pressure, SPO2, and ECG. The physician inserts the bronchoscope through the upper airways noting any abnormalities. The vocal cords are visualized, and the structure and function are noted. The needle-catheter or dye marker delivery tool is pre-marked and a tool-limit mark is placed on the proximal side of the tool. Navigate and reach the desired targeted tumor(s). The syringe is loaded with the desired dye marker volume. Advance the bronchoscope into the tracheobronchial tree, noting any abnormalities. The syringe and/or catheter is loaded with the desired dye marker volume or fiducial marker. The marker delivery tool is inserted into the catheter channel. Imaging (fluroscopy, ultrasound, or other) is used to verify placement and position of the delivery catheter or dye marker tool. The dye marker is injected into the soft lung tissue at target locations. Typically, a median of 4 fiducial markers are placed. The needle catheter or dye marker delivery tool is removed. All steps in previous points are repeated until all targeted lesions and all markers have been placed.

Lungs and Pleura

INTRODUCTION AND REMOVAL

●**32552**   Removal of indwelling tunneled pleural catheter with cuff

⊙●**32553**   Placement of interstitial device(s) for radiation therapy guidance (eg, fiducial markers, dosimeter), percutaneous, intra-thoracic, single or multiple

▶(Report supply of device separately)◀

▶(For imaging guidance, see 76942, 77002, 77012, 77021)◀

▶(For percutaneous placement of interstitial device[s] for intra-abdominal, intrapelvic, and/or retroperitoneal radiation therapy guidance, use 49411)◀

✎ Rationale

In 2005, code 32550 was established (originally 32019, then renumbered to 32550 in 2009) to describe insertion of a tunneled catheter into the pleural space for drainage and management of pleural effusions. Initially, placement of an indwelling tunneled pleural catheter was commonly performed for the management of malignant pleural effusion (MPE) at the end of a patient's life. Since its inception, however, the catheter has been employed to resolve other types of pleural effusions such as noninfected benign pleural effusion, recurrent pleural effusion of unknown etiology, and trapped lung with pleural effusion. Removal of the catheter following resolution of the pleural effusion improves the quality of the patient's life by removing the possibility of infection or other complications.

The technique of insertion and management of the tunneled pleural catheter with cuff requires multiple incisions and subcutaneous tunneling of the indwelling pleural catheter through multiple incisions in the thorax into the pleural space. Code 32550 does not include the incisions and dissection required to remove the catheter and cuff. For 2010, code 32552 has been established to describe removal of an indwelling tunneled pleural catheter with a cuff. In accordance with the addition of this "removal" code, the heading for this subsection has been revised to indicate introduction and removal.

Code 32553 has been established to describe placement of percutaneous, intrathoracic placement of interstitial devices, such as fiducial markers or dosimeters. These interstitial devices are placed for the purpose of radiation therapy guidance. There is an "(s)" in the word device(s), which indicates that code 32553 is reported one time, regardless of the number of devices placed. Moderate sedation is performed in support of this procedure, and is included in code 32553. This is indicated by the moderate sedation symbol (⊙). Supply of the interstitial device(s) is reported separately. This is reflected in the instructional note that follows code 32553. Imaging guidance is not included in code 32553. For this reason, a cross-reference note has been added directing users to codes 76942, 77002, 77012, and 77021 for imaging guidance. An additional cross-reference has been added directing users to code 49411 for percutaneous placement of interstitial device(s) for intraabdominal, intrapelvic, and/or retroperitoneal radiation therapy guidance.

Clinical Example (32552)

A 65-year-old female with metastatic breast cancer undergoing chemotherapy had a tunneled pleural catheter inserted 8 weeks ago for a malignant pleural effusion. Patient records indicate that catheter drainage progressively slowed and ceased. Review of chest X-ray has demonstrated resolution of her effusion and re-expansion of the lung. She presents today for surgical removal of the catheter.

Description of Procedure (32552)

Administer conscious sedation if the patient is unduly anxious. Infiltrate the catheter exit site and cuff site with the appropriate local anesthesia. Make a small incision around the catheter exit site and, if necessary, the cuff site. Dissect around the catheter and cuff sites to loosen the catheter from the surrounding tissue. Grasp and gently remove the entire catheter from within the chest. Confirm that the entire catheter is removed. Suture the exit site of the catheter. Apply sterile dressings.

Clinical Example (32553)

A 65-year-old woman with metastatic breast cancer undergoing chemotherapy had a tunneled pleural catheter inserted 8 weeks ago for a malignant pleural effusion.

⊘=Modifier 51 Exempt   ⊙=Moderate Sedation   ✚=Add-on Code   ✗=FDA approval pending

Patient records indicate that catheter drainage progressively slowed and ceased. Review of chest X-ray has demonstrated resolution of her effusion and re-expansion of the lung. She presents today for surgical removal of the catheter.

Description of Procedure (32553)

Moderate sedation is administered if the patient is unduly anxious. The catheter exit site and cuff site are infiltrated with the appropriate local anesthesia. A small incision is made around the catheter exit site and, if necessary, the cuff site. Dissection is performed around the catheter and cuff sites to loosen the catheter from the surrounding tissue. The entire catheter is grasped and gently removed from within the chest. Removal of the entire catheter is confirmed. The exit site of the catheter is sutured. Sterile dressings are applied.

DESTRUCTION

▶The instillation of a fibrinolytic agent may be performed multiple times per day over the course of several days. Code 32561 should be reported only once on the initial day treatment. Code 32562 should be reported only once on each subsequent day of treatment.◀

▲**32560**   Instillation, via chest tube/catheter, agent for pleurodesis (eg, talc for recurrent or persistent pneumothorax)

▶(For chest tube insertion, use 32551)◀

●**32561**   Instillation(s), via chest tube/catheter, agent for fibrinolysis (eg, fibrinolytic agent for break up of multiloculated effusion); initial day

▶(For chest tube insertion, use 32551)◀

●**32562**   subsequent day

▶(For chest tube insertion, use 32551)◀

🖎 Rationale

The Lungs and Pleura/Destruction section has been updated to reflect current practice in the performance of pleurodesis and fibrinolysis procedures. Pleurodesis is performed by instilling an agent into the pleural space to get the visceral pleura of the lung to stick to the parietal pleura of the chest wall so the lung won't collapse down. Fibrinolysis is the instillation of an agent into the pleural space to break up debris or fibrin within the chest thus freeing up an entrapped lung. Fibrinolysis may take place more than once per day and over a course of several days.

The agent used may be a chemical such as talc, or a nonchemical agent such as tissue plasminogen activator (tPA), a fibrinolytic enzyme.

Code 32560 has been editorially revised to specify the instillation of an agent for pleurodesis through a chest tube or catheter. Codes 32561 and 35262 have been established to describe the instillation of an agent for fibrinolysis.

Both pleurodesis and fibrinolysis are performed via chest tube or catheter. Placement of the chest tube or catheter is separately reported with code 32551.

Instructional notes have been added following codes 32560, 32561, and 32562 directing users to code 32551 for chest tube or catheter placement.

New guidelines have been added following the Destruction heading to explain that instillation of the fibrinolytic agent may occur more than one time per day over a period of several days; however, the service is reported once per day. Code 32561 is reported one time for the initial day of treatment, and code 32561 is reported once per each subsequent day of treatment.

In addition, instillation of fibrinolytic chemicals may be performed by a different physician from the physician who places the catheter or chest tube (eg, emergency room physician or radiologist).

 ### Clinical Example (32561)

A 57-year-old diabetic female presents with right lower lobe pneumonia and a complicated parapneumonic effusion. A chest tube was previously placed for drainage. A chest computed tomography (CT) scan confirms several sizable loculations. Instillation of fibrinolysis through the existing chest tube is recommended.

Description of Procedure (32561)

The patient is positioned. The connection between the chest tube and drainage unit is prepared and draped in sterile fashion. Clamps are placed on either side of the connection, and the tube is disconnected from the drainage hose. A syringe containing the fibrinolytic agent is inserted into the chest tube, the clamp is removed from the tube, and the fibrinolytic agent is injected into the thoracic cavity. The clamp is replaced on the chest tube, which is reconnected to the drainage unit. The patient is sequentially moved to each of six positions to distribute the fibrinolytic agent throughout the pleural cavity for 2 hours. The clamp is then removed and suction is reinstituted.

Clinical Example (32562)

A 57-year-old diabetic female presents with right lower lobe pneumonia and a complicated parapneumonic effusion through a previously placed chest tube. A chest computed tomography (CT) scan confirms several sizable loculations. Instillation of fibrinolysis is recommended. The patient had an initial treatment with a fibrinolytic agent with only a partial response and thus requires subsequent treatments through the existing chest tube.

Description of Procedure (32562)

The patient is positioned. The connection between the chest tube and drainage unit is prepared and draped in sterile fashion. Clamps are placed on either side of the connection, and the tube is disconnected from the drainage hose. A syringe containing the fibrinolytic agent is inserted into the chest tube, the clamp is removed from the tube, and the fibrinolytic agent is injected into the thoracic cavity. The clamp is replaced on the chest tube, which is reconnected to the drainage unit. The patient is sequentially moved to each of six positions to distribute the fibrinolytic agent throughout the pleural cavity for 2 hours. The clamp is then removed and suction is reinstituted.

⊘=Modifier 51 Exempt   ⊙=Moderate Sedation   ✚=Add-on Code   ✗=FDA approval pending

Cardiovascular System

Heart and Pericardium

PACEMAKER OR PACING CARDIOVERTER-DEFIBRILLATOR

⊙▲**33216**   Insertion of a single transvenous electrode, permanent pacemaker or cardioverter-defibrillator

⊙▲**33217**   Insertion of 2 transvenous electrodes, permanent pacemaker or cardioverter-defibrillator

(Do not report 33216-33217 in conjunction with 33214)

►(For insertion or replacement of a cardiac venous system lead, see 33224, 33225)◄

⊙▲**33223**   Revision of skin pocket for cardioverter-defibrillator

✍ Rationale

Editorial revisions have been made to codes 33216, 33217, and 33223 to clarify the procedures described by these codes. The changes reflect the number of electrodes inserted, rather than the type of device (eg, single, dual, or multiple cardioverter-defibrillator). Codes 33216 and 33217 have been editorially revised to distinguish insertion of a single electrode from insertion of two electrodes. Code 33217 has been changed from an indented code to a parent code to accommodate these changes. Code 33223 has been editorially revised to remove the specification of single or dual chamber, as the device may be a single, dual, or multiple-lead device.

A cross-reference note has been added following code 33217 directing users to codes 33224 and 33225 for insertion or replacement of a cardiac venous system lead.

TRANSPOSITION OF THE GREAT VESSELS

●**33782**   Aortic root translocation with ventricular septal defect and pulmonary stenosis repair (ie, Nikaidoh procedure); without coronary ostium reimplantation

►(Do not report 33782 in conjunction with 33412, 33413, 33608, 33681, 33770, 33771, 33778, 33780, 33920)◄

●**33783**   with reimplantation of 1 or both coronary ostia

✍ Rationale

Two new codes, 33782 and 33783, have been established to report aortic root translocation with ventricular septal defect and pulmonary stenosis repair for children requiring repair of transposition of the great arteries with ventricular septal defect and pulmonary stenosis. Code 33782 has been established to describe the Nikaidoh procedure performed without coronary ostium reimplantation. Code 33783 has been established to report when 1 or both of the coronary ostia are reimplanted. A parenthetical note has been added following code 33782 to restrict its use with other cardiac repairs, including aortic reconstruction or repair codes, cardiac anomaly repairs, and great artery transposition repairs.

Clinical Example (33782)

A 14-month-old boy was born with mild cyanosis and a heart murmur. Echocardiography at birth revealed transposition of the great arteries (discordant ventricular-arterial connections) with ventricular septal defect and left ventricular outflow tract obstruction. The child's oxygen saturation on room air was 85% at birth and remained between 80 and 90% throughout the first 14 months of life. At age 14 months, the oxygen saturations began to fall to 70%, and the child was referred for surgical intervention secondary to falling oxygen saturation levels. The child's clinical and echocardiographic data were reviewed at a Joint Cardiology and Cardiac Surgery conference and the decision was made to proceed with a Nikaidoh procedure (aortic root translocation over the left ventricle).

Description of Procedure (33782)

Under general endotracheal anesthesia, in the supine position, the patient is prepared and draped in standard aseptic fashion. A skin incision is made via standard median sternotomy. The sternum is divided in the midline. Cardiac cannulae are placed. Cardiopulmonary bypass is initiated. Snares are snugged down on the caval cannulae allowing for complete heart bypass. The aorta is mobilized, as are the proximal coronary arteries. With the heart still perfused, the aortic root is dissected off the right ventricle with the coronaries intact. The aorta is crossclamped and cold cardioplegic solution is injected into the aortic root. The ascending aorta is divided just below the crossclamp. The pulmonary artery is opened longitudinally with the incision carried down across the pulmonary annulus to the ventricular septal defect (VSD) thus creating unobstructed left ventricular outflow. The septal muscle is excised as necessary. The aortic root is now translocated posteriorly with the back wall sewn to the remnant of the pulmonary valve annulus. A patch is used to close the VSD, which superiorly attaches to the anterior wall of the proximal aortic root thus providing unobstructed flow from the left ventricle to the aorta. The pulmonary bifurcation is widely mobilized and brought anterior to the distal ascending aorta (the LeCompte Maneuver). An end-to-end anastomosis is performed between the proximal ascending aorta and the distal ascending aorta. Right ventricular to pulmonary artery continuity is established either with a valved conduit or by attaching the posterior wall of the main pulmonary artery remnant to the right ventricle and roofing it with a nonvalved patch. Air is evacuated from the cardiac chambers, and the crossclamp is released. After satisfactory rewarming and resuscitation, the child is then weaned from cardiopulmonary bypass. The cannulae are removed, and the sites are secured. Chest tubes and temporary pacing wires are placed. The sternum is closed with wires; the abdominal fascia, skin, and subcutaneous tissue are closed in layers.

Clinical Example (33783)

A 12-month-old girl was born with mild cyanosis and a heart murmur. Echocardiography at birth revealed transposition of the great arteries (discordant ventricular-arterial connections) with ventricular septal defect and left ventricular outflow tract obstruction. The child's oxygen saturation on room air was 90% at birth and remained between 80 and 90% throughout the first year of life. At 12 months of age, the oxygen saturation started to fall to the 70 to 80% range. The child was referred for surgical intervention secondary to falling oxygen saturation levels. The child's clinical and echocardiographic data were reviewed at a Joint Cardiology and Cardiac Surgery conference, and the decision was made to proceed with a Nikaidoh procedure (aortic root translocation over the left ventricle). At operation, the surgeon identified a pattern of coronary artery branching necessitating individual transfer of the coronary arteries, with coronary artery button re-implantation after suitable coronary artery mobilization.

Description of Procedure (33783)

Under general endotracheal anesthesia, in the supine position, the patient is prepared and draped in standard aseptic fashion. A skin incision is made via standard median sternotomy. The sternum is divided in the midline. Cardiac cannulae are placed. Cardiopulmonary bypass is initiated. Snares are snugged down on the caval cannulae allowing for complete heart bypass. The aorta is mobilized, as are the proximal coronary arteries. The aorta is crossclamped and cold cardioplegic solution is injected into the aortic root. The ascending aorta is divided just below the crossclamp. The coronary ostia are excised from the aortic root with an oval of aortic tissue and mobilized. The aortic root is dissected off the right ventricle. The pulmonary artery is opened longitudinally with the incision carried down across the pulmonary annulus to the ventricular septal defect (VSD) thus creating unobstructed left ventricular outflow. The septal muscle is excised as necessary. The aortic root is now translocated posteriorly with the back wall sewn to the remnant of the pulmonary valve annulus. A patch is used to close the VSD, which superiorly attaches to the anterior wall of the proximal aortic root thus providing unobstructed flow from the left ventricle to the aorta. The previously excised coronary buttons are transferred back to the translocated aortic root either using the original coronary button harvest sites in the aortic root or creating new defects for transfer and closing the original harvest sites. The pulmonary bifurcation is widely mobilized and brought anterior to the distal ascending aorta (the LeCompte Maneuver). An end-to-end anastomosis is performed between the proximal ascending aorta and the distal ascending aorta. Right ventricular to pulmonary artery continuity is established either with a valved conduit or by attaching the posterior wall of the main pulmonary artery remnant to the right ventricle and roofing it with a non-valved patch. Air is evacuated from the cardiac chambers, and the crossclamp is released. After satisfactory rewarming and resuscitation, the child is then weaned from cardiopulmonary bypass. The cannulae are removed, and the sites are secured. Chest tubes and temporary pacing wires are placed. The sternum is closed with wires; the abdominal fascia, skin, and subcutaneous tissue are closed in layers.

CARDIAC ASSIST

▶The insertion of a ventricular assist device (VAD) can be performed via percutaneous (0048T) or transthoracic (33975, 33976, 33979) approach. The location of the ventricular assist device may be intracorporeal or extracorporeal.

Removal of a ventricular assist device (33977, 33978, 33980, 0050T) includes removal of the entire device, including the cannulas.

Replacement of a ventricular assist device pump includes the removal of the pump and insertion of a new pump, connection, de-airing, and initiation of the new pump.

Replacement of the entire ventricular assist device system, ie, pump(s) and cannulas, is reported using the insertion codes. Removal of the ventricular assist device system being replaced is not separately reported.◄

►(For implantation or removal of ventricular assist device, extracorporeal, percutaneous transseptal access, see 0048T, 0050T. For replacement of a ventricular assist device, extracorporeal, percutaneous transseptal access, use 33999)◄

●**33981**   Replacement of extracorporeal ventricular assist device, single or biventricular, pump(s), single or each pump

●**33982**   Replacement of ventricular assist device pump(s); implantable intracorporeal, single ventricle, without cardiopulmonary bypass

●**33983**   implantable intracorporeal, single ventricle, with cardiopulmonary bypass

Rationale

Codes 33981-33983 have been established in the Ventricular Assist Devices/ Cardiac Assist section to report replacement of ventricular assist devices, as well as new guidelines to instruct the user how to report the new codes. Ventricular assist devices have been used on a short-term basis to help patients recovering from heart surgery or myocardial infarction. More recently, however, ventricular assist devices are being used on a long-term basis for patients with heart disease such as congestive heart failure. Long-term use makes ventricular assist devices vulnerable to mechanical failure, which requires the devices to be replaced. Codes 33981-33983 have been established to describe the work involved in replacing a ventricular assist device, as this work has not been adequately described in the CPT code set prior to 2010. Codes 33981-33983 include the removal of the existing pump as well as the replacement.

Code 33981 describes the replacement of a single or biventricular pump of an extracorporeal ventricular assist device and is reported for each pump replaced. Code 33982 describes replacement of single ventricle pump of an implantable, intracorporeal ventricular assist device. The procedure described by code 33982 is performed without the use of cardiopulmonary bypass. Code 33983 describes the same procedure as code 33982; however, the procedure is performed with cardiopulmonary bypass. The cross-reference note following the new guidelines has been revised to direct the user to the appropriate codes for implantation, removal, and replacement of an extracorporeal ventricular assist device with percutaneous transseptal access.

Clinical Example (33981)

A 50-year-old patient with life-limiting ventricular dysfunction presents with mechanical failure of his ventricular assist device (VAD). He is scheduled for device pump replacement.

⊘=Modifier 51 Exempt   ⊙=Moderate Sedation   ✚=Add-on Code   ✗=FDA approval pending

Description of Procedure (33981)

Inflow and outflow cannulas are clamped. The assist device pump is removed and inspected. A new ventricular assist device pump is physically connected to the inflow and outflow cannulas. The pump is primed and de-aired to prevent gas embolization. The device is activated to support the circulation and its flow characteristics varied to ensure that adequate flow rates are achievable and that there is unobstructed inflow and outflow. During the process of VAD initiation, the patient's intravascular volume and vasoactive drug therapy are adjusted to achieve satisfactory, stable cardiovascular function and end-organ perfusion.

Clinical Example (33982)

A 50-year-old patient with life-limiting ventricular dysfunction presents with mechanical failure of his ventricular assist device (VAD). He is scheduled for device pump replacement.

Description of Procedure (33982)

A reoperative median sternotomy is performed, and the patient is fully anticoagulated. The implanted VAD is dissected free from surrounding scar tissue, avoiding injury to vital structures. The dissection is extended to permit ready access to the great vessels and the right heart for urgent cannulation to institute cardiopulmonary bypass should it be necessary. VAD flow rates are gradually reduced, and the patient is carefully weaned from its assistance with adjustment of intravascular volume and inotropic agents. Inflow and outflow cannulas are clamped, and the assist device pump is removed and inspected. A new VAD is physically connected to the inflow and outflow cannulas. The device is primed and de-aired to prevent gas embolization. The device pump is activated to support the circulation and its flow characteristics varied to ensure that adequate flow rates are achievable and that there is unobstructed inflow and outflow. During the process of VAD initiation, the patient's intravascular volume and vasoactive drug therapy are adjusted to achieve satisfactory, stable cardiovascular function and end-organ perfusion. Hemostasis is achieved and the sternotomy closed over drains.

Clinical Example (33983)

A 50-year-old patient with life-limiting ventricular dysfunction presents with mechanical failure of his ventricular assist device (VAD). He is scheduled for device pump replacement.

Description of Procedure (33983)

A reoperative median sternotomy is performed, and the patient is fully anticoagulated. The implanted VAD is dissected free from surrounding scar tissue, avoiding injury to vital structures. The dissection is extended to permit ready access to the great vessels and the right heart. (The patient does not tolerate weaning from the VAD, and is therefore cannulated for cardiopulmonary bypass.) Cardiopulmonary bypass is initiated, the inflow and outflow VAD cannulas are clamped, and the assist device is removed and inspected. A new VAD pump is physically connected to the inflow and outflow cannulas. The pump is primed and de-aired to prevent gas embolization. The device is activated to support the circulation and its flow characteristics varied to ensure that adequate flow rates are achievable and that there is unobstructed inflow and outflow. During the process of VAD initiation, the patient's intravascular volume and vasoactive drug therapy are adjusted to achieve satisfactory, stable cardiovascular function and end-organ perfusion. Hemostasis is achieved. The sternotomy is closed over drains.

VASCULAR INJECTION PROCEDURES

Intra-Arterial—Intra-Aortic

36120   Introduction of needle or intracatheter; retrograde brachial artery

36140   extremity artery

(For insertion of arteriovenous cannula, see 36810-36821)

▶(36145 has been deleted. To report see 36147, 36148)◀

⊙●**36147**   Introduction of needle and/or catheter, arteriovenous shunt created for dialysis (graft/fistula); initial access with complete radiological evaluation of dialysis access, including fluoroscopy, image documentation and report (includes access of shunt, injection[s] of contrast, and all necessary imaging from the arterial anastomosis and adjacent artery through entire venous outflow including the inferior or superior vena cava)

▶(If 36147 indicates the need for a therapeutic intervention requiring a second catheterization of the shunt, use 36148)◀

▶(Do not report 36147 in conjunction with 75791)◀

✚⊙●**36148**   additional access for therapeutic intervention (List separately in addition to code for primary procedure)

▶(Use 36148 in conjunction with 36147)◀

36215   Selective catheter placement, arterial system; each first order thoracic or brachiocephalic branch, within avascular family

✚**36218**   additional second order, third order, and beyond, thoracic or brachiocephalic branch, within a vascular family (List in addition to code for initial second or third order vessel as appropriate)

(Use 36218 in conjunction with 36216, 36217)

▶(For angiography, see 36147, 75600-75774, 75791)◀

Venous

⊙▲**36481**   Percutaneous portal vein catheterization by any method

✍ Rationale

Arteriovenous shunt code 36145 has been deleted. To reflect current clinical practice, code 36147 and add-on code 36148 have been established to report arteriovenous shunt imaging.

In support of the establishment of codes 36147 and 36148, radiology code 75791 has been added to describe the performance of a radiological evaluation through an already existing access into the shunt or from an access that is not a direct puncture of the shunt.

⊘=Modifier 51 Exempt   ⊙=Moderate Sedation   ✚=Add-on Code   ✗=FDA approval pending

Parenthetical notes have been added to direct the user (1) to report codes 36147 and 36148 for arteriovenous shunt imaging; (2) that if code 36147 indicates the need for a therapeutic intervention requiring a second catheterization of the shunt, then code 36148 should be reported; (3) to not report code 36147 with 75791; and (4) to report code 36148 in conjunction with code 36147.

The cross-reference notes following codes 36218 and 36870 have been updated to include these new codes. The second cross-reference following code 36870 has been revised to direct the use of codes 36147 and 75791 to report radiological supervision and interpretation.

Code 36481 has been revised with the addition of the moderate sedation symbol (⊙). Moderate sedation is inherently performed with percutaneous portal vein catheterization and should not be reported separately.

Clinical Example (36147)

A 65-year-old male with end-stage renal disease (ESRD) is referred for evaluation because of increased difficulty puncturing the arteriovenous (AV) shunt for dialysis. He has been on hemodialysis for 5 years, and this is his second AV shunt. He has an AV fistula in the left upper arm and was most recently studied 10 months ago, at which time a 2-cm stenosis of the arteriovenous anastomosis and immediate outflow was found and treated with balloon angioplasty.

Description of Procedure (36147)

The patient is positioned. The intravenous setup is checked, and moderate sedation is administered. Local anesthesia is applied to the entry site. The arteriovenous shunt is punctured, and the sheath is placed. Angiography is performed to include the entire length of the graft and all outflow veins to the level of the superior vena cava. (Compression may be applied to allow for visualization of the arterial anastomosis.) Technical personnel are directed throughout. Interpretation of the imaging of all views is obtained. The sheath and any necessary catheters and wires are removed from the body. Hemostasis is obtained by direct compression.

Clinical Example (36148)

A patient with end-stage renal disease (ESRD) is referred for a study of a dialysis access (either graft or fistula) that is not performing well. The patient is seen in an angiographic laboratory. The arteriovenous (AV) shunt is punctured under local anesthesia, and a diagnostic study of the AV shunt is performed (CPT code 36147). The diagnostic study demonstrates a significant stenosis just below the puncture site that requires balloon angioplasty. A second puncture is required to reach the lesion.

Description of Procedure (36148)

Local anesthesia is applied to the second entry site. The AV shunt is punctured, and a sheath is placed. Moderate sedation is monitored. Required interventions are performed (reported separately). The sheath and any necessary catheters and wires are removed from the body. Hemostasis is obtained by direct compression.

HEMODIALYSIS ACCESS, INTERVASCULAR CANNULATION FOR EXTRACORPOREAL CIRCULATION, OR SHUNT INSERTION

▶(36834 has been deleted. To report an arteriovenous access fistula or graft revision, use 36832)◀

36835 Insertion of Thomas shunt (separate procedure)

⊙**36870** Thrombectomy, percutaneous, arteriovenous fistula, autogenous or nonautogenous graft (includes mechanical thrombus extraction and intra-graft thrombolysis)

(Do not report 36870 in conjunction with 36593)

▶(For catheterization, see 36147, 36148)◀

▶(For radiological supervision and interpretation, see 36147, 75791)◀

Rationale

Code 36834 has been deleted as this service is already described under 36832. An instructional note has been added to direct users to code 36832 for revision of an arteriovenous fistula or graft.

In accordance with the deletion of code 36145 and the establishment of codes 36147 and 36148, the cross-reference following code 36870 has been revised.

PORTAL DECOMPRESSION PROCEDURES

⊙▲**37183** Revision of transvenous intrahepatic portosystemic shunt(s) (TIPS) (includes venous access, hepatic and portal vein catheterization, portography with hemodynamic evaluation, intrahepatic tract recanulization/dilatation, stent placement and all associated imaging guidance and documentation)

(Do not report 75885 or 75887 in conjunction with 37183)

▶(For repair of arteriovenous aneurysm, use 36832)◀

Rationale

Code 37183 has been revised with the addition of the moderate sedation symbol (⊙). Moderate sedation is inherently performed with the transvenous intrahepatic portosystemic shunt(s) (TIPS) revision procedure and should not be reported separately.

In accordance with the deletion of code 36834, the cross-reference following code 37183 has been revised with the replacement of code 36834 with code 36832.

LIGATION

▲**37760** Ligation of perforator veins, subfascial, radical (Linton type), including skin graft, when performed, open,1 leg

(For endoscopic procedure, use 37500)

●**37761** Ligation of perforator vein(s), subfascial, open, including ultrasound guidance, when performed, 1 leg

▶(For bilateral procedure, report 37761 with modifier 50)◀

⃠=Modifier 51 Exempt   ⊙=Moderate Sedation   ✛=Add-on Code   ✗=FDA approval pending

►(Do not report 37760, 37761 in conjunction with 76937, 76942, 76998, 93971)◄

►(For endoscopic ligation of subfascial perforator veins, use 37500)◄

🖎 Rationale

Code 37761 has been established to report ligation of subfascial perforator veins. In support of the addition of code 37761, code 37760 has been editorially revised for consistency with the CPT nomenclature conventions, to clarify that it includes placement of a skin graft, when performed. The phrase "1 leg" was added to code 37760 to indicate that this is a unilateral procedure.

Two instructional notes have been added following code 37761 to: (1) instruct the use of modifier 50 with code 37761 for bilateral procedures; and (2) to preclude reporting codes 37760 and 37761 in conjunction with code 76937, 76942, 76998 or 93971. A cross-reference has been added to direct the user to code 37500 for endoscopic ligation of subfascial perforator vein.

Clinical Example (37761)

A 50-year-old female presents with her third medial left-leg ulcer. It measures 3 x 3 cm and is deep and painful. She has palpable pedal pulses and pigmentary scarring in the gaiter distribution of the extremity. A left greater saphenous vein ligation and stripping was performed 1 year earlier, which improved but did not completely relieve her symptoms. Duplex scanning reveals large incompetent perforating veins just cephalad to the ulcer. Open ligation of the perforators is undertaken.

Description of Procedure (37761)

The skin of the lower extremity is incised 1 cm from the marked perforator, with care taken to avoid chronically scarred regions. The subcutaneous tissue is dissected using retraction to expose the fascia and the perforating vein. The fascia is incised with care taken not to injure the vein, and the vein is isolated. A ligature is placed around the vein, and the vein is ligated. The fascia is closed with interrupted sutures. These steps are repeated for each vein to be treated. The wound(s) are copiously irrigated with sterile saline. Electrocautery or suture ligation is used to achieve final hemostasis at all sites. Subcutaneous tissues are closed in multiple layers. The skin is closed.

Hemic and Lymphatic Systems

General

BONE MARROW OR STEM CELL SERVICES/PROCEDURES

38240	Bone marrow or blood-derived peripheral stem cell transplantation; allogenic
38241	autologous
38242	allogeneic donor lymphocyte infusions

(For bone marrow aspiration, use 38220)

(For modification, treatment, and processing of bone marrow or blood-derived stem cell specimens for transplantation, use 38210-38213)

▶(For cryopreservation, freezing, and storage of blood-derived stem cells for transplantation, use 38207)◀

▶(For thawing and expansion of blood-derived stem cells for transplantation, see 38208, 38209)◀

 Rationale

The cross-references following code 38242 have been editorially revised to clarify that codes 38207, 38208, and 38209 should be used for freezing and thawing of bone marrow/stem cells harvest and preservation prior to therapeutic transplant or re-infusion, and not codes 88240 and 88241, which are intended to be used for freezing or thawing small amounts of tissue to be sent to another facility for diagnostic testing.

Mediastinum and Diaphragm

Diaphragm

REPAIR

39502   Repair, paraesophageal hiatus hernia, transabdominal, with or without fundoplasty, vagotomy, and/or pyloroplasty, except neonatal

▶(For laparoscopic paraesophageal hernia repair, see 43281, 43282)◀

39520   Repair, diaphragmatic hernia (esophageal hiatal); transthoracic

▶(For laparoscopic paraesophageal hernia repair, see 43281, 43282)◀

39530   combined, thoracoabdominal

 Rationale

In support of the establishment of codes 43281 and 43282, cross-references have been added following 39502 and 39520 directing the users to 43281 and 43282 for reporting laparoscopic paraesophageal hernia repair.

Digestive System

Palate and Uvula

EXCISION, DESTRUCTION

42104   Excision, lesion of palate, uvula; without closure

42106   with simple primary closure

42107   with local flap closure

⊘=Modifier 51 Exempt   ⊙=Moderate Sedation   ✚=Add-on Code   ✗=FDA approval pending

▶(For skin graft, see 14040-14302)◀

42120 Resection of palate or extensive resection of lesion

▶(For reconstruction of palate with extraoral tissue, see 14040-14302, 15050, 15120, 15240, 15576)◀

 Rationale

In accordance with the establishment of codes 14301 and 14302, the cross-reference following codes 42107 and 42120 have been revised to expand the code range and to support the establishment of these services.

Pharynx, Adenoids, and Tonsils

EXCISION, DESTRUCTION

▲**42894** Resection of pharyngeal wall requiring closure with myocutaneous or fasciocutaneous flap or free muscle, skin, or fascial flap with microvascular anastamosis

(When combined with radical neck dissection, use also 38720)

(For limited pharyngectomy with radical neck dissection, use 38720 with 42890)

▶(For flap used for reconstruction, see 15732, 15734, 15756, 15757, 15758)◀

 Rationale

Code 42894 has been revised to reflect use of this code for fasciocutaneous (fascia and skin) flaps, free muscle, skin, or fascial flaps as well as myocutaneous flaps (muscle and skin). This is due to the fact that, although the resection of the pharyngeal wall may be the same, many of these defects that are currently being repaired using this procedure are currently being reconstructed using fasciocutaneous flaps, which may be pedicled and may utilize microvascular anastomosis. In addition, a cross-reference has been included to direct users to the appropriate code to use to identify flaps used for reconstruction (15732, 17534, 15756, 15757, or 15758), since flaps provided for reconstruction require different work effort from flaps used to close the resection site of the pharyngeal wall.

Esophagus

LAPAROSCOPY

⊙**+43273** Endoscopic cannulation of papilla with direct visualization of common bile duct(s) and/or pancreatic duct(s) (List separately in addition to code(s) for primary procedure)

▶(Use 43273 in conjunction with 43260-43265, 43267-43272)◀

 Rationale

Code 43262 may be reported in conjunction with code 43273. To reflect this, the parenthetical note following code 43273 has been revised to include code 43262 within the range.

●43281 Laparoscopy, surgical, repair of paraesophageal hernia, includes fundoplasty, when performed; without implantation of mesh

●43282   with implantation of mesh

▶(For transthoracic paraesophageal hernia repair, use 39520. For transabdominal paraesophageal hernia repair, use 39502)◀

▶(Do not report 43281, 43282 in conjunction with 43280, 43450, 43453, 43456, 43458, 49568)◀

🖎 Rationale

Codes 43281 and 43282 have been established to report repair of paraesophageal via the laparoscopic approach, without implantation of mesh (43281), and with implantation of mesh (43282). The main purpose in establishing these codes was to identify the difference in both clinical setting and work involved with mesh placement for a paraesophageal hernia repair. While it is typical to include fundoplication as a core component of the repair, the use of mesh is much more variable. The patient's condition and surgeon's preference may determine whether mesh is used or not. Placement of mesh adds significantly to the intra-service work involved in the procedure, often adding as much as an hour to the operative time.

A cross-reference has been added to direct users to the open procedure code 39520 for transthoracic paraesophageal hernia and to code 39502 for transabdominal paraesophageal hernia repair. An exclusionary parenthetical note has also been added to restrict the use of codes 43281 and 43282 when a laparoscopic fundoplication procedure (43280), dilation of esophagus procedure (43450, 43453, 43456, 43458), or implantation of mesh or other prosthesis for open procedure (49568) is performed.

🩺 Clinical Example (43281)

A 64-year-old female presents with dysphagia, reflux, and intermittent chest pain. A work-up including an upper gastrointestinal series, endoscopy, and computed tomography (CT) scan of the chest and abdomen demonstrates a type III paraesophageal hernia with more than 50% of the stomach present in the chest. She undergoes laparoscopic repair without implantation of mesh.

Description of Procedure (43281)

Under general anesthesia, surgical laparoscopy is performed. Pneumoperitoneum is established to distend the abdomen, and the laparoscope is introduced. Gas flow and intra-abdominal pressure are carefully monitored so as not to impair ventilation or venous return. Four to six trocar ports are sited through the anterior abdominal wall above the umbilicus. The viscera are inspected. An orogastric tube may be placed to decompress the stomach if it will pass. The liver is retracted to allow visualization of the esophageal hiatus. The stomach is gently retracted into the abdomen to assess its degree of tethering in the thorax. The peritoneum overlying the right crus is incised, and the plane along the hernia sac is developed. The dissection is extended anteriorly and laterally to the left crus. The base of the crural confluence is dissected free of adhesions to the sac. The hernia sac is carefully dissected into the mediastinum with caudal traction. The interfaces between the pleura, pericardium, spine, and aorta are developed as the dissection is carried

⊘=Modifier 51 Exempt   ⊙=Moderate Sedation   ✚=Add-on Code   ✗=FDA approval pending

cephalad to the top of the hernia sac. The sac contents are completely reduced back into the abdominal cavity. The hernia sac is then excised taking care to avoid injury to stomach and vagal trunks. An esophageal dilator may be placed transorally. The esophagus is identified and dissected circumferentially and along its mediastinal course in order to reduce tension, allowing the gastroesophageal junction to rest comfortably within the abdominal cavity. Care is taken to identify and preserve the vagus nerves. The gastro-splenic ligament and the short gastric vessels are divided if necessary. The retro-esophageal window is developed, and the esophagus is retracted caudally. The crural pillars are then approximated with sutures. Anterior reinforcement of the diaphragm is performed with sutures as needed, the tightness of the repair being gauged visually or by the presence of the bougie or other device. Partial or total fundoplasty is then performed with sutures. (Additional sutures may be placed to attach the gastric fundus and/or body to the diaphragm.) The operative field is carefully inspected to ensure hemostasis. Esophageal tubes are removed as per surgeon preference. The liver retractor and trocars are removed. The wounds are closed.

Clinical Example (43282)

A 72-year-old female with episodes of postprandial chest pain and abdominal pain is found to have a large type III paraesophageal hernia with organoaxial volvulus. She undergoes laparoscopic repair, including implantation of mesh.

Description of Procedure (43282)

Under general anesthesia, surgical laparoscopy is performed. Pneumoperitoneum is established to distend the abdomen, and the laparoscope is introduced. Gas flow and intra-abdominal pressure are carefully monitored so as not to impair ventilation or venous return. Four to six trocar ports are sited through the anterior abdominal wall above the umbilicus. The viscera are inspected. An orogastric tube may be placed to decompress the stomach if it will pass. The liver is retracted to allow visualization of the esophageal hiatus. The stomach is gently retracted into the abdomen to assess its degree of tethering in the thorax. The peritoneum overlying the right crus is incised, and the plane along the hernia sac is developed. The dissection is extended anteriorly and laterally to the left crus. The base of the crural confluence is dissected free of adhesions to the sac. The hernia sac is carefully dissected into the mediastinum with caudal traction. The interfaces between the pleura, pericardium, spine, and aorta are developed as the dissection is carried cephalad to the top of the hernia sac. The sac contents are completely reduced back into the abdominal cavity. The hernia sac is then excised taking care to avoid injury to stomach and vagal trunks. An esophageal dilator may be placed transorally. The esophagus is identified and dissected circumferentially and along its mediastinal course in order to reduce tension, allowing the gastroesophageal junction to rest comfortably within the abdominal cavity. Care is taken to identify and preserve the vagus nerves. The gastro-splenic ligament and the short gastric vessels are divided if necessary. The retro-esophageal window is developed, and the esophagus is retracted caudally. If possible the crural pillars are approximated with sutures. Anterior reinforcement of the diaphragm is performed with sutures as needed, the tightness of the repair being gauged visually or by the presence of the bougie or other device. Determine if mesh reinforcement of the repair is necessary. A relaxing incision may be created in the diaphragm. A suitably sized, shaped, and trimmed piece of synthetic or biologic mesh prosthesis is introduced into the abdomen; positioned appropriately in the hiatal region; and fixed with stitches, tacks, staples, or other devices. Partial or total fundoplasty is then performed with sutures. Additional sutures may be placed to attach the gastric fundus and/or body to the diaphragm. The operative field is carefully inspected to ensure hemostasis. Esophageal tubes are removed as per surgeon preference. The liver retractor and then trocars are removed. The wounds are closed.

Stomach

INTRODUCTION

43760   Change of gastrostomy tube, percutaneous, without imaging or endoscopic guidance

▶(To report fluoroscopically guided replacement of gastrostomy tube, use 49450)◀

▲**43761**   Repositioning of a naso- or oro-gastric feeding tube, through the duodenum for enteric nutrition

 Rationale

Code 43761 has been editorially revised to clarify its use for reporting repositioning of the naso- or oro-gastric feeding tube through the duodenum. The cross-reference following 43760 has been revised to clarify its use for replacement of a gastrostomy tube.

BARIATRIC SURGERY

Laparoscopy

43770   Laparoscopy, surgical, gastric restrictive procedure; placement of adjustable gastric restrictive device (eg, gastric band and subcutaneous port components)

43774   removal of adjustable gastric restrictive device and subcutaneous port components

(For removal and replacement of both gastric band and subcutaneous port components, use 43659)

●**43775**   longitudinal gastrectomy (ie, sleeve gastrectomy)

▶(For open gastric restrictive procedure, without gastric bypass, for morbid obesity, other than vertical-banded gastroplasty, use 43843)◀

OTHER PROCEDURES

43842   Gastric restrictive procedure, without gastric bypass, for morbid obesity; vertical-banded gastroplasty

43843   other than vertical-banded gastroplasty

▶(For laparoscopic longitudinal gastrectomy [ie, sleeve gastrectomy], use 43775)◀

⊘=Modifier 51 Exempt   ⊙=Moderate Sedation   ✚=Add-on Code   ✗=FDA approval pending

✍ Rationale

Code 43775 has been established to report a longitudinal gastrectomy (ie, sleeve gastrectomy) performed via a laparoscopy. The longitudinal (or sleeve) gastrectomy originated from the duodenal switch procedure performed as part of a complex operation known as a biliopancreatic diversion with duodenal switch (BPD-DS) or performed as a first stage procedure on morbid obese patients who later undergo a more complicated surgery (Roux-en-Y gastric bypass or BPD-DS).

Laparoscopic sleeve gastrectomy (LSG) is now being used as a primary single-stage restrictive procedure achieved by staple placement, which is reportable with code 43775.

A cross-reference note has been added following code 43775 to direct the use of code 43843 when this procedure is performed by an open technique. Another cross-reference note, directing the use of code 43775 for the laparoscopic technique, has been added under the open gastric restrictive procedure code 43843.

🩺 Clinical Example (43775)

A 43-year-old female presents with a life-long history of obesity and a diet history that confirms morbid obesity (ie, BMI greater than 40). She has been refractory to medical weight loss management and elects to undergo laparoscopic longitudinal gastrectomy.

Description of Procedure (43775)

Under general anesthesia, surgical laparoscopy is performed. Pneumoperitoneum is established to distend the abdomen, and the laparoscope is introduced. Gas flow and intra-abdominal pressure are carefully monitored so as not to impair ventilation or venous return. Four to six trocar ports are sited through the anterior abdominal wall above the umbilicus. The viscera are inspected. An oro-gastric tube may be placed to decompress the stomach. The liver is retracted to allow visualization of the stomach to the esophageal hiatus. The Angle of His is exposed by dissecting the peritoneal attachments. From a site approximately 4- to 6-cm proximal to the pylorus, the gastrocolic ligament is opened and divided cephalad along the greater curvature. The dissection and division are carried through the gastro-splenic ligament and the short gastric vessels until the Angle of His is reached. The posterior attachments of the stomach to the lesser sac are then dissected to free the lesser curvature. A bougie, or wide bore tube, is passed though the mouth into the stomach. With laparoscopic visualization, the bougie is positioned along the lesser curvature. Starting proximal to the pylorus and staying parallel to the bougie, the greater curve of the stomach is then divided longitudinally with several firings of an endoscopic stapler until the Angle of His is reached. Care is taken to exclude the entire fundus of the stomach and to not impinge on the gastroesophageal junction. (The staple line may be over sewn or otherwise sealed per surgeon preference.) Staple line integrity is checked to exclude leaks. The resected stomach segment is placed in a retrieval bag and extracted with enlargement of one of the trocar site incisions. The extraction site is closed at the fascia. The operative field is carefully inspected to ensure good hemostasis. A drain may be placed per surgeon preference along the gastric staple line. The liver retraction is released, and the trocars are removed. The incisions are closed.

Rectum

EXCISION

45160   Excision of rectal tumor by proctotomy, transsacral or transcoccygeal approach

▶(45170 has been deleted. To report excision of rectal tumor, transanal approach, see 45171, 45172)◀

(For transanal endoscopic microsurgical [ie, TEMS] excision of rectal tumor, use 0184T)

●45171   Excision of rectal tumor, transanal approach; not including muscularis propria (ie, partial thickness)

●45172   including muscularis propria (ie, full thickness)

▶(For destruction of rectal tumor, transanal approach, use 45190)◀

DESTRUCTION

45190   Destruction of rectal tumor (eg, electrodesiccation, electrosurgery, laser ablation, laser resection, cryosurgery) transanal approach

▶(For excision of rectal tumor, transanal approach, see 45171, 45172)◀

 Rationale

Codes 45171 and 45172 have been established to report excision of rectal tumor using a transanal approach. In order to provide more granularity and capture the variable work, the procedural services have been split into two codes. Specifically, code 45171 is reported for partial-thickness excision of rectal wall tumors, which are typically small polyps or benign tumors that are too close to the anal verge to be amenable to endoscopic excision; and code 45172 is reported for full-thickness excision of rectal wall tumors, which are generally larger and may be benign or malignant. When full thickness excision procedures are performed, a patient will typically be kept in a facility to monitor for leakage, bleeding, and/or urinary retention that sometimes occurs postoperatively.

This service was previously reported with code 45170, which has been deleted. A cross-reference has been added following code 45172 to direct users to code 45190 for destruction of rectal tumor using a transanal approach. In addition, a cross-reference has also been added following code 45190 to direct users to codes 45171 and 45172 for excision of rectal tumor using a transanal approach.

 Clinical Example (45171)

A 70-year-old male presents with rectal bleeding. Clinical and diagnostic studies confirm a small 2.5-cm benign tumor of the posterior rectal wall with the lower margin 3 to 4 cm from the anal verge. He undergoes a transanal partial-thickness excision of the tumor.

Description of Procedure (45171)

A retractor system is utilized to evert the anal canal. A large anal retractor or rectal speculum is placed, and a local anesthetic agent with epinephrine is injected into the submucosal plane of the lesion. Stay sutures are placed 1 cm proximal and 1 cm distal to the lesion. A 1-cm margin is outlined around the entire lesion. A local anesthetic is injected into the submucosal plane under the lesion to elevate the lesion off of the underlying muscular layer. An energy source (eg, electric cautery or harmonic scalpel) is utilized to excise the entire tumor. This is performed circumferentially around the lesion along the margin. The lesion is removed and sent to pathology. Hemostasis is obtained, and the defect is closed.

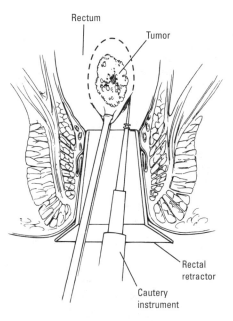

Rectum

Tumor

Rectal retractor

Cautery instrument

 Clinical Example (45172)

A 75-year-old male presents with rectal bleeding and watery diarrhea. Clinical and diagnostic studies confirm a large tumor of the posterior rectal wall with the lower margin 4 cm from the anal verge. He undergoes a transanal full thickness excision of the tumor.

Description of Procedure (45172)

The patient is placed into a prone jackknife position. A retractor system is utilized to evert the anal canal. A large anal retractor or rectal speculum is placed, and a local anesthetic agent with epinephrine is injected into the submucosal plane of the lesion. Stay sutures are placed 1 cm proximal and 1 cm distal to the lesion. A 1-cm or greater margin is outlined around the entire lesion. An energy source (eg, electric cautery, harmonic scalpel) is utilized to begin the full thickness excision of the tumor. The posterior rectal wall is transected through the mucosa, muscular layer, lamina propria, and then through the rectal mesentery. This is performed circumferentially around the lesion along the margin. The lesion is removed and sent to pathology. Hemostasis is obtained, and the defect is closed.

ENDOSCOPY

Proctosigmoidoscopy is the examination of the . . .

Sigmoidoscopy is the examination of the . . .

Colonoscopy is the examination of the . . .

For an incomplete colonoscopy, with full . . .

Surgical endoscopy always includes diagnostic endoscopy.

▶For computed tomographic colonography, see 74261-74263.◀

45300   Proctosigmoidoscopy, rigid; diagnostic, with or without collection of specimen(s) by brushing or washing (separate procedure)

 Rationale

In support of the addition of CT colonography codes 74261-74263, the Endoscopy guidelines have been revised to include these services.

Anus

▶For incision of thrombosed external hemorrhoid, use 46083. For ligation of internal hemorrhoid(s), see 46221, 46945, 46946. For excision of internal and/or external hemorrhoid(s), see 46250-46262, 46320. For injection of hemorrhoid(s), use 46500. For destruction of internal hemorrhoid(s) by thermal energy, use 46930. For destruction of hemorrhoid(s) by cryosurgery, use 46999. For hemorrhoidopexy, use 46947.◀

INCISION

(For subcutaneous fistulotomy, use 46270)

46020   Placement of seton

EXCISION

▲**46200**   Fissurectomy, including sphincterotomy, when performed

▶(46210, 46211 have been deleted. To report, use 46999)◀

46220   ▶Code is out of numerical sequence. See 46200-46288◀

▲**46221**   Hemorrhoidectomy, internal, by rubber band ligation(s)

#▲**46945**   Hemorrhoidectomy, internal, by ligation other than rubber band; single hemorrhoid column/group

#▲**46946**   2 or more hemorrhoid columns/groups

#▲**46220**   Excision of single external papilla or tag, anus

▲**46230**   Excision of multiple external papillae or tags, anus

#▲**46320**   Excision of thrombosed hemorrhoid, external

▲**46250**   Hemorrhoidectomy, external, 2 or more columns/groups

▶(For hemorrhoidectomy, external, single column/group, use 46999)◀

▲**46255**   Hemorrhoidectomy, internal and external, single column/group;

46257   with fissurectomy

⊘=Modifier 51 Exempt   ⊙=Moderate Sedation   ✚=Add-on Code   ✔=FDA approval pending

▲46258   with fistulectomy, including fissurectomy, when performed

▲46260   Hemorrhoidectomy, internal and external, 2 or more columns/groups;

46261   with fissurectomy

▲46262   with fistulectomy, including fissurectomy, when performed

46270   Surgical treatment of anal fistula (fistulectomy/fistulotomy); subcutaneous

▲46275   intersphincteric

▲46280   transsphincteric, suprasphincteric, extrasphincteric or multiple, including placement of seton, when performed

46285   second stage

46288   Closure of anal fistula with rectal advancement flap

46320   ▶Code is out of numerical sequence. See 46200-46288◀

INTRODUCTION

46500   Injection of sclerosing solution, hemorrhoids

46505   Chemodenervation of internal anal sphincter

REPAIR

46706   Repair of anal fistula with fibrin glue

●46707   Repair of anorectal fistula with plug (eg, porcine small intestine submucosa [SIS])

46760   Sphincteroplasty, anal, for incontinence, adult; muscle transplant

46761   levator muscle imbrication (Park posterior anal repair)

46762   implantation artificial sphincter

#46947   Hemorrhoidopexy (eg, for prolapsing internal hemorrhoids) by stapling

DESTRUCTION

46930   Destruction of internal hemorrhoid(s) by thermal energy (eg, infrared coagulation, cautery, radiofrequency)

▶(46934-46936 have been deleted) ◀

▶(46937, 46938 have been deleted. To report, use 45190)◀

46945   ▶Code is out of numerical sequence. See 46200-46288◀

46946   ▶Code is out of numerical sequence. See 46200-46288◀

46947   ▶Code is out of numerical sequence. See 46700-46947◀

✍ Rationale

A large number of editorial changes have been made to the codes included in the Digestive System/Anus section of the CPT codebook. The editorial changes reflect revisions that address issues such as notation of procedures that are ordinarily performed together, services that are rarely performed, or services that have been relocated for placement with codes that are more closely related to that particular procedure.

Guidelines for the Anus section have been added to clarify the intent of use for particular codes included in this section. These include the appropriate code to use for incision of thrombosed external hemorrhoids (46083), the codes to use to identify ligation of internal hemorrhoid(s) (46221, 46945, 46946), the correct codes to use for excision of internal and/or external hemorrhoid(s) (46250-46262, 46320), the code to use for injection of hemorrhoid(s) (46500), and the appropriate coding for destruction of internal hemorrhoid(s) by thermal energy (46930). The correct code for identification of destruction of hemorrhoid(s) by cryosurgery is 46999. Code 46947 should be reported for hemorrhoidopexy.

Code 46200 has been revised with the removal of the phrase "with or without." This is due to the fact that spincterotomy is typically performed with this procedure.

Codes 46210 and 46211 have been deleted, as they are both procedures that are rarely performed in current practice. As a result, a parenthetical note directs users to report the unlisted code (46999) in order to identify these procedures when provided.

The language for code 46221 has been editorially revised to include language that more specifically identifies the procedure performed.

With the resequencing of codes 46945 and 46946, two reference notes have been added (where the codes would have been found numerically) to direct the user to the appropriate code range (46200-46288) for their current placement, which is non-sequential. Codes 46945 and 46946 appear with the number symbol (#) to indicate that these codes are out of numerical sequence.

Codes 46945 and 46946 for reporting internal hemorrhoidectomy procedure performed using other than rubber band ligation has been relocated from the suture section as this procedure does not involve use of sutures. In addition, language included in the code descriptor indicates that the codes should be utilized according to the number of columns addressed during the procedure (an illustration of "columns" has been included in the CPT codebook). Subsequently, since no codes were left in the Suture Section, the Suture heading was deleted. Therefore, these codes have been relocated to the "Excision" section.

With the resequencing of code 46220, a reference note has been added (where the code would have been found numerically) to direct the user to the appropriate code range (46200-46288) for its current placement, which is non-sequential. Code 46220 appears with a number symbol (#) to indicate that it is out of numerical sequence.

Code 46220 has been relocated to be placed with other procedure codes that are more closely related to this procedure. In addition, because the excision of papilla or tags involves similar work, this code has been revised to reflect an excision procedure of a single external papilla or tag.

Code 46230 has been revised to reflect use for excision of multiple external papillae or tags of the anus. Because the excision of papilla or tags involves similar work, the language for this code has been revised to complement the language for code 46220, allowing use of that code to identify single papilla or tag removal and code 46230 to identify removal of multiple tags or papillae. With the resequencing of code 46320, a reference note has been added (where the code would have been found numerically) to direct the user to the appropriate code range (46200-46288) for its current placement, which is non-sequential. Code 46320 appears with a number symbol (#) to indicate that it is out of numerical sequence.

Code 46250 has been revised to note "two or more columns" to identify what is meant by "complete." As a result, a cross-reference note has been included to direct users to the unlisted code 46999 to identify removal of a single external column via hemorrhoidectomy.

Code 46255 (and indented codes 46257 and 46258) has been editorially revised to reflect use of the more descriptive phrase "single columns/groups." This phrase has replaced the word "single." In addition, code 46258 has been revised with the removal of the phrase "with or without" in accordance with current coding language convention.

Codes 46260-46262 have similarly been revised to reflect the number of columns addressed for the procedure, as well as to align with current coding convention.

The parenthetical note that previously followed code 46262 has now been included as part of the section guidelines.

Code 46275 has been revised replacing the term "submuscular" with the term "intersphincteric" to more specifically identify the service being provided.

Code 46280 has been revised to be more descriptive regarding the procedures included as part of the "complex" surgical treatment of an anal fistula. For this code, the term "complex" has been replaced with the phrase "transsphincteric, suprasphincteric, extrasphincteric."

The cross-reference note following code 46500, hemorrhoid excision, destruction, ligation, and hemorrhoidopexy has been removed. As a result, instead of using a cross-reference note to identify this information, the instruction has been added to the section guidelines.

Code 46707 has been established with the conversion of Category III code 0170T to Category I status to report repair of an anorectal fistula with a plug. As a result, a cross-reference has replaced code 0170T to direct users to use of code 46707 for this procedure.

The repair procedure identified by code 46707 is a new surgical modality that provides a minimally invasive, sphincter-sparing option for treating anal fistulae.

This procedure involves the placement into the fistula tract (and anchoring with sutures) of an acellular xenogeneic "plug" (derived from porcine small intestine submucosa) that spans the entire length of the fistula tract from the internal to the external opening. This plug is then anchored into place with sutures at both the internal and external openings of the fistula. The "plug" (this same porcine-derived material is used in a number of other different FDA-cleared devices for wound healing, soft tissue repair, hernia repair, dura mater replacement, etc.) offers support for fistula tract healing and closure.

The cross-references that followed codes 46930 and 46947 have been removed and replaced with instruction language included in the section guidelines.

Codes 46937 and 46938 have been deleted. The cryosurgery services identified by these codes are more appropriately reported using code 45190.

 Clinical Example (46707)

A 44-year-old male presents with a 3-month history of perianal itching, pain, and drainage. Four months ago he had a perianal abscess incised and drained. Physical exam reveals an external os (opening) in the posterior anal space with drainage of mucus with no signs of acute infection or recurrent abscess. Upon anoscopy there is an internal os directly in the midline at the dentate line. The diagnosis of a transsphincteric fistula of the deep posterior anal space is confirmed. Repair of the anal fistula with a cellular xenogeneic plug is performed.

Description of Procedure (46707)

Under anesthesia, a Hill-Ferguson rectal retractor is placed into the anus, and isolation and identification of the internal os is made by passing a series of fistula probes through the fistula tract into the anus. The fistula tract is thoroughly cleaned, irrigated, and debrided. At this time the cellular xenogenic plug is placed in normal saline for 5 to 7 minutes. A large fistula probe is then passed through the external opening and advanced through the tract until it extends through the internal opening. A suture is passed through the tail of the soaked plug. The plug is then pulled into the fistula tract and drawn through the tract until the wider end is tightly aligned with the internal opening, with the "tail" extending distally through the external opening. The internal end of the plug is sutured into place, being careful to also close the internal opening of the fistula tract. Excess "tail" protruding from the external opening is trimmed off, and the distal end of the plug is sutured to the skin at the external opening, being careful to leave this open for drainage. A long acting local anesthetic is injected into the perianal area for comfort postoperatively.

Liver

OTHER PROCEDURES

⊙▲**47382**   Ablation, 1 or more liver tumor(s), percutaneous, radiofrequency

⊘=Modifier 51 Exempt   ⊙=Moderate Sedation   ✚=Add-on Code   ✗=FDA approval pending

Rationale

Code 47382 has been revised with the addition of the moderate sedation symbol (⊙), as moderate sedation is an inherent component of percutaneous radiofrequency ablation of liver tumor procedures.

Biliary Tract

INTRODUCTION

⊙▲47525 Change of percutaneous biliary drainage catheter

 Rationale

Code 47525 has been revised with the addition of the moderate sedation symbol (⊙), as moderate sedation is an inherent component when changing a percutaneous biliary drainage catheter procedure.

Abdomen, Peritoneum, and Omentum

INTRODUCTION, REVISION, REMOVAL

⊙●49411 Placement of interstitial device(s) for radiation therapy guidance (eg, fiducial markers, dosimeter), percutaneous, intra-abdominal, intra-pelvic (except prostate), and/or retroperitoneum, single or multiple

▶(Report supply of device separately)◀

▶(For imaging guidance, see 76942, 77002, 77012, 77021)◀

▶(For percutaneous placement of interstitial device[s] for intra-thoracic radiation therapy guidance, use 32553)◀

Rationale

Code 49411 has been established to describe interstitial device (eg, fiducial marker, dosimeter) placement using a percutaneous, intra-abdominal, intrapelvic, and/or retroperitoneal approach. The interstitial device(s) is placed for the purpose of radiation therapy guidance. Code 49411 is reported one time, regardless of the number of devices placed. This is indicated with the "(s)" in the word "device(s)."

An instructional note has been added to instruct the user to report the supply of the interstitial device separately. Two additional cross-reference notes have been added following code 49411. One note directs users to codes 76942, 77002, 77012, and 77021 for imaging guidance. The second directs users to code 32553 for percutaneous placement of interstitial devices for radiation therapy guidance into the thorax.

Clinical Example (49411)

A 71-year-old female presents with an unresectable adenocarcinoma in the head of the pancreas. She has gold tracking fiducial implants inserted using a percutaneous approach.

Description of Procedure (49411)

Check the patient's intravenous setup. Supervise the positioning of the patient into a supine position. Administer moderate sedation. Prepare and drape the abdomen. Confirm tumor localization. Apply local anesthesia to the three needle entry sites. Introduce preloaded gold fiducial markers into the periphery of the tumor in a triangular array. Confirm that the placement of the markers is within 2 mm of the tumor margin. Verify that complications such as bleeding and hematoma have not occurred.

Replacement

49450   Replacement of gastrostomy or cecostomy (or other colonic) tube, percutaneous, under fluoroscopic guidance including contrast injection(s), image documentation and report

▶(To report a percutaneous change of a gastrostomy tube without imaging or endoscopic guidance, use 43760)◀

 Rationale

The cross-reference following code 49450 has been added to direct the use of code 43760 for percutaneous change of a gastrostomy tube when imaging guidance is not performed.

Urinary System

Kidney

EXCISION

⊙▲**50200**   Renal biopsy; percutaneous, by trocar or needle

 Rationale

Code 50200 has been revised with the addition of the moderate sedation symbol (⊙), as moderate sedation is an inherent component of a percutaneous renal biopsy using a trocar or needle.

Bladder

URODYNAMICS

▶The following section (51725-51792) lists procedures that may be used separately or in many and varied combinations.◀

51725   Simple cystometrogram (CMG) (eg, spinal manometer)

▲**51726**   Complex cystometrogram (ie, calibrated electronic equipment);

●**51727**   with urethral pressure profile studies (ie, urethral closure pressure profile), any technique

●**51728**   with voiding pressure studies (ie, bladder voiding pressure), any technique

⊘=Modifier 51 Exempt   ⊙=Moderate Sedation   ✚=Add-on Code   ✗=FDA approval pending

●51729   with voiding pressure studies (ie, bladder voiding pressure) and urethral pressure profile studies (ie, urethral closure pressure profile), any technique

#✛▲51797   Voiding pressure studies, intra-abdominal (ie, rectal, gastric, intraperitoneal) (List separately in addition to code for primary procedure)

▶(Use 51797 in conjunction with 51728, 51729)◀

51741   Complex uroflowmetry (eg, calibrated electronic equipment)

▶(51772 has been deleted. To report urethral pressure profile studies, see 51727, 51729)◀

51792   Stimulus evoked response (eg, measurement of bulbocavernosus reflex latency time)

▶(51795 has been deleted. To report bladder voiding pressure studies, see 51728, 51729)◀

51797   ▶Code is out of numerical sequence. See 51725-51798◀

Rationale

Codes 51727, 51728, and 51729 have been established to allow reporting of combinations of services that are usually provided together for urodynamic studies. To accommodate these additions, certain codes have been deleted (codes 51772 and 51795), and code 51726 has been revised. Code 51726 is now a parent code that should be used to report the use of complex cystometrogram (specifically use of calibrated electronic equipment) with (1) the urethral pressure profile study (that is, the urethral closure pressure profile previously identified by code 51772 and now identified by code 51727), (2) the voiding pressure study (ie, the bladder voiding pressure study previously identified by code 51795 and now identified by code 51728), or (3) both a voiding pressure study and urethral pressure profile study, identified by code 51729. As a result, codes 51727-51729 have been included as indented codes for code 51726 to note that these procedures are typically performed together. Code 51726 has also been retained to allow reporting of the complex cystometrogram as an independent service. Code 51797 has also been revised to identify the specific intra-abdominal voiding pressure studies performed. Parenthetical notes direct users to the appropriate codes to use to identify the services represented by the deleted procedure codes. A reference note has been added to direct the user to the appropriate code range (51725-51798) for placement of the out of sequence code 51797. Code 51797 appears with a number symbol (#) to indicate that it is out of numerical sequence.

Clinical Example (51727)

A 66-year-old female complains of urinary stress incontinence 6 months after undergoing an anti-incontinence operation.

Description of Procedure (51727)

Note: This is an interactive examination between the patient and the examiner. The procedural steps vary considerably depending upon the cystometric findings.

Infuse fluid into the bladder, and record bladder sensations and bladder volume at predefined physiological landmarks. Wait for involuntary detrusor contractions as the bladder fills, and record the volume and pressure measurements. If involuntary detrusor contractions occur (evidenced by voiding around the catheter), the bladder should be emptied. (In some instances, the examination needs to be repeated when the patient is in sitting and/or standing positions.) If involuntary detrusor contractions are not demonstrated, assist the patient to a sitting and/or standing position and repeat the infusion. When ready to measure urethral measure profile, begin to withdraw the catheter through the urethra, and record bladder sensations and bladder volume at predefined physiologic landmarks. (Each rise in urethral pressure must be accounted for by careful observation and annotated.) When intra-urethral pressure is at its maximum, have the patient do a sustained Valsalva maneuver and several coughs. Record changes to urethral pressures. Check the patient for stress incontinence.

Clinical Example (51728)

A 69-year-old male complains of urinary frequency, urgency, and weak stream. His postvoid residual urine is 210 mL.

Description of Procedure (51728)

Note: This is an interactive examination between the patient and the examiner. The procedural steps vary considerable depending upon the cystometric findings.

Infuse fluid into the bladder, and record bladder sensations and bladder volume at predefined physiologic landmarks. Wait for involuntary detrusor contractions as the bladder fills, and record the volume and pressure measurements. If involuntary detrusor contractions occur (evidenced by voiding around the catheter), the bladder should be emptied. (In some instances, the examination needs to be repeated when the patient is in sitting and/or standing positions.) If involuntary detrusor contractions are not demonstrated, assist the patient to a sitting and/or standing position and repeat the infusion. Ask the patient to try to void when he feels full. (Each rise in vesical pressure must be accounted for by careful observation to distinguish detrusor contractions from rises in abdominal pressure.) If detrusor contractions are not demonstrated, assist the patient with provocative maneuvers such as turning on running water or helping him to relax. If the patient is still unable to void, terminate the examination. Monitor voiding to determine peak voiding pressure. Assess abdominal straining and the quality of the detrusor contraction. Calculate residual urine volume after voiding is completed.

Clinical Example (51729)

A 72-year-old male who had a post-radical retropubic prostatectomy 2 years ago complains of urinary frequency, weak stream, and urinary incontinence. His postvoid residual urine is 208 mL.

Description of Procedure (51729)

Note: This is an interactive examination between the patient and the examiner. The procedural steps vary considerably depending upon the cystometric findings.

Infuse fluid into the bladder, and record bladder sensations and bladder volume at predefined physiologic landmarks. Wait for involuntary detrusor contractions as the bladder fills, and record the volume and pressure measurements. If involuntary detrusor contractions occur (evidenced by voiding around the catheter), the bladder should be emptied. (In some instances, examination needs to be repeated

⊘=Modifier 51 Exempt   ⊙=Moderate Sedation   ✚=Add-on Code   ✗=FDA approval pending

when the patient is in sitting and/or standing positions.) If involuntary detr·
contractions are not demonstrated, assist the patient to a sitting and/or standing position and repeat the infusion. Ask the patient to try to void when he feels
full. (Each rise in vesical pressure must be accounted for by careful observation
to distinguish detrusor contractions from rises in abdominal pressure.) If detrusor
contractions are not demonstrated, assist the patient with provocative maneuvers
such as turning on running water or helping him to relax. When ready to measure
urethral pressure profile, begin to withdraw the catheter through the urethra, and
record bladder sensations and bladder volume at predefined physiologic landmarks.
(Each rise in urethral pressure must be accounted for by careful observation and
annotated.) When intra-urethral pressure is at its maximum, have the patient do
a sustained Valsalva maneuver and several coughs. Record changes to urethral
pressures. Check the patient for stress incontinence. Monitor voiding to determine
peak voiding pressure. Assess abdominal straining and the quality of the detrusor
contraction. Calculate residual urine volume after voiding is completed.

TRANSURETHRAL SURGERY

Urethra and Bladder

▲**52282**   Cystourethroscopy, with insertion of permanent urethral stent

▶(For placement of temporary prostatic urethral stent, use 53855)◀

 Rationale

In support of the establishment of code 53855, which describes insertion of a temporary prostatic urethral stent, code 52282 has been editorially revised to specify
insertion of a *permanent* stent in order to distinguish a temporary stent from a
permanent stent. A cross-reference has been added following code 52282 directing
users to code 53855 for placement of a temporary prostatic urethral stent.

Urethra

OTHER PROCEDURES

(53853 has been deleted. To report, use 55899)

●**53855**   Insertion of a temporary prostatic urethral stent, including urethral measurement

▶(For insertion of permanent urethral stent, use 52282)◀

 Rationale

Category III code 0084T, which described insertion of a temporary prostatic
urethral stent, has been deleted and converted to a Category I code (53855).
The procedure is now performed frequently enough to warrant Category I status.
Category I code 53855 has been established to report insertion of a temporary
prostatic urethral stent, including urethral measurement. A cross-reference has
been added following code 53855 directing users to code 52282 for insertion of
a permanent urethral stent.

Clinical Example (53855)

A 70-year-old male presents to his urologist for an evaluation of continuing lower urinary tract symptoms caused by prostatic enlargement. It is determined the patient is a candidate for a minimally invasive prostatic therapy. Two to five days following the minimally invasive therapy, the patient presents with temporary worsening symptoms (eg, decreased voided volume, increase in post-void residual urine, and urinary retention). A temporary prostatic urethral stent is placed to manage voiding dysfunction during the healing phase. (Prostatic thermotherapy, when performed, should be reported separately.)

Description of Procedure (53855)

The length of the urethra from the bladder neck to the distal side of the external sphincter is measured using the measurement device. The appropriate length stent is selected to accommodate the patient's anatomical requirements and is prepared for insertion. The stent and insertion tool is inserted into the urethra until the distal tip and balloon are positioned in the bladder. The balloon is inflated. The urethral stent is then positioned in the prostatic urethra and deployed. The insertion tool is slowly withdrawn from the urethra. The stent's retrieval tether may be trimmed such that the distal end is just inside the urethra's meatus.

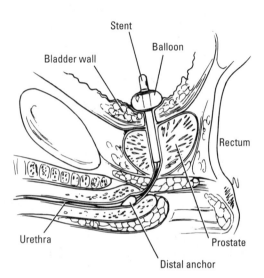

Male Genital System

Prostate

OTHER PROCEDURES

▲**55873**   Cryosurgical ablation of the prostate (includes ultrasonic guidance and monitoring)

▲**55876**   Placement of interstitial device(s) for radiation therapy guidance (eg, fiducial markers, dosimeter), percutaneous, prostate, single or multiple

Rationale

In accordance with the addition of the establishment of the percutaneous interstitial device placement codes 32555 and 49411, the language in codes 55873 and 55876 have been editorially revised to be consistent with the language in the new codes.

 **Clinical Example (55873)**

A 62-year-old man with clinically localized prostate cancer, having considered all available treatment options, has elected to have cryosurgical ablation of the prostate. **Note:** Placement of a suprapubic tube (trocar technique) is included in the work of this procedure, as well as all postoperative care for 90 days.

Description of Procedure (55873)

The patient is in the dorsal lithotomy position. A cystoscopy is performed. The skin of the perineum and suprapubic area is prepared and draped, and the bladder is palpated. The bladder is filled in a retrograde fashion using a syringe or catheter. A trocar puncture is made into the bladder. A guidewire is introduced into the bladder through the sheath once the trocar itself is removed. A skin incision is made to facilitate catheter advancement over the guidewire. A suprapubic tube is placed. This accomplished, the guidewire is removed, the balloon is inflated, return checked through the catheter port, and the catheter is sutured to the skin. A guidewire is then placed into the bladder through the urethra, and a urethral warming device is advanced into the bladder over the guidewire. The guidewire is then removed. The transrectal ultrasound probe is positioned in the rectum. Multiple needle passes are made into the prostate through the perineum. The stylet of each needle is removed, and an angle-tipped wire is advanced through the needle into the prostate. The needle sheath is then removed. The process is repeated multiple times until all needles have been replaced with angle-tipped wires. A small incision is made on the perineum where each guidewire enters the skin to facilitate the passage of a series of sequential dilators. Using these dilators, a tract is made through the perineum and pelvic floor into the prostate. Finally, multiple cryosurgical probes are placed over the guidewires and into the prostate under ultrasonic guidance. The cryoprobes are cooled to the appropriate setting. The initial freeze takes approximately 15 minutes followed by 15 minutes of thaw time. The second freeze time is approximately 15 minutes followed by 15 minutes of thaw time. The growth and regression of the iceball is monitored with ultrasound. A second freeze is routinely done. A third freeze may be done in the area of the urethral diaphragm and prostatic apex by withdrawing the posterior probes. After all areas are treated, the cryoprobes are thawed and removed. The cryoprobe sheath sites in the perineum may be closed with sutures. A compression dressing is applied.

Female Genital System

Vagina

REPAIR

57295	Revision (including removal) of prosthetic vaginal graft; vaginal approach
57296	open abdominal approach

▶(For laparoscopic approach, use 57426)◀

Rationale

In accordance with the establishment of code 57426 to describe the revision of a prosthetic vaginal graft using a laparoscopic approach, a cross-reference note has been added following codes 57295 and 57296 directing users to code 57426 when a laparoscopic approach is used to perform revision of a prosthetic vaginal graft.

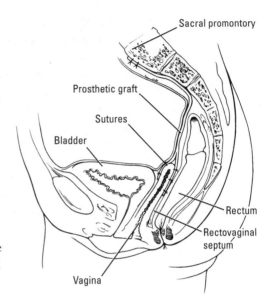

▶ENDOSCOPY/LAPAROSCOPY◀

57425 Laparoscopy, surgical, colpopexy (suspension of vaginal apex)

●**57426** Revision (including removal) of prosthetic vaginal graft, laparoscopic approach

▶(For vaginal approach, see 57295. For open abdominal approach, see 57296)◀

Rationale

The Endoscopy heading in the Vagina section has been revised to include "Laparoscopy," because laparoscopic procedures are listed in this section. Code 57426 has been established to describe revision of a prosthetic vaginal graft using a laparoscopic approach. Prosthetic vaginal graft revision is necessary due to infection. Currently, codes 57295 and 57296 describe revision of prosthetic vaginal graft using vaginal approach and open abdominal approach respectively. However, the laparoscopic approach is also widely performed. Code 57426 includes removal of a prosthetic vaginal graft, when performed. A cross-reference note has been added to instruct users to codes 57295 and 57296 when a vaginal or open abdominal approach is used for this procedure.

Clinical Example (57426)

A 67-year-old gravida 3 para 3 female presents complaining of vaginal discharge, discomfort, and painful intercourse. She underwent abdominal sacral colpopexy using mesh approximately 1 year ago, which was uncomplicated. Her past medical history is negative. Her pertinent physical examination reveals mesh eroding through the apex of the vagina. Vaginal apical support is adequate. The surgeon decides that excision is necessary and performs this via the laparoscopic route.

Description of Procedure (57426)

Access to the pelvis is achieved via laparoscopic approach. The vaginal tissue may be elevated by the surgeon's free hand introduced vaginally or by an instrument placed within the vaginal cavity. The graft is identified and the peritoneum is opened over it. Sharp dissection at the area of graft attachment to the vagina is performed. Care is taken not to dissect too deeply to avoid entering the bladder or rectum. The vaginal epithelium is dissected sharply around the eroding mesh, creating a plane between the vaginal epithelium and the endopelvic fascia.

This dissection is taken circumferentially approximately 2 cm, and the graft and attached tissue is removed. All of the eroding material is excised sharply, with care taken to avoid the rectum, bladder, and small bowel. Once excision is complete, the remaining edges of the endopelvic fascia are re-approximated with delayed absorbable suture, and the vaginal epithelium is closed in layers. The portion of the graft that is attached to the presacral ligament is identified. Sharp dissection is completed with care taken to avoid the significant vasculature here. The graft is removed, as are the permanent sutures that were used to attach it. Skin wounds or vaginal mucosa are re-approximated. Irrigation is carried out, and a urinary catheter is placed to complete the procedure.

Maternity Care and Delivery

►ANTEPARTUM AND FETAL INVASIVE SERVICES◄

►(For fetal intrauterine transfusion, use 36460)◄

►(For unlisted fetal invasive procedure, use 59897)◄

59000   Amniocentesis; diagnostic

(For radiological supervision and interpretation, use 76946)

59076   Fetal shunt placement, including ultrasound guidance

✐ Rationale

The Maternity Care and Delivery/Antepartum Services subheading has been revised to include fetal invasive services to more accurately describe the procedures listed in this section. Two new cross-reference notes have been added following the subheading to direct users to code 36460 for fetal intrauterine transfusions, and code 59897 for unlisted fetal invasive procedure. The cross-reference note following code 59076 has been relocated above code 59000, as this instruction does not apply solely to code 59076.

OTHER PROCEDURES

▲**59897**   Unlisted fetal invasive procedure, including ultrasound guidance, when performed

✐ Rationale

Code 59897 describes an unlisted laparoscopic procedure performed for maternity care and delivery, which includes ultrasound guidance when performed. To clarify that code 59897 may be reported whether ultrasound guidance is used or not, the descriptor has been editorially revised to indicate ultrasound guidance, when performed.

Skull, Meninges, and Brain

STEREOTACTIC RADIOSURGERY (CRANIAL)

Cranial stereotactic radiosurgery is a distinct . . .

Cranial stereotactic radiosurgery is typically performed . . .

Codes 61796 and 61797 involve stereotactic . . .

Codes 61798 and 61799 involve stereotactic . . .

Do not report codes 61796-61800 in . . .

Codes 61796-61799 include computer-assisted planning. Do . . .

▶(For intensity modulated beam delivery plan and treatment, see 77301, 77418. For stereotactic body radiation therapy see 77373, 77435)◀

+61795   Stereotactic computer-assisted volumetric (navigational) procedure, intracranial, extracranial, or spinal (List separately in addition to code for primary procedure)

Spine and Spinal Cord

STEREOTACTIC RADIOSURGERY (SPINAL)

Spinal stereotactic radiosurgery is a distinct . . .

Spinal stereotactic radiosurgery is typically performed . . .

Stereotactic spinal surgery is only used . . .

Codes 63620, 63621 include computer-assisted planning. . . .

▶(For intensity modulated beam delivery plan and treatment, see 77301, 77418. For stereotactic body radiation therapy see 77373, 77435)◀

63620   Stereotactic radiosurgery (particle beam, gamma ray, or linear accelerator); 1 spinal lesion

Rationale

The cross-references following introductory guidelines of the Stereotactic Radiosurgery sections for cranial (61795-61800) and spinal (63620-63621) procedures have been revised to instruct the use of code 77373 or 77435 for stereotactic body radiation therapy of non-cranial/non-spinal lesions.

NEUROSTIMULATORS (SPINAL)

Codes 63650-63688 apply to both simple . . .

▶Codes 63650, 63655, and 63661-63664 describe the operative placement, revision, replacement, or removal of the spinal neurostimulator system components to provide spinal electrical stimulation.

      ⊘=Modifier 51 Exempt   ⊙=Moderate Sedation ✛=Add-on Code ⋏=FDA approval pending

A neurostimulator system includes an implanted neurostimulator, external controller, extension, and collection of contacts. Multiple contacts or electrodes (4 or more) provide the actual electrical stimulation in the epidural space.

For percutaneously placed neurostimulator systems (63650, 63661, 63663), the contacts are on a catheter-like lead. An array defines the collection of contacts that are on one catheter.

For systems placed via an open surgical exposure (63655, 63662, 63664), the contacts are on a plate or paddle-shaped surface.

Do not report 63661 or 63663 when removing or replacing a temporary percutaneously placed array for an external generator.◀

63650 Percutaneous implantation of neurostimulator electrode array, epidural

▶(63660 has been deleted. To report, see 63661-63664)◀

●**63661** Removal of spinal neurostimulator electrode percutaneous array(s), including fluoroscopy, when performed

●**63662** Removal of spinal neurostimulator electrode plate/paddle(s) placed via laminotomy or laminectomy, including fluoroscopy, when performed

●**63663** Revision including replacement, when performed, of spinal neurostimulator electrode percutaneous array(s), including fluoroscopy, when performed

▶(Do not report 63663 in conjunction with 63661, 63662 for the same spinal level)◀

●**63664** Revision including replacement, when performed, of spinal neurostimulator electrode plate/paddle(s) placed via laminotomy or laminectomy, including fluoroscopy, when performed

▶(Do not report 63664 in conjunction with 63661, 63662 for the same spinal level)◀

✐ Rationale

Four new codes—63661, 63662, 63663, and 63664—have been established to report the removal and the revision of a spinal neurostimulator electrode percutaneous array(s) and plate/paddle(s) procedures. Codes 63661-63664 will allow differentiation of the services and work involved in revision and replacement procedures compared to the removal and the difference in services for a percutaneous electrode when compared to a "plate/paddle" electrode array procedure. These services also include fluoroscopy when performed; therefore, fluoroscopy is considered an inclusive component and should not be separately reported.

Code 63660 was previously used to report these services; however, it was too broad and did not capture the intensity of the work involved in the revision and in the removal of a percutaneous electrode and so has been deleted. The Spine and Spinal Cord – Neurostimulator guidelines have also been revised to include these services. An exclusionary parenthetical note has been added to restrict use of codes 63663 and 63664 when removal of spinal neurostimulator electrode percutaneous array(s) (63661) and removal of spinal neurostimulator electrode plate/paddle(s) placed via laminotomy or laminectomy (63662) are performed.

Clinical Example (63661)

A 54-year-old male underwent a previous implantation of a dorsal column spinal stimulator for pain control, which provided good coverage and control of pain in the affected area initially. Over time, the stimulator no longer provided coverage to the affected area despite revision; thus the thoracic epidural stimulator array is to be removed.

Description of Procedure (63661)

The anchoring site of the previous stimulator lead in the thoracolumbar spine is localized. The overlying soft tissue structures are anesthetized to the level of the lamina with local anesthetic. A midline incision is created, and soft tissues are dissected to expose the lead. The lead is cut at the site and removed from the epidural space via gentle traction. An image is obtained to document removal of the lead. (**Note:** Removal of the implanted spinal neurostimulator pulse generator or receiver is a separately reportable procedure [CPT code 63688]). The overlying tissues are closed, and the site is bandaged.

Clinical Example (63662)

A 56-year-old female underwent a previous implantation of a plate/paddle dorsal column spinal stimulator for pain control, which provided good coverage and control of pain in the affected area. Over time, the stimulator no longer provided coverage to the affected area despite revision; thus the plate/paddle is to be removed.

Description of Procedure (63662)

Under anesthesia, the anchoring site of the previous stimulator lead in the thoracolumbar spine is localized. The overlying soft tissue structures are anesthetized using local anesthesia to the level of the lamina. A midline incision is created, and soft tissues are dissected to expose the lead. Removal of scar tissue and additional bone around the prior laminectomy site, along with dissection of the epidural space, are performed to access and remove the preexisting paddle lead in the epidural space via gentle traction. An image is obtained to document the removal of the paddle lead. (**Note:** Removal of the implanted spinal neurostimulator pulse generator or receiver is a separately reportable procedure [CPT code 63688]). The pre-existing paddle lead is disconnected from the connector to the electrodes of the pulse generator or receiver. The paddle lead is removed from the anchoring site. The incision is closed, and dressings are applied.

Clinical Example (63663)

A 54-year-old male underwent a previous implantation of a dorsal column spinal stimulator for pain control, which provided good coverage and control of pain in the affected area. The patient suffered a fall, after which the stimulator no longer provided coverage to the affected area. The thoracic epidural stimulator array is to be repositioned to once again cover the affected area.

Description of Procedure (63663)

The anchoring site of the previous stimulator lead in the thoracolumbar spine is localized, and the overlying soft tissue structures are anesthetized to the level of the lamina. A midline incision is created, and soft tissues are dissected to expose the lead. The lead is cut at the site and removed from the epidural space via gentle traction. Using fluoroscopic guidance, a needle is advanced into the epidural space using a loss of resistance technique. Epidural location is confirmed with a percutaneous probe. A percutaneous electrode array is guided into the epidural space through the needle and advanced toward the midthoracic spine. The exposed end of the electrode array is attached to an external stimulator unit. Under guidance from the surgeon, a technician out of the operating field tests various electrode combinations, and the lead(s) is/are physically relocated by the surgeon until the patient indicates that the dermatomal areas of his typical pain have been covered with paresthesias generated by the stimulator. The external unit is detached, the needle and stylet are removed, and the lead(s) is/are anchored to the fascia. (**Note:** Insertion or replacement of the implanted spinal neurostimulator pulse generator or receiver is a separately reportable procedure [CPT code 63685]). The electrode array is attached to the neurostimulator pulse generator or receiver electrode connectors and anchored in place. An image is obtained to document final placement. The incision is closed and dressings are applied.

Clinical Example (63664)

A 56-year-old female underwent a previous implantation of a dorsal column spinal stimulator for pain control, which provided good coverage and control of pain in the affected area. The lead has fractured, and the stimulator no longer provides coverage to the affected area. The plate/paddle electrode is to be removed and replaced to once again cover the affected area.

Description of Procedure (63664)

Under anesthesia, the anchoring site of the previous stimulator lead in the thoracolumbar spine is localized. The overlying soft tissue structures are anesthetized to the level of the lamina. A midline incision is created, and soft tissues are dissected to expose the lead. Scar tissue and additional bone removal around the prior laminectomy site, along with dissection of the epidural space, are performed to access and remove the preexisting paddle lead in the epidural space via gentle traction. A new paddle lead is placed through this laminectomy site using fluoroscopic guidance. The exposed end of the electrode array is attached to an external stimulator unit. Under guidance from the surgeon, a technician out of the operating field tests various electrode combinations, and the lead is physically relocated by the surgeon until the patient indicates that the dermatomal areas of her typical pain have been covered with paresthesias generated by the stimulator. (**Note:** Insertion or replacement of the implanted spinal neurostimulator pulse generator or receiver is a separately reportable procedure [CPT code 63685]). The paddle lead is attached to the neurostimulator pulse generator or receiver electrode connectors. The lead is anchored to the fascia. An image is obtained to document final placement. The incision is closed, and the sites are dressed.

Extracranial Nerves, Peripheral Nerves, and Autonomic Nervous System

INTRODUCTION/INJECTION OF ANESTHETIC AGENT (NERVE BLOCK), DIAGNOSTIC OR THERAPEUTIC

▶(For destruction by neurolytic agent or chemodenervation, see 62280-62282, 64600-64681)◀

▶(For epidural or subarachnoid injection, see 62310-62319)◀

▶(Codes 64479-64495 are unilateral procedures. For bilateral procedures, use modifier 50)◀

▶(For fluoroscopic guidance and localization for needle placement and injection in conjunction with 64479-64484, use 77003)◀

Somatic Nerves

64400   Injection, anesthetic agent; trigeminal nerve, any division or branch

64449   lumbar plexus, posterior approach, continuous infusion by catheter (including catheter placement)

(Do not report 64449 in conjunction with 01996)

64450   other peripheral nerve or branch

64455   Injection(s), anesthetic agent and/or steroid, plantar common digital nerve(s) (eg, Morton's neuroma)

(Do not report 64455 in conjunction with 64632)

▶(Codes 64470-64476 have been deleted. To report, see 64490-64495)◀

▶Paravertebral Spinal Nerves and Branches◀

▶(Image guidance [fluoroscopy or CT] and any injection of contrast are inclusive components of 64490-64495. Imaging guidance and localization are required for the performance of paravertebral facet joint injections described by codes 64490-64495. If imaging is not used, report 20550-20553. If ultrasound guidance is used, report 64999)◀

▶(For bilateral procedures, use modifier 50)◀

▶(For injection of the T12-L1 joint, or nerves innervating that joint, use 64493)◀

●**64490**   Injection(s), diagnostic or therapeutic agent, paravertebral facet (zygapophyseal) joint (or nerves innervating that joint) with image guidance (fluoroscopy or CT), cervical or thoracic; single level

+●**64491**   second level (List separately in addition to code for primary procedure)

+●**64492**   third and any additional level(s) (List separately in addition to code for primary procedure)

▶(Do not report 64492 more than once per day)◀

▶(Use 64491, 64492 in conjunction with 64490)◀

●**64493**   Injection(s), diagnostic or therapeutic agent, paravertebral facet (zygapophyseal) joint (or nerves innervating that joint) with image guidance (fluoroscopy or CT), lumbar or sacral; single level

+●**64494**   second level (List separately in addition to code for primary procedure)

⊘=Modifier 51 Exempt   ⊙=Moderate Sedation   ✚=Add-on Code   ✗=FDA approval pending

+●64495   third and any additional level(s) (List separately in addition to code for primary procedure)

▶(Do not report 64495 more than once per day)◀

▶(Use 64494, 64495 in conjunction with 64493)◀

▶Autonomic Nerves◀

64505   Injection, anesthetic agent; sphenopalatine ganglion

 Rationale

The cross-reference immediately following code 64450 stating: "(For phenol destruction, see 64622-64627)," has caused some confusion among users. The cross-reference appears to have had an inadvertent limitation to the use of phenol in the Neurolytic Destruction section, which otherwise does not define specific neurolytic agents to inject, the most commonly used ones being alcohol or phenol or botulism toxin. In order to eliminate this confusion, the cross-references following code 64450 have been moved above the Somatic subsection as instructional cross-references to be applied to the entire section. The cross-references have been further revised to clarify the use of phenol in the Neurolytic Destruction section.

In an effort to allay confusion about the reporting of facet joint and facet joint nerve injections, some changes have been made in the Nervous System section. The new subheading Paravertebral Spinal Nerves and Branches has been added in the Extracranial Nerves, Peripheral Nerves, and Autonomic Nervous System, Introduction/Injection of Anesthetic Agent (Nerve Block), Diagnostic or Therapeutic subsection. Codes 64470-64476 have been deleted. Codes 64490-64495 have been established in the new subsection to report paravertebral spinal facet or nerve injections. The new series of codes reflect multiple level injections and include injection of contrast during fluoroscopic guidance and localization.

Several parenthetical notes have been added to instruct that (1) image guidance (fluoroscopy or CT) and any injection of contrast are inclusive components of codes 64490-64495; (2) imaging guidance and localization are required for the performance of paravertebral facet joint or nerve injections described by codes 64490-64495; (3) if imaging is not used, report codes 20550-20553; (4) if ultrasound guidance is used, code 64999 should be reported; (5) modifier 50 should be used for bilateral procedures; and (6) injections in the T12-L1 joint or nerves innervating that joint should be reported with code 64493.

Code 64490 is reported for injections into the paravertebral facet joints or nerves innervating the joint at the cervical or thoracic level. Code 64490 is reported for a single or the initial level treated.

Add-on code 64491 is reported for injections at the second cervical or thoracic level treated.

Add-on code 64492 is reported for injections at the third and any additional cervical or thoracic level(s) treated. Two instructional notes have been added following code 64492 to indicate that (1) code 64492 should not be reported more than once per day, and (2) codes 64491 and 64492 should be used in conjunction with code 64490.

Code 64493 is reported for injections at the paravertebral facet joints or nerves innervating the joint at the lumbar or sacral level. Code 64493 is reported for a single or the initial level treated.

Add-on code 64494 is reported for injections at the second lumbar or sacral level treated.

Add-on code 64495 is reported for injections at the third and any additional lumbar or sacral level(s) treated. Two instructional notes have been added following code 64495 to indicate that (1) code 64495 should not be reported more than once per day, and (2) codes 64494 and 64495 should be used in conjunction with code 64493.

In accordance with the revisions in the Somatic Nerves system subsection, the subheading Sympathetic Nerves was changed to Autonomic Nerves.

Clinical Example (64490)

A 67-year-old female has chronic neck pain radiating toward her right shoulder. She has no neurological symptoms or weakness in her arms. Based on her exam findings and imaging studies and due to her failure with conservative treatment and persistent pain, diagnostic testing with cervical facet blocks under fluoroscopic guidance on the right at the C4-C5 level is indicated. This testing will be performed by blocking the right C4 and C5 medial branch nerves that innervate the C4-C5 facet joint.

Description of Procedure (64490)

The patient is monitored with continuous pulse oximetry, blood pressure, and electrocardiography. A C-arm fluoroscopy machine is rotated and adjusted until the targeted facet joint and the bony landmarks corresponding to the right C4 and C5 medial branch nerves (that innervate the right C4-C5 facet joint) are optimally visualized. Initially, the C4 medial branch nerve is targeted. The skin and subcutaneous tissues are anesthetized with 1 cc of 1% lidocaine. A spinal needle is then directed toward the lateral facet pillar and groove under intermittent fluoroscopic guidance. Care is taken to avoid vital neural structures or blood vessels. Appropriate positioning of the needle tip is confirmed with multiple fluoroscopic views, including A-P and lateral projections. Non-ionic contrast is injected to confirm appropriate spread around the targeted nerve and exclude any vascular, epidural, or intrathecal spread. Next, anesthetic is slowly infiltrated around the C4 medial branch nerve, after which the needle is removed. With the patient still prepared and draped, the fluoroscopic machine is re-oriented inferiorly, and the entire procedure repeated to block the C5 medial branch nerve. Bandages are applied, and the patient is taken to the recovery area.

Note: Imaging guidance (fluoroscopy or computed tomography) is included in this code.

Clinical Example (64491)

A 67-year-old female has chronic neck pain radiating toward her right shoulder. She has no neurological symptoms or weakness in her arms. Based on her exam findings and imaging studies and due to her failure with conservative treatment

and persistent pain, diagnostic testing with cervical facet blocks under fluoroscopic guidance on the right at the C4-C5 and C5-C6 levels is indicated. This
testing will be performed by blocking the right C4, C5, and C6 medial branch
nerves that innervate the C4-C5 and C5-C6 facet joints.

Description of Procedure (64491)

After injections are placed at the C4-C5 joint's medial branch nerves, and with
the patient still prepared and draped, the fluoroscopic machine is reoriented
inferiorly, and the entire procedure is repeated to block the C5-C6 joint's medial
branch nerves.

Note: Imaging guidance (fluoroscopy or computed tomography) is included in this
code. CPT code 64491 includes only the work associated with injection of the
second level.

Clinical Example (64492)

A 67-year-old female has chronic neck pain radiating toward her right shoulder.
She has no neurological symptoms or weakness in her arms. Based on her exam
findings and imaging studies and due to her failure with conservative treatment
and persistent pain, diagnostic testing with cervical facet blocks under fluoroscopic guidance on the right at the C4-C5, C5-C6, and C6-C7 levels is indicated.
This testing will be performed by blocking the right C4, C5, C6, and C7 medial
branch nerves that innervate the C4-C5, C5-C6, and C6-C7 facet joints.

Description of Procedure (64492)

After injections are placed at the C4 and C5 joints' medial branch nerves, and
with the patient still prepared and draped, the fluoroscopic machine is re-oriented
inferiorly, and the entire procedure is repeated to block the C6-C7 joint's medial
branch nerves.

Note: Imaging guidance (fluoroscopy or computed tomography) is included in this
code. CPT code 64492 includes only the work associated with injection of the
third and any additional levels.

Clinical Example (64493)

A 66-year-old male has chronic right low back pain with radiation toward his buttock, limiting his ability to stand and walk for more than 10 minutes. Based on his
exam findings and imaging studies and due to his failure with conservative care,
diagnostic testing with a lumbar facet block under fluoroscopic guidance on the
right at the L3-L4 level is indicated.

Description of Procedure (64493)

The patient is monitored with continuous pulse oximetry, blood pressure, and
electrocardiography monitors. The C-arm fluoroscopy machine is rotated and
adjusted until the targeted facet joint (L3-L4) is optimally viewed. The skin and
subcutaneous tissues are infiltrated with anesthetic. A spinal needle is then
directed toward the facet joint under intermittent fluoroscopic guidance. Care
is taken not to inadvertently injure vital neural structures or blood vessels. Once
the joint is cannulated, non-ionic contrast is infiltrated to confirm intra-articular
spread and exclude any intra-vascular spread. A mixture containing steroid

mixed with anesthetic is then slowly infiltrated into the facet joint. The needle is removed, a bandage applied, and the patient taken to the recovery area.

Note: Imaging guidance (fluoroscopy or computed tomography) is included in this code.

⚕ Clinical Example (64494)

A 66-year-old male has chronic right low back pain with radiation toward his buttock, limiting his ability to stand and walk for more than 10 minutes. He has no radicular pain or weakness in his legs. Based on his exam findings and imaging studies and due to his failure with conservative care, diagnostic testing with lumbar facet blocks under fluoroscopic guidance on the right at the L3-L4 and L4-L5 levels is indicated.

Description of Procedure (64494)

After an injection of the L3-L4 facet joint, and with the patient still prepared and draped, the C-arm fluoroscopy machine is re-oriented and the entire procedure repeated at the L4-L5 facet joint.

Note: Imaging guidance (fluoroscopy or computed tomography) is included in this code. CPT code 64494 includes only the work associated with injection of the second level.

⚕ Clinical Example (64495)

A 66-year-old male has chronic right low back pain with radiation toward his buttock, limiting his ability to stand and walk for more than 10 minutes. He has no radicular pain or weakness in his legs. Based on his exam findings and imaging studies and due to his failure with conservative care, diagnostic testing with lumbar facet blocks under fluoroscopic guidance on the right at the L3-L4, L4-L5, and L5-S1 levels is indicated.

Description of Procedure (64495)

After injections at the L3-L4 and L4-L5 joints, and with the patient still prepped and draped in the prone position, the C-arm fluoroscopy machine is re-oriented and the entire procedure is repeated the L5-S1 facet joint.

Note: Imaging guidance (fluoroscopy or computed tomography) is included in this code. CPT code 64495 includes only the work associated with injection of the third and any additional levels.

Eye and Ocular Adnexa

Anterior Segment

OTHER PROCEDURES

+66990   Use of ophthalmic endoscope (List separately in addition to code for primary procedure)

▶(66990 may be used only with codes 65820, 65875, 65920, 66985, 66986, 6703
67041, 67042, 67043, 67112, 67113)◀

Posterior Segment

RETINA OR CHOROID

Repair

67113   Repair of complex retinal detachment (eg, proliferative vitreoretinopathy, stage C-1 or greater, diabetic traction retinal detachment, retinopathy of prematurity, retinal tear of greater than 90 degrees), with vitrectomy and membrane peeling, may include air, gas, or silicone oil tamponade, cryotherapy, endolaser photocoagulation, drainage of subretinal fluid, scleral buckling, and/or removal of lens

(To report vitrectomy, pars plana approach, other than in retinal detachment surgery, see 67036-67043)

▶(For use of ophthalmic endoscope with 67113, use 66990)◀

🖉 Rationale

The inclusionary list of procedures which can be used in conjunction with the ophthalmic endoscopy add-on procedure code 66990 has been revised to include code 67113 (complex repair of retinal detachment). A parenthetical note below code 67113 has also been added to direct the use of code 66990 for use of the ophthalmic endoscope.

Prophylaxis

Codes 67141, 67145 include treatment at one or more sessions that may occur at different encounters. These codes should be reported once during a defined treatment period.

Repetitive services. The services listed below . . .

The following descriptors are intended to . . .

67141   Prophylaxis of retinal detachment (eg, retinal break, lattice degeneration) without drainage, 1 or more sessions; cryotherapy, diathermy

🖉 Rationale

The reference to codes 67208-67220, 67227, 67228, and 67229 has been deleted from the Prophylaxis guidelines and moved to the new guidelines in the Destruction subsection, as these codes describe destruction procedures.

Destruction

▶Codes 67208, 67210, 67218, 67220, 67227, 67228, 67229 include treatment at one or more sessions that may occur at different encounters. These codes should be reported once during a defined treatment period.◀

67208   Destruction of localized lesion of retina (eg, macular edema, tumors), 1 or more sessions; cryotherapy, diathermy

Rationale

The reference to codes 67208-67220, 67227, 67228, and 67229 previously included in the introductory guidelines under the subheading of Prophylaxis within the Posterior Segment, Eye and Ocular Adnexa subsection have been relocated to appear under the more directly related subheading of Destruction.

Auditory System

External Ear

REPAIR

(For suture of wound or injury of external ear, see 12011-14302)

⊙**69300**   Otoplasty, protruding ear, with or without size reduction

Rationale

In accordance with the establishment of codes 14301 and 14302, the cross-reference preceding code 69300, has been revised to expand the code range and support the establishment of these services.

⊘=Modifier 51 Exempt   ⊙=Moderate Sedation   ✚=Add-on Code   ✔=FDA approval pending

Radiology

The most significant revisions to the Radiology section are the addition of a series of codes for CT colonography diagnostic and screening procedures, cardiac magnetic imaging codes and guidelines.

In addition, a series of new codes for CT and CTA of the heart, and myocardial perfusion and cardiac blood pool imaging studies have been added.

Radiology

Chest

71250   Computed tomography, thorax; without contrast material

71260   with contrast material(s)

71270   without contrast material, followed by contrast material(s) and further sections

▶(For cardiac computed tomography of the heart, see 75571-75574)◀

71275   Computed tomographic angiography, chest (noncoronary), with contrast material(s), including noncontrast images, if performed, and image postprocessing

(For coronary artery computed tomographic angiography including calcification score and/or cardiac morphology, use 75574)

 Rationale

In support of the deletion of codes 0144T-0151T, the cross-reference following code 71270 has been revised to include the appropriate codes to report cardiac computed tomography of the heart.

In support of the deletion of 0146T-0149T, the cross-reference following code 71275 has been revised to include the appropriate code to report coronary artery computed tomography angiography and/or cardiac morphology.

Spine and Pelvis

72192   Computed tomography, pelvis; without contrast material

72193   with contrast material(s)

72194   without contrast material, followed by contrast material(s) and further sections

(To report 3D rendering, see 76376, 76377)

▶(For computed tomographic colonography, diagnostic, see 74261-74262. For computed tomographic colonography, screening, use 74263)◀

▶(Do not report 72192-72194 in conjunction with 74261-74263)◀

 Rationale

In support of the addition of CT colonography codes 74261, 74262, and 74263, the parenthetical note following code 72194 has been revised to reference these services. In addition, an exclusionary note has been added instructing users not to report codes 72192-72194 in conjunction with codes 74261, 74262, and 74263.

▲72291   Radiological supervision and interpretation, percutaneous vertebroplasty,or vertebral augmentation, or sacral augmentation (sacroplasty), including cavity creation, per vertebral body or sacrum; under fluoroscopic guidance

▲72292   under CT guidance

(For procedure, see 22520-22525, 0200T, 0201T)

🖎 Rationale

In support of the establishment of Category III codes 0200T and 0201T, the radio-logical codes 72291 and 72292 have been revised with the addition of "or sacrum" to be consistent with the intent of these codes. In addition, the cross-reference following code 72292 has been revised to reference the new Category III codes.

Abdomen

74150   Computed tomography, abdomen; without contrast material

74160   with contrast material(s)

74170   without contrast material, followed by contrast material(s) and further sections

(To report 3D rendering, see 76376, 76377)

▶(For computed tomographic colonography, diagnostic, see 74261-74262. For computed tomographic colonography, screening, use 74263.)◀

▶(Do not report 74150-74170 in conjunction with 74261-74263)◀

🖎 Rationale

In support of the addition of CT colonography codes 74261, 74262, and 74263, the cross-reference following code 74170 has been revised to reference these services. Additionally, an exclusionary parenthetical note has been added directing users not to report codes 74150-74157 in conjunction with codes 74261, 74262, and 74263.

Gastrointestinal Tract

●74261   Computed tomographic (CT) colonography, diagnostic, including image postprocessing; without contrast material

●74262   with contrast material(s) including non-contrast images, if performed

▶(Do not report 74261, 74262 in conjunction with 72192-72194, 74150-74170, 74263, 76376, 76377)◀

●74263   Computed tomographic (CT) colonography, screening, including image postprocessing

▶(Do not report 74263 in conjunction with 72192-72194, 74150-74170, 74261, 74262, 76376, 76377)◀

⊘=Modifier 51 Exempt   ⊙=Moderate Sedation   ✚=Add-on Code   𝒩 =FDA approval pending

✍🏻 Rationale

In support of the deletion of codes 0066T and 0067T, Category I codes 74261, 74262, and 74263 and parenthetical notes have been established to describe CT colonography.

Diagnostic CT colonography is described by two codes, 74261 and 74262, and is distinguished by the non-use or use of IV contrast. Code 74261 is intended to report diagnostic CT colonography, including image postprocessing, without contrast material. Code 74262 is intended to report diagnostic CT colonography, with contrast material(s) including non-contrast images, if performed. A parenthetical note has been added to preclude reporting codes 74261 and 74262 in conjunction with certain radiological services.

Screening CT colonography is described by code 74263. Code 74263 is intended to report CT colonography, including image postprocessing. Code 74263 includes interpretation of the entire examination. A parenthetical note has been added to preclude reporting code 74263 in conjunction with certain radiological services.

In the Surgery/Digestive System section, an introductory note has been added to the Rectum/Endoscopy guidelines directing the use of codes 74261, 74262, and 74263 for CT colonography. In addition, the parenthetical notes following codes 72194, 74170, 76376, and 76377 have been updated to reflect these changes.

🩺 Clinical Example (74261)

A 60-year-old female presents with abdominal discomfort, iron deficiency anemia, and guaiac-positive stools. Optical colonoscopy was unsuccessful due to extreme redundancy of the colon.

Description of Procedure (74261)

Supervise the insertion of a rectal tube and the instillation of room air or carbon dioxide. Review the 2D (scout) topogram of the abdomen and pelvis to ensure adequate colonic distention for each acquisition. Supervise the acquisition of thin section, low-dose 2D CT images and review for adequacy. After ensuring continued adequate colonic distention, supervise the acquisition of thin section, low-dose 2D CT images in the second position, typically prone, and review for adequacy. Instruct the technologist to acquire any additional images as needed. Perform interactive manipulations of 3D image datasets (eg, volume rendered, endoluminal, and/or flythrough views) with correlative multiplanar 2D reconstructions of datasets from all positions. Modify and perform additional targeted 3D reconstructions as necessary. Interpret both the supine and prone images of the colon (including decubitus, if performed) using 2D and 3D reconstructions, including 3D endoluminal views, integrated with 2D multiplanar reformations and source images, and compare to pertinent prior imaging studies. Dictate a report for the patient's medical record.

🩺 Clinical Example (74262)

A 60-year-old female presents with abdominal discomfort, iron deficiency anemia, and guaiac-positive stools. Optical colonoscopy was unsuccessful due to extreme redundancy of the colon.

Description of Procedure (74262)

Supervise the insertion of a rectal tube and the instillation of room air or carbon dioxide. Review the 2D (scout) topogram of the abdomen and pelvis to ensure adequate colonic distention for each acquisition. Supervise the acquisition of thin section, low-dose 2D CT images and review for adequacy. After ensuring continued adequate colonic distention, supervise the acquisition of thin section, low-dose 2D CT images in the second position, typically prone, and review for adequacy. Instruct the technologist to acquire any additional images as needed. When an indeterminate polypoid lesion is identified, supervise the administration of intravenous iodinated contrast and the targeted re-acquisition of 2D images of the colon. Interpret the 2D postcontrast images to differentiate an enhancing soft tissue lesion from adherent stool. Perform interactive manipulations of 3D image datasets (eg, volume rendered, endoluminal, and/or flythrough views) with correlative multiplanar 2D reconstructions of datasets from all positions. Modify and perform additional targeted 3D reconstructions as necessary. Interpret both the supine and prone images of the colon (including decubitus, if performed) using 2D and 3D reconstructions, including 3D endoluminal views, integrated with 2D multiplanar reformations and source images, and compare to pertinent prior imaging studies. Dictate a report for the patient's medical record.

 Clinical Example (74263)

A 50-year-old female without signs or symptoms presents for colorectal cancer screening.

Description of Procedure (74263)

Supervise the insertion of a rectal tube and the instillation of room air or carbon dioxide. Review the 2D (scout) topogram of the abdomen and pelvis to ensure adequate colonic distention for each acquisition. Supervise the acquisition of thin section, low-dose 2D CT images and review for adequacy. After ensuring continued adequate colonic distention, supervise the acquisition of thin section, low-dose 2D CT images in the second position, typically prone, and review for adequacy. Instruct the technologist to acquire any additional images as needed. Perform interactive manipulations of 3D image datasets (eg, volume rendered, endoluminal, and/or flythrough views) with correlative multiplanar 2D reconstructions of datasets from all positions. Modify and perform additional targeted 3D reconstructions as necessary. Interpret both the supine and prone images of the colon (including decubitus, if performed) using 2D and 3D reconstructions, including 3D endoluminal views, integrated with 2D multiplanar reformations and source images, and compare to pertinent prior imaging studies. Dictate a report for the patient's medical record.

Heart

▶Cardiac magnetic imaging differs from traditional magnetic resonance imaging (MRI) in its ability to provide a physiologic evaluation of cardiac function. Traditional MRI relies on static images to obtain clinical diagnoses based upon anatomic information. Improvement in spatial and temporal resolution has expanded the application from an anatomic test and includes physiologic evaluation of cardiac function. Flow and velocity assessment for valves and intracardiac shunts is performed in addition to a function and morphologic evaluation. Use 75559 with 75565 to report flow with pharmacologic wall motion stress evaluation without contrast. Use 75563 with 75565 to report flow with pharmacologic perfusion stress with contrast.

Cardiac MRI for velocity flow mapping can be reported in conjunction with 75557, 75559, 75561, or 75563.

Listed procedures may be performed independently or in the course of overall medical care. If the physician providing these services is also responsible for diagnostic workup and/or follow-up care of the patient, see appropriate sections also. Only one procedure in the series 75557-75563 is appropriately reported per session. Only one add-on code for flow velocity can be reported per session.

▶Cardiac MRI studies may be performed at rest and/or during pharmacologic stress. Therefore, the appropriate stress testing code from the 93015-93018 series should be reported in addition to 75559 or 75563.◀

Cardiac computed tomography (CT) and coronary computed tomographic angiography (CTA) include the axial source images of the pre-contrast, arterial phase sequence, and venous phase sequence (if performed), as well as the two-dimensional and three-dimensional reformatted images resulting from the study, including cine review. Contrast enhanced cardiac CT and coronary CTA codes 75571-75574 include any quantitative assessment when performed as part of the same encounter. Report only one computed tomography heart service per encounter.◀

(For separate injection procedures for vascular . . .

(For cardiac catheterization procedures, see 93501-93556)

▶(75552-75556 have been deleted. To report, see 75557, 75559, 75561, 75563, 75565)◀

75557   Cardiac magnetic resonance imaging for morphology and function without contrast material;

75559   with stress imaging

75561   Cardiac magnetic resonance imaging for morphology and function without contrast material(s), followed by contrast material(s) and further sequences;

75563   with stress imaging

▶(75558, 75560, 75562, 75564 have been deleted. To report flow velocity, use 75565)◀

+●75565   Cardiac magnetic resonance imaging for velocity flow mapping (List separately in addition to code for primary procedure)

▶(Use 75565 in conjunction with 75557, 75559, 75561, 75563)◀

▶(Do not report 75557, 75559, 75561, 75563, 75565 in conjunction with 76376, 76377)◀

✍🏻 Rationale

Add-on code 75565 has been established to report cardiac magnetic resonance imaging for velocity flow mapping. Previously, cardiac magnetic resonance imaging codes 75558, 75560, 75562, and 75564 were used to report these services. For CPT 2010, codes 75558, 75560, 75562, and 75564 have been deleted. An instructional note has been added following code 75565, directing users to report code 75565 with cardiac magnetic resonance imaging codes 75557, 75559, 75561, and 75563. The existing cross-reference has been revised by deleting code 75564 and adding codes 75559, 75561, 75563, and 75565.

In support of the establishment of code 75565, the cardiac magnetic imaging guidelines have been revised to clarify that add-on code 75565 should be used to report flow velocity measurements, to describe the inclusive components of cardiac computed tomography (CT), coronary computed tomographic angiography, and to indicate that only one computed tomography heart service should be reported per encounter. The parenthetical note immediately following the guidelines has been revised to reflect the appropriate range of codes to report for these services.

Clinical Example (75565)

A 55-year-old male presents with heart failure, an enlarged cardiac silhouette on chest X-ray, and an eccentric jet of aortic regurgitation echocardiography. He is undergoing cardiac magnetic resonance imaging to evaluate ventricular size and function. Flow velocity quantification is also requested.

Description of Procedure (75565)

Supervise the set-up of flow quantification scan planes. Scan using flow protocols to obtain data to quantify valve function. Adjust the parameters to optimize data accuracy. Analyze the velocity/flow data on an independent workstation. Calculate the regurgitation fraction, gradients, or shunt ratio using the velocity/flow data obtained.

●**75571** Computed tomography, heart, without contrast material, with quantitative evaluation of coronary calcium

●**75572** Computed tomography, heart, with contrast material, for evaluation of cardiac structure and morphology (including 3D image postprocessing, assessment of cardiac function, and evaluation of venous structures, if performed)

●**75573** Computed tomography, heart, with contrast material, for evaluation of cardiac structure and morphology in the setting of congenital heart disease (including 3D image postprocessing, assessment of LV cardiac function, RV structure and function and evaluation of venous structures, if performed)

●**75574** Computed tomographic angiography, heart, coronary arteries and bypass grafts (when present), with contrast material, including 3D image postprocessing (including evaluation of cardiac structure and morphology, assessment of cardiac function, and evaluation of venous structures, if performed)

Rationale

Codes 0144T, 0145T, 0146T, 0147T, 0148T, 0149T, 0150T, and 0151T, which previously described cardiac computed tomography (CT) and coronary computed tomographic angiography (CTA), have been deleted. These procedures are now performed frequently enough to warrant Category I status. Category I codes 75571, 75572, 75573, and 75574 have been established to report these services.

In an effort to clearly define these services and to clarify that these services are reported per encounter, new guidelines have been added in the Radiology section.

◯=Modifier 51 Exempt   ◉=Moderate Sedation   ✦=Add-on Code   ⋈=FDA approval pending

For consistency, cross-references have been added in the Category III section directing users to these new codes. The cross-reference following code 71270 has been updated to reflect the new codes. The exclusionary notes following codes 76376 and 76377 were revised by adding the new codes, indicating that codes 76376 and 76377 should not be reported with codes 75571, 75572, 75573, and 75574.

Clinical Example (75571)

A 45-year-old male presents for evaluation. He is asymptomatic. His family history is significant for coronary disease with his father having suffered a myocardial infarction at the age of 58. A lipid profile is as follows: total cholesterol 245 mg/dL, LDL cholesterol 156 mg/dL, HDL cholesterol 34 mg/dL, and triglycerides 190 mg/dL. A risk assessment calculates a 10% risk of coronary disease over the next 10 years. A calcium score is ordered to help support the initiation of therapy with lipid-lowering agents.

Description of Procedure (75571)

The physician describes the procedure to the patient and obtains informed consent where applicable. The physician reviews the scout views of the area to be imaged, axial images of the heart for adequacy prior to transfer to the workstation, and post-processed images for the presence of calcified coronary atherosclerosis. The physician quantifies coronary artery calcium using dedicated software that determines the score, the calcified volume, and the mass of calcium. The physician compares the amount of calcium detected for each individual patient with databases of population data stratified for age, gender, and ethnicity, and interprets source images for correlation with the post-processed images and for the presence of coexisting disease. Finally, the physician compares and correlates the findings with pertinent available prior studies and creates a report for the patient's medical record.

Clinical Example (75572)

A 66-year-old female is seen for treatment of atrial fibrillation. A 48-hour monitor now shows her to be in atrial fibrillation approximately 12% of the time. Radiofrequency ablation is planned to isolate the pulmonary veins and eliminate the focus of atrial fibrillation. A cardiac computed tomography scan is ordered by the electrophysiologist to identify the number, location, and morphology of the pulmonary veins as they enter the left atrium, the contours of the endoluminal surface of the left atrium, and the location of the esophagus in relation to the pulmonary veins.

Description of Procedure (75572)

The physician describes the procedure to the patient and obtains informed consent where applicable. The physician reviews the scout views of the area to be imaged and non-contrast CT images to localize the vascular phase sequence and to screen those patients who are not candidates for the arterial phase component of the study. The physician supervises the administration of low- or iso-osmolar contrast material as well as the administration of intravenous (IV) medication to lower the heart rate and to control heart rhythm when necessary. The physician manages the patient's pacemaker function and rate when applicable. The physician reviews the arterial phase CT images to ensure adequate anatomic coverage and prescribes and reviews venous phase images as necessary. The physician creates, interprets, and annotates 2D reconstructions of the vasculature. The physician creates 3D reconstructions of the vasculature and associated myocardium and adjusts the projection of the 3D reconstructions to optimize visualization of the anatomy or pathology. The physician interprets the axial source images of the pre-contrast, arterial phase, and venous phase sequences, as well as the 2D and 3D reformatted images resulting from the study, including cine review. The physician compares the study results to all pertinent available prior studies and dictates a report for the patient's medical record.

Clinical Example (75573)

A 12-year-old male presents for evaluation. As an infant he underwent bilateral modified Blalock-Taussig shunts for Tetralogy of Fallot with pulmonary atresia. Subsequent to that he underwent total repair that included an aortic homograft Rastelli conduit from the right ventricle to the pulmonary arteries. Echocardiography reveals pulmonary pressures that are 65% of systemic pressures. There is minimal Rastelli valve stenosis but marked insufficiency and right ventricular enlargement. Bilateral peripheral pulmonary artery stenosis is suspected but branch pulmonary arteries are not visualized on echocardiography. The patient is referred for cardiac computed tomography to measure right ventricular volume to determine whether he is a candidate for pulmonic valve replacement and to define branch pulmonary arteries to rule out significant peripheral pulmonary stenosis.

Description of Procedure (75573)

The physician describes the procedure to the patient and the patient's parents and obtains informed consent where applicable. The physician reviews the scout views of the area to be imaged and non-contrast CT images to localize the vascular phase sequence. The physician supervises the administration of low- or iso-osmolar contrast material and appropriately modifies the contrast protocol to ensure adequate cardiac chamber opacification. The physician reviews the enhanced phase CT images to ensure adequate anatomic coverage and prescribes and reviews delayed images as necessary. The physician evaluates multiphasic reconstructions to identify the end-systole and end-diastole and to determine the boundary between the myocardium and blood pool. The physician quantitatively determines the ventricular volumes of the heart using dedicated cardiac function analysis software available on the workstation. The physician calculates the ejection fraction, stroke volume, and/or cardiac output of both left and right ventricles and creates, interprets, and annotates 2D reconstructions of the heart and adjacent structures. The physician creates 3D reconstructions of the heart and adjacent structures and adjusts the projection of the 3D reconstructions to optimize visualization of the anatomy or pathology. The physician interprets the axial source images of the pre-contrast, arterial phase, and venous phase sequences, as well as the 2D and 3D reformatted images resulting from the study, including cine review. The physician compares the study results to all pertinent available prior studies.

Clinical Example (75574)

A 52-year-old female presents for evaluation and possible treatment for chest pain. The pain is described as a retrosternal tightness that radiates to her left shoulder. Her physician determines that she is at intermediate risk for coronary artery disease. Stress evaluations in the past have been nondiagnostic. She is referred for a cardiac computed tomography angiography for evaluation of her coronary anatomy and left ventricular function.

Description of Procedure (75574)

The physician describes the procedure to the patient and obtains informed consent where applicable. The physician reviews the scout views of the area to be imaged, the axial images of the heart for adequacy prior to transfer to the workstation, and the post-processed images for the presence of calcified coronary atherosclerosis. Coronary artery calcium is quantified using dedicated software that determines the score, the calcified volume, and the mass of calcium. Next, the amount of calcium detected is compared to databases of population data stratified for age and gender. The physician reviews non-contrast CT images to localize the vascular phase sequence and to screen those patients who are not candidates for the arterial phase component of the study. The physician oversees the administration of intravenous (IV) medication to lower the heart rate and control heart rhythm when necessary. The physician manages pacemaker function and rate when applicable. The physician supervises the administration of low- or iso-osmolar contrast material and appropriately modifies the contrast protocol to ensure adequate cardiac chamber opacification. The physician evaluates multiphasic reconstructions to identify the end-systole and end-diastole and to determine the boundary between the myocardium and blood pool. The physician quantitatively determines ventricular volumes of the heart using dedicated cardiac function analysis software available on the workstation. The physician calculates the ejection fraction, stroke volume, and/or cardiac output of both left and right ventricles. The physician reviews the arterial phase CT images to ensure adequate anatomic coverage and prescribes and reviews delayed and venous phase images as necessary. The physician creates, interprets, and annotates 2D reconstructions of the vasculature. The physician creates 3D reconstructions of the vasculature and associated myocardium and adjusts the projection of the 3D reconstructions to optimize visualization of the anatomy or pathology. The physician interprets the axial source images of the pre-contrast, arterial, and venous phase sequences, as well as the 2D and 3D reformatted images resulting from the study, including cine review. The physician compares the study results to all pertinent available prior studies.

Vascular Procedures

AORTA AND ARTERIES

+75774 Angiography, selective, each additional vessel studied after basic examination, radiological supervision and interpretation (List separately in addition to code for primary procedure)

(Use 75774 in addition to code for specific initial vessel studied)

▶(For angiography, see 36147, 75600-75774, 75791)◀

Rationale

The cross-reference following code 75774 has been revised to direct users to the appropriate codes to report angiography.

▶(75790 has been deleted. To report, see 36147, 75791)◀

●**75791** Angiography, arteriovenous shunt (eg, dialysis patient fistula/graft), complete evaluation of dialysis access, including fluoroscopy, image documentation and report (includes injections of contrast and all necessary imaging from the arterial anastomosis and adjacent artery through entire venous outflow including the inferior or superior vena cava), radiological supervision and interpretation

▶(Do not report 75791 in conjunction with 36147, 36148)◀

▶(For introduction of catheter, if necessary, see 36140, 36215-36217, 36245-36247)◀

▶(Use 75791 only if radiological evaluation is performed through an already existing access into the shunt or from an access that is not a direct puncture of the shunt)◀

▶(For radiological evaluation with needle/catheter introduction, AV dialysis shunt, complete procedure, use 36147)◀

 Rationale

In support of the establishment of code 36147 and add-on code 36148, radiology code 75791 has been established to describe the performance of a radiological evaluation through an already existing access site into the shunt or from an access site that is not a direct puncture of the shunt.

An note has been added following code 75791 instructing users not to report code 75791 in conjunction with codes 36147 and 36148. In addition, a parenthetical note has been added, instructing users to report 75791 only if radiological evaluation is performed through an already-existing access into the shunt or from an access that is not a direct puncture of the shunt. Two cross-references have been added, directing users to codes 36140, 36215-36217, and 36245-36247 for introduction of a catheter and code 36147 for a complete radiological evaluation with needle/catheter introduction of an AV dialysis shunt. A parenthetical note has also been added indicating that code 75790 has been deleted and directing users to the appropriate codes.

Clinical Example (75791)

A patient with end-stage renal disesase (ESRD) is found to have poor flows during dialysis with clotting of the needle such that dialysis cannot be completed. The patient is sent to the angiographic suite with needles in place for a diagnostic study to evaluate the arteriovenous shunt.

Description of Procedure (75791)

Angiography is performed to include the entire length of the graft and all outflow veins to the level of the superior vena cava. Compression may be applied to allow visualization of the arterial anastomosis. Technical personnel are directed throughout. Interpretation of the imaging of all views is obtained.

Other Procedures

76376   3D rendering with interpretation and reporting of computed tomography, magnetic resonance imaging, ultrasound, or other tomographic modality; not requiring image postprocessing on an independent workstation

(Use 76376 in conjunction with code[s] for base imaging procedure[s])

▶(Do not report 76376 in conjunction with 31627, 70496, 70498, 70544-70549, 71275, 71555, 72159, 72191, 72198, 73206, 73225, 73706, 73725, 74175, 74185, 74261-74263, 75557, 75559, 75561, 75563, 75565, 75571-75574, 75635, 76377, 78000-78999, 0159T)◀

76377   requiring image postprocessing on an independent workstation

(Use 76377 in conjunction with code[s] for base imaging procedure[s])

▶(Do not report 76377 in conjunction with 70496, 70498, 70544-70549, 71275, 71555, 72159, 72191, 72198, 73206, 73225, 73706, 73725, 74175, 74185, 74261-74263, 75557, 75559, 75561, 75563, 75565, 75571-75574, 75635, 76376, 78000-78999, 0159T)◀

✍🏻 Rationale

In support of the establishment of codes 31627, 74261-74263, 75565, and 75571-75574, and the deletion of codes 75564, 0066T, 0067T, and 0144T-0151T, the exclusionary notes following codes 76376 and 76377 have been revised to reflect these changes.

Diagnostic Ultrasound

Ultrasonic Guidance Procedures

+76937   Ultrasound guidance for vascular access requiring ultrasound evaluation of potential access sites, documentation of selected vessel patency, concurrent realtime ultrasound visualization of vascular needle entry, with permanent recording and reporting (List separately in addition to code for primary procedure)

▶(Do not use 76937 in conjunction with 37760, 37662, or 76942)◀

76942   Ultrasonic guidance for needle placement (eg, biopsy, aspiration, injection, localization device), imaging supervision and interpretation

▶(Do not report 76942 in conjunction with 37760, 37761, 43232, 43237, 43242, 45341, 45342, or 76975)◀

✍🏻 Rationale

The parenthetical notes following codes 76937 and 76942 have been revised by expanding the list of codes that should not be reported in conjunction with codes 76937 and 76942.

76950   Ultrasonic guidance for placement of radiation therapy fields

>▶(For placement of interstitial device[s] for radiation therapy guidance, see 31627, 32553, 49411, 55876)◄

 Rationale

In support of the establishment of interstitial device placement codes 31627, 32553, and 49411, a cross-reference has been added following code 76950 directing users to these new codes, as well as existing interstitial device placement in the prostate code 55876 for placement of interstitial devices for radiation therapy guidance.

Other Procedures

76998   Ultrasonic guidance, intraoperative

>▶(Do not report 76998 in conjunction with 36475-36479, 37760, 37761, 47370-47382)◄

 Rationale

In support of the establishment of code 37761 and the editorial revision of code 37760, the note following code 76998 has been revised to instruct users not to report code 76998 in conjunction with 37760 and 37761.

Radiologic Guidance

Fluoroscopic Guidance

▲**77003**   Fluoroscopic guidance and localization of needle or catheter tip for spine or paraspinous diagnostic or therapeutic injection procedures (epidural, transforaminal epidural, subarachnoid, or sacroiliac joint), including neurolytic agent destruction

(Injection of contrast during fluoroscopic guidance . . .

(Fluoroscopic guidance for subarachnoid puncture for . . .

(For epidural or subarachnoid needle or . . .

(For sacroiliac joint arthrography, see 27096, . . .

>▶(For paravertebral facet joint injection, see 64490-64495. For transforaminal epidural needle placement and injection, see 64479-64484)◄

 Rationale

In support of the establishment of paravertebral facet injection codes 64490-64495, code 77003 has been revised by deleting the phrase paravertebral facet joint. The cross-reference regarding facet injections following code 77003 has also been revised to direct users to these codes.

Ø=Modifier 51 Exempt   ⊙=Moderate Sedation   ✚=Add-on Code   ✗=FDA approval pending

Computed Tomography Guidance

77014   Computed tomography guidance for placement of radiation therapy fields

▶(For placement of interstitial device[s] for radiation therapy guidance, see 31627, 32553, 49411, 55876)◀

✐ Rationale

In support of the establishment of interstitial device placement codes 31627, 32553, and 49411, the cross-reference following code 77014 has been revised to include the new codes for placement of interstitial devices for radiation therapy guidance.

Radiation Oncology

Medical Radiation Physics, Dosimetry, Treatment Devices, and Special Services

77336   Continuing medical physics consultation, including assessment of treatment parameters, quality assurance of dose delivery, and review of patient treatment documentation in support of the radiation oncologist, reported per week of therapy

●**77338**   Multi-leaf collimator (MLC) device(s) for intensity modulated radiation therapy (IMRT), design and construction per IMRT plan

▶(Do not report 77338 more than once per IMRT plan)◀

▶(For immobilization in IMRT treatment, see 77332-77334)◀

▶(Do not report 77338 in conjunction with 0073T, compensator based IMRT)◀

✐ Rationale

Code 77338 was established to report multi-leaf collimator (MLC) design and construction for intensity modulated radiation therapy (IMRT). The descriptor includes the phrase "per IMRT plan" to indicate that multi-leaf collimator device design and construction should be reported one time only per course of treatment, regardless of the number of plan adjustments.

Code 77338 was added to the CPT code set to capture the physician work associated with the design and fabrication of the device; the practice expense associated with staff (physics and dosimetrists); and the equipment used to design, analyze and fabricate the device.

Three exclusionary parenthetical notes were added to instruct the user (1) to not report code 77338 more than once per IMRT plan, (2) to not report code 77338 in conjunction with code 0073T, and (3) to report codes 77332-77334 for IMRT treatment.

⚕ Clinical Example (77338)

Following clinical treatment planning (77261-77263), simulation (77280-77290), and creation of the treatment isodose for a nine-field intensity-modulated radiation

---

therapy (IMRT) plan (77301), a 65-year-old male with stage T2a, N0, M0 adeno-carcinoma of the prostate (who will be treated with IMRT) presents for the design and construction of the nine custom multi-leaf collimator (MLC) devices required for delivery of the IMRT treatment.

Description of Procedure (77338)

Physician work on the MLC treatment device begins after the intensity modu-lated plan (77301) has been generated. This plan will have achieved satisfactory compliance with the prescribed tumor and normal tissue dose specifications by modulating the intensity of the radiation beam through separate beam positions/angles (typically nine). This dose modulation per beam angle is displayed as flu-ence maps. The physician work for the IMRT device is associated with the work of converting the fluence map for each beam into a series of small segments shaped by MLCs and the ongoing revision and adjustments to these devices to ensure that the final device shape achieves the necessary dose modulation from each beam.

The physician reviews with the dosimetrist the combination of beam angles and MLC segments that have been generated to produce the intended cross-sectional beam intensity profile. For each modulated beam, the dosimetrist operates the planning software to provide a digitally reconstructed radiograph that represents the maximum aperture of each MLC-shaped field. For each individual beam, the physician and dosimetrist consider the component segments (typically around 20–30 per beam), taking into consideration both the pertinent anatomic relation-ships (eg, avoidance of unintended entrance or exit dose to a structure remote from the tumor that was not accounted for in the initial planning) and practical considerations (eg, avoidance of the need for the patient to be immobilized for an excessive length of time or other obvious inefficiency in treatment delivery, such as the removal of very small segments that contribute minimal dose). This is repeated for each beam angle. The entire set of MLC segment combinations (the IMRT treatment device) has to be evaluated by the radiation oncologist, as modification of any one might require compensatory modification of the others to achieve the required fluence.

As modifications occur, the physician reviews these with the physicist and then the dosimetrist, who recalculates the desired dose distribution based on the modi-fied MLC patterns. The final device is then generated and shaped using the MLC shaper and uploaded into the information system platform.

After the final device is uploaded into the information system, the physician reviews each device in the information system for accurate transfer of information, electronically approves the composite MLC device, and authorizes its release to the treatment machine for use throughout the specified course of therapy.

Stereotactic Radiation Treatment Delivery

⊙▲77371   Radiation treatment delivery, stereotactic radiosurgery (SRS), complete course of treatment of cranial lesion(s) consisting of 1 session; multi-source Cobalt 60 based

    ⊘=Modifier 51 Exempt ⊙=Moderate Sedation ✚=Add-on Code ✗=FDA approval pending

Rationale

Code 77371 has been revised with the addition of the moderate sedation symbol (⊙), as moderate sedation is an inherent component of this procedure.

Radiation Treatment Delivery

(Radiation treatment delivery [77401-77416] recognizes the technical component and the various energy levels)

▶(For intra-fraction localization and tracking of target, use 0197T)◀

77401 Radiation treatment delivery, superficial and/or ortho voltage

 Rationale

In support of the establishment of code 0197T, a cross-reference preceding code 77401 has been added to direct the user to the appropriate code to report.

77421 Stereoscopic X-ray guidance for localization of target volume for the delivery of radiation therapy

(Do not report 77421 in conjunction with 77432, 77435)

▶(For placement of interstitial device[s] for radiation therapy guidance, see 31627, 32553, 49411, 55876)◀

 Rationale

In support of the establishment of interstitial device placement codes 31627, 32553, and 49411, the cross-reference following code 77421 has been revised to include the new codes for placement of interstitial devices for radiation therapy guidance and to remove the specific reference to the prostate.

Clinical Brachytherapy

77785 Remote afterloading high dose rate radionuclide brachytherapy; 1 channel

77786 2–12 channels

77787 over 12 channels

▶(Do not report 77785-77787 in conjunction with Category III code 0182T)◀

 Rationale

A parenthetical note has been added following code 77787 instructing users not to report codes 77785, 77786, and 77787 in conjunction with code 0182T.

Nuclear Medicine

Diagnostic

CARDIOVASCULAR SYSTEM

▶Myocardial perfusion and cardiac blood pool imaging studies may be performed at rest and/or during stress. When performed during exercise and/or pharmacologic stress, the appropriate stress testing code from the 93015-93018 series should be reported in addition to 78451-78454, 78472-78492.◀

●**78451** Myocardial perfusion imaging, tomographic (SPECT) (including attenuation correction, qualitative or quantitative wall motion, ejection fraction by first pass or gated technique, additional quantification, when performed); single study, at rest or stress (exercise or pharmacologic)

●**78452** multiple studies, at rest and/or stress (exercise or pharmacologic) and/or redistribution and/or rest reinjection

●**78453** Myocardial perfusion imaging, planar (including qualitative or quantitative wall motion, ejection fraction by first pass or gated technique, additional quantification, when performed); single study, at rest or stress (exercise or pharmacologic)

●**78454** multiple studies, at rest and/or stress (exercise or pharmacologic) and/or redistribution and/or rest reinjection

78456 Acute venous thrombosis imaging, peptide

78457 Venous thrombosis imaging, venogram; unilateral

78458 bilateral

78459 Myocardial imaging, positron emission tomography (PET), metabolic evaluation

(For myocardial perfusion study, see 78491-78492)

▶(78460-78465 have been deleted. To report, see 78451-78454)◀

78466 Myocardial imaging, infarct avid, planar; qualitative or quantitative

78472 Cardiac blood pool imaging, gated equilibrium; planar, single study at rest or stress (exercise and/or pharmacologic), wall motion study plus ejection fraction, with or without additional quantitative processing

(For assessment of right ventricular ejection fraction by first pass technique, use 78496)

78473 multiple studies, wall motion study plus ejection fraction, at rest and stress (exercise and/or pharmacologic), with or without additional quantification

▶(Do not report 78472, 78473 in conjunction with 78451-78454, 78481, 78483, 78494)◀

▶(78478, 78480 have been deleted. To report, see 78451-78454)◀

78481 Cardiac blood pool imaging (planar), first pass technique; single study, at rest or with stress (exercise and/or pharmacologic), wall motion study plus ejection fraction, with or without quantification

78483 multiple studies, at rest and with stress (exercise and/or pharmacologic), wall motion study plus ejection fraction, with or without quantification

---

⊘=Modifier 51 Exempt   ☉=Moderate Sedation   ✚=Add-on Code   ✎=FDA approval pending

(For cerebral blood flow study, use 78610)

▶(Do not report 78481-78483 in conjunction with 78451–78454)◀

Rationale

As part of the AMA RUC five year review workgroup analysis of potentially misvalued codes, the myocardial perfusion codes were identified for review. The Center for Medicare and Medicaid Services (CMS) claims data found that providers reported wall motion and ejection fraction more than 90 percent of the time myocardial perfusion imaging was performed. To eliminate potential duplication of work, and since the wall motion and ejection fraction are typically performed during the majority of myocardial perfusion studies, the codes have been combined and simplified.

Therefore, Nuclear Medicine myocardial perfusion codes, 78460, 78461, 78464, 78465, 78478, and 78480 have been deleted. Codes 78451–78454 have replaced codes 78460, 78461, 78464, and 78465, to clarify that when wall motion and ejection fraction are determined, they should be considered as part of the myocardial perfusion study and should not be separately reported.

The Nuclear Medicine/Cardiovascular System introductory guidelines have been updated to include codes 78451–78454, to omit codes 78460–78465, and to direct users to the appropriate codes for stress test codes when myocardial perfusion and cardiac blood pool imaging studies are performed during exercise and/or pharmacologic stress.

Parenthetical notes have been added following codes 78473 and 78483 to instruct that when wall motion and ejection fraction are assessed by a first pass technique during a myocardial perfusion study, they are part of the myocardial perfusion study and should not be separately reported, since they are a part of the performed base procedure. In addition, cross-reference notes have been added following codes 78459 and 78473, which direct users to the appropriate codes in lieu of deleted codes 78460, 78461, 78464, 78465, 78478, and 78480.

These codes were established to more accurately capture the actual services that are typically performed for these studies. The new myocardial perfusion codes, include any method to determine the left ventricular ejection fraction and wall motion when performing services described in codes 78451-78454, whether it is from the gated SPECT data or from first pass data upon injection of the radiopharmaceutical for the myocardial perfusion study

In establishing the new combination codes describing wall motion/ejection fraction and myocardial perfusion services, it is recognized that exercise or rest first pass could be performed along with myocardial perfusion studies. The focus in establishing these combination codes is to emphasize that when wall motion and ejection fraction are assessed by any method as part of a myocardial perfusion study, they are considered as part of the myocardial perfusion study and should not be separately reported, since they are a part of the base procedure when performed.

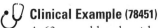

Clinical Example (78451)

A 60-year-old male with two prior myocardial infarctions and congestive heart failure has been determined by angiography examination to have disease in three vessels. A resting myocardial perfusion scan is ordered to assess viable tissue for a possible coronary artery bypass graft.

Description of Procedure (78451)

The study consists of acquiring either a stress or a rest tomographic (SPECT) data set, synchronized (gated) to the patient's electrocardiogram when performed. The physician verifies the completeness and adequacy of the data before completion of the study and may order additional imaging if necessary.

The images are reviewed for artifacts and abnormal extracardiac distribution. Three tomographic data sets are reviewed and re-reconstructed, if necessary. The physician compares the three tomographic views for differences or similarities that would suggest ischemia or scar. Qualitative assessment of ventricular wall function and perfusion are made in a standardized manner, with each segment scored on a semi-quantitative scale. Wall motion is qualitatively scored for motion and thickening. This occurs in a standardized segment model for the data set with each segment scored as normal, mildly hypokinetic, moderately hypokinetic, severely hypokinetic, akinetic, or dyskinetic. Attention is paid to the assessment of regional myocardial function and to the percent of myocardium that is regionally dysfunctional in order to judge the amount of underlying myocardial scar (or stress-induced ischemia). The extent and severity of perfusion defects and their relationship to vascular geographic territories are noted.

When performed, wall motion and thickening quantitative data are generated and reviewed for the image set. The segmental wall motion data are compared to the perfusion images to generate a clinically relevant wall motion analysis for the individual patient. When performed, left ventricular ejection fraction is reported after confirming the correctness of the regions of interest that were selected for the calculation. Digital data of perfusion and ventricular function are reviewed after the qualitative assessment, in part to refine the qualitative impression. Results are compared with relevant prior studies. A report is dictated for the patient's medical record.

Clinical Example (78452)

A 62-year-old male has hypertension, hyperlipidemia, and a family history of coronary artery disease. He has been experiencing atypical chest pain and advancing shortness of breath while walking. His resting electrocardiogram is abnormal, showing sinus rhythm, possible inferior wall myocardial infarction, and nonspecific ST-T wave abnormalities. He is referred for a stress and rest myocardial perfusion study with wall motion and ejection fraction evaluation.

Description of Procedure (78452)

The study consists of acquisition of a stress and a rest (and/or redistribution) tomographic (SPECT) data sets, synchronized (gated) to the patient's electrocardiogram when performed. The physician verifies the completeness and adequacy of the data sets before completion of the study and may order additional imaging if necessary.

⊘=Modifier 51 Exempt   ⊙=Moderate Sedation   ✛=Add-on Code   ⁄=FDA approval pending

The images are reviewed for artifacts and abnormal extracardiac distribution. Three tomographic data sets are reviewed for each acquisition, and re-reconstructed, if necessary. The physician compares the tomographic data sets for differences or similarities that would suggest ischemia or scar. Qualitative assessment of ventricular wall function and perfusion are made in a standardized manner, with each segment scored on a semi-quantitative scale. Wall motion is qualitatively scored for motion and thickening. This occurs in a standardized segment model for the data set with each segment scored as normal, mildly hypokinetic, moderately hypokinetic, severely hypokinetic, akinetic, or dyskinetic. Attention is paid to the assessment of regional myocardial function and to the percent of myocardium that is regionally dysfunctional in order to judge the amount of underlying myocardial scar (or stress-induced ischemia). The extent and severity of perfusion defects and their relationship to vascular geographic territories are noted.

When performed, wall motion and thickening quantitative data are generated and reviewed. The segmental wall motion data are compared to the perfusion images to generate a clinically relevant wall motion analysis for the individual patient. When performed, left ventricular ejection fraction is noted after confirming the correctness of the regions of interest that were selected for the calculation. Digital data of perfusion and ventricular function are reviewed after the qualitative assessment, in part to refine the qualitative impression. Results are compared with relevant prior studies. A report is dictated for the patient's medical record.

Clinical Example (78453)

A 63-year-old female with hypertension and hypercholesterolemia has been experiencing chest discomfort and shortness of breath. She has significant arthritis of her upper extremities and back and difficulty with positioning when lying down. Resting electrocardiogram shows sinus rhythm and non-specific ST-T wave abnormalities. She is referred for a stress myocardial perfusion study, which, if completely normal, will not require a rest study.

Description of Procedure (78453)

The study consists of a single study acquisition of either a stress or rest set of planar images, synchronized (gated) to the patient's electrocardiogram when performed. The physician verifies the completeness and adequacy of the data before completion of the study and may order additional imaging if necessary.

The planar images are reviewed for artifacts and abnormal extracardiac distribution. The cardiac images that are acquired in at least three different projections (eg, anterior, left anterior oblique, and lateral) are reviewed. The physician compares the acquisition data sets for differences or similarities that would suggest ischemia or scar. Qualitative assessment of myocardial perfusion is made in a standardized manner, with each segment scored on a semi-quantitative scale. Qualitative assessment of left ventricular global function is made, when performed. Wall motion is qualitatively scored for motion and thickening, when performed. This occurs in a standardized segment model for each data set with each segment scored as normal, mildly hypokinetic, moderately hypokinetic, severely hypokinetic, akinetic, or dyskinetic. Attention is paid to the assessment of regional myocardial function and to the percent of myocardium that is regionally dysfunctional in order to judge the amount of underlying myocardial scar (or stress-induced ischemia). The extent and severity of perfusion defects and their relationship to vascular geographic territories are noted.

When performed, wall motion and thickening quantitative data are generated and reviewed. The segmental wall motion data are compared to the perfusion images to generate a clinically relevant wall motion analysis for the individual patient. When performed, left ventricular ejection fraction is noted after confirming the correctness of the regions of interest that were selected for the calculation. Digital data of perfusion and ventricular function are reviewed after the qualitative assessment, in part to refine the qualitative impression. Results are compared with relevant prior studies. A report is dictated for the patient's medical record.

Clinical Example (78454)

A 64-year-old male with cigarette use and hypertension has been experiencing chest pain and shortness of breath. He has significant arthritis and difficulty with positioning when lying down. Resting electrocardiogram shows sinus rhythm and non-specific ST-T wave abnormalities. He is referred for stress myocardial perfusion study.

Description of Procedure (78454)

The study consists of acquisition of both stress and rest (or redistribution) planar image sets, synchronized (gated) to the patient's electrocardiogram when performed. The physician verifies the completeness and adequacy of the images before completion of the study and may order additional imaging if necessary.

The planar images are reviewed for artifacts and abnormal extracardiac distribution. The cardiac images that are acquired in at least three different projections (eg, anterior, left anterior oblique, and lateral) for both rest and stress sets of images are reviewed. The physician compares the acquisition data sets for differences or similarities that would suggest ischemia or scar. Qualitative assessment of myocardial perfusion is made in a standardized manner, with each segment scored on a semi-quantitative scale. Qualitative assessment of left ventricular global function is made, when performed. Wall motion is qualitatively scored for motion and thickening, when performed. This occurs in a standardized segment model for each data set with each segment scored as normal, mildly hypokinetic, moderately hypokinetic, severely hypokinetic, akinetic, or dyskinetic. Attention is paid to the assessment of regional myocardial function and to the percent of myocardium that is regionally dysfunctional in order to judge the amount of underlying myocardial scar (or stress-induced ischemia). The extent and severity of perfusion defects and their relationship to the vascular geographic territories are noted.

When performed, wall motion and thickening quantitative data are generated and reviewed. The segmental wall motion data are compared to the perfusion images to generate a clinically relevant wall motion analysis for the individual patient. When performed, left ventricular ejection fraction is noted after confirming the correctness of the regions of interest that were selected for the calculation. Digital data of perfusion and ventricular function are reviewed after the qualitative assessment, in part to refine the qualitative impression. Results are compared with relevant prior studies. A report is dictated for the patient's medical record.

RESPIRATORY SYSTEM

78580   Pulmonary perfusion imaging, particulate

▶(Do not report 78580 in conjunction with 78451-78454)◀

 Rationale

In support of the establishment of codes 78451-78454, a parenthetical note has been added following code 78580, instructing users not to report code 78580 in conjunction with codes 78451-78454.

Pathology and Laboratory

The Chemistry subsection has the most number of changes of the Pathology and Laboratory section. These changes consist of several new codes, numerous editorial revisions, and a resequenced code to accommodate the appropriate placement of a Vitamin D procedure.

Pathology and Laboratory

Organ or Disease-Oriented Panels

These panels were developed…

These panel components are not…

▶Do not report two or more panel codes that include any of the same constituent tests performed from the same patient collection. If a group of tests overlaps two or more panels, report the panel that incorporates the greater number of tests to fulfill the code definition and report the remaining tests using individual test codes (eg, do not report 80047 in conjunction with 80053)◀

80047   Basic metabolic panel (Calcium, ionized)

This panel must include the following:

Calcium, ionized (82330)

Carbon dioxide (82374)

Chloride (82435)

Creatinine (82565)

Glucose (82947)

Potassium (84132)

Sodium (84295)

Urea Nitrogen (BUN) (84520)

80048   Basic metabolic panel (Calcium, total)

This panel must include the following:

Calcium, total (82310)

Carbon dioxide (82374)

Chloride (82435)

Creatinine (82565)

Glucose (82947)

Potassium (84132)

Sodium (84295)

Urea nitrogen (BUN) (84520)

80053   Comprehensive metabolic panel

This panel must include the following:

Albumin (82040)

Bilirubin, total (82247)

Calcium, total (82310)

Carbon dioxide (bicarbonate) (82374)

Chloride (82435)

Creatinine (82565)

Glucose (82947)

Phosphatase, alkaline (84075)

Potassium (84132)

Protein, total (84155)

Sodium (84295)

Transferase, alanine amino (ALT) (SGPT) (84460)

Transferase, aspartate amino (AST) (SGOT) (84450)

Urea nitrogen (BUN) (84520)

▲80055   Obstetric panel

This panel must include the following:

Blood count, complete (CBC), automated and automated differential WBC count (85025 or 85027 and 85004)

OR

Blood count, complete (CBC), automated (85027) and appropriate manual differential WBC count (85007 or 85009)

Hepatitis B surface antigen (HBsAg) (87340)

Antibody, rubella (86762)

Syphilis test, non-treponemal antibody; qualitative (eg, VDRL, RPR, ART) (86592)

Antibody screen, RBC, each serum technique (86850)

Blood typing, ABO (86900) AND

Blood typing, Rh (D) (86901)

▶(When syphilis screening is performed using a treponemal antibody approach [86780], do not use 80055. Use the individual codes for the tests performed in the obstetric panel)◀

80076   Hepatic function panel

This panel must include the following:

Albumin (82040)

Bilirubin, total (82247)

Bilirubin, direct (82248)

⊘=Modifier 51 Exempt   ⊙=Moderate Sedation   ✚=Add-on Code   ⨰=FDA approval pending

Phosphatase, alkaline (84075)

Protein, total (84155)

Transferase, alanine amino (ALT) (SGPT) (84460)

Transferase, aspartate amino (AST) (SGOT) (84450)

 Rationale

The introductory language in the Organ or Disease-Oriented Panels subsection of the Pathology and Laboratory section was editorially revised to clarify that users should not report multiple panel codes that include any of the same constituent analytes performed from the same patient collection. In accordance with this change, the parenthetical notes following panel codes 80047, 80048, 80053, and 80076 were deleted. The term "analytes" was changed to "tests" in the guidelines and the phrase "(eg, do not report 80047 in conjunction with 80053)" was added at the end of the guidelines. All references to code 82310 found in the panel codes were corrected to state, "Calcium, total," because this reflects the correct descriptor for this code.

In support of revised Syphillis test code 86592, code 86592 has been updated in panel code 80055. In addition, an instructional note has been added following panel code 80055. The instructional parenthetical note instructs users not to report code 80055 when Syphilis test is performed using a treponemal approach (code 86780). Use the individual codes for the tests performed in the obstetric panel.

Chemistry

▲**82306**   Vitamin D; 25 hydroxy, includes fraction(s), if performed

▶(82307 has been deleted. For 25 hydroxy vitamin D, use 82306)◀

#▲**82652**   1, 25- dihydroxy, includes fraction(s), if performed

82441   Chlorinated hydrocarbons, screen

(Chlorpromazine, use 84022)

(Cholecalciferol [Vitamin D], use 82306)

82651   Dihydrotestosterone (DHT)

82652   ▶Code is out of numerical sequence. See 82000-84999◀

 Rationale

In the Chemistry section, a reference has been added to direct users to the appropriate code range (82000–84999) for the placement of the out-of-sequence code 82652. Code 82652 will appear with a number symbol (#) to indicate that it is out of numerical sequence. Codes 82306 and 82652 have been revised to clarify reporting Vitamin D and to accurately describe the current methodology of Vitamin D testing. In support of the revision of these codes, code 82307 has been deleted.

🩺 Clinical Example (82306)

A 56-year-old female presents with muscle pain and weakness whose diet is suspected to be low in vitamin D. Laboratory tests are ordered to assess possible vitamin D deficiency.

🩺 Clinical Example (82652)

A 46-year-old established female patient under treatment for sarcoidosis presented with nausea, vomiting, excessive thirst, abnormal heart rhythms, and elevated heartbeat. During the last office visit, the disease appeared under control with corticosteroids. The patient exhibited poor skin turgor shown by the hand skin not returning to the normal position after pinching. The patient had not urinated for 9 hours. Lab tests were ordered to assess possible vitamin D deficiency. The patient was transported to the hospital with an elevated 1,25-dihydroxy-vitamin D level of 90 pg/mL indicating a vitamin D production by the sarcoid macrophages.

▲82784   Gammaglobulin (immunoglobulin); IgA, IgD, IgG, IgM, each

▲82785   IgE

(For allergen specific IgE, see 86003, 86005)

▲82787   immunoglobulin subclasses (eg, IgG1, 2, 3, or 4), each

(Gamma-glutamyltransferase [GGT], use 82977)

✍ Rationale

Code 82784 has been editorially revised to add "(immunoglobulin)" to the code's descriptor. The indented code 82785 has also been revised as a result of this change, and it has a revised symbol (▲) indicating this.

Code 82787 has been editorially revised to add "eg" to the code descriptor's parenthetical note to signify that the list of examples is not comprehensive.

▲83516   Immunoassay for analyte other than infectious agent antibody or infectious agent antigen; qualitative or semiquantitative, multiple step method

▲83518   qualitative or semiquantitative, single step method (eg, reagent strip)

▲83519   quantitative, by radioimmunoassay (eg, RIA)

▲83520   quantitative, not otherwise specified

✍ Rationale

The descriptors of codes 83516, 83518, 83519, and 83520 as a group were not consistent with customary CPT nomenclature. Therefore, these codes have been revised to reduce confusion and clarify their meaning and intent.

Code 83516 has been revised by relocating the semicolon after the word "antigen" so that the phrase "qualitative or semiquantitative, multiple step method" now applies only to code 83516. Code 83518 has been revised to describe a qualitative or semiquantitative test using a single-step method. Code 83519 has been revised by replacing the phrase "radiopharmaceutical technique" with "radioimmunoassay," and by changing it to indent status within the 83516 family of codes. Code 83520 has been revised by specifying that it is a quantitative test.

83887	Nicotine

Codes 83890-83914 are intended for....

Codes 83890-83914 are coded by procedure . . .

Code separately for each procedure used . . .

When molecular diagnostic procedures are performed . . .

Each nucleic acid preparation may include . . .

►(For microbial identification, see 87149, 87150, 87152, 87153, 87470-87801)◄

(For array technology using more than . . .

83890	Molecular diagnostics; molecular isolation or extraction, each nucleic acid type (ie, DNA or RNA)
83970	Parathormone (parathyroid hormone)
▲**83986**	pH; body fluid, not otherwise specified
●**83987**	exhaled breath condensate

(For blood pH, see 82800, 82803)

✍ Rationale

Code 83987 has been established in support of archived Category III code 0140T for laboratory analysis of the pH of exhaled breath condensate, a test used to differentiate gastroesophageal reflux (GER) in asthmatic symptoms.

With the establishment of code 83987, code 83986 has been revised to a parent (without indentation) code. In addition to this revision, the term "except blood" has been removed and the phrase "not otherwise specified" added to the code's descriptor.

The first cross-reference preceding code 83890 has been editorially revised with the addition of codes 87149, 87150, 87152, and 87153.

🩺 Clinical Example (83987)

A 9-year-old boy presents with unresolved chronic cough. He had been coughing persistently for 6 months. Evaluation showed him to not be clinically allergic. Spirometry was normal. During the preceding months he had failed therapeutic trials with amoxicillin, azithromycin, prednisone, inhaled steroids, beta agonists, and montelukast.

Description of Procedure (83987)

The respiratory therapist demonstrated the exhaled breath condensate self-collection technique to both the child and the mother. A breath specimen collection kit with six disposable collectors was then provided to the patient, and he and his mother were sent home.

Over the next two days the patient performed all six breath specimen collections, each immediately following a new and bothersome coughing episode. All six specimens were then sent together to the laboratory.

The laboratory performed the gas-standardized pH test on each specimen. Dissolved carbon dioxide was removed, and the pH was measured using a sensitive electrode specifically for low ionic-strength fluids. Any pH reading below 7.4 was considered abnormally acidic.

Two of the six specimens associated with cough were abnormally acidic, indicating an acid-related etiology of the patient's cough. The physician initiated omeprazole BID dosing at 20 mg, exercise, and reflux-limiting diet. Upon follow-up four weeks later the cough had resolved.

84144   Progesterone

(Progesterone receptor assay, use 84234)

(For proinsulin, use 84206)

●**84145**   Procalcitonin (PCT)

 Rationale

Category III code 0194T has been converted to Category I code 84145 for reporting procalcitonin. In support of the deletion of code 0194T, a cross-reference has been added in the Category III section directing users to code 84145 for procalcitonin.

Clinical Example (84145)

A 57-year-old male with a history of chronic obstructive pulmonary disease (COPD) presents with mild cough and minimal shortness of breath.

Description of Procedure (84145)

Chest X-ray reveals mild hyperinflation and possible atelectasis. The white blood cell count is 8.9 k/μl. The patient reports some improvement after the first nebulization treatment with beta-agonists. The patient is referred to the observation unit for treatment of a COPD exacerbation. A procalcitonin level is obtained.

●**84431**   Thromboxane metabolite(s), including thromboxane if performed, urine

▶(For concurrent urine creatinine determination, use 84431 in conjunction with 82570)◀

⊘=Modifier 51 Exempt   ⊙=Moderate Sedation   ✚=Add-on Code   ✗=FDA approval pending

Rationale

Code 84431 has been established to report the total level of thromboxane production using urine as specimen to identify the individual who is taking aspirin but remains at risk of a cardiovascular event. Thromboxane is a vasoconstrictor and a potent hypertensive agent, and it facilitates platelet aggregation. Aspirin therapy acts by inhibiting the ability of the COX enzyme to synthesize the precursors of thromboxane within platelets. Low-dose, long-term aspirin use irreversibly blocks the formation of thromboxane A2 in platelets, producing an inhibitory effect on platelet aggregation. This anticoagulant property makes aspirin useful for reducing the incidence of heart attacks.

In support of the establishment of code 84431, an instructional parenthetical note has been added instructing users to report code 84431 in conjunction with code 82570. A cross-reference has been added following code 85576 directing users to code 84431 for urine testing of thromboxane metabolite(s).

Clinical Example (84431)

A 52-year-old apparently healthy postmenopausal female with a family history of cardiovascular disease (mother died at age 58 of a myocardial infarction, and father suffered a stroke at age 65) presents for her annual physical examination. She has been on 81 mg aspirin (ASA) daily for the past 12 months as recommended by her physician during a previous visit.

The physical exam was normal except for mild overweight and borderline hypertension. The patient is not a smoker and is physically active. Her fasting blood glucose, total cholesterol, HDL, and LDL levels are normal. Due to the family history, the physician orders an 11dhTxB2 test, including a urine creatinine test to normalize 11dhTxB2 and to determine if the ASA is showing the intended effect by lowering her thromboxane levels to ≤1500 pg 11dhTxB2/mg creatinine.

Description of Procedure (84431)

A urine sample is collected, and a urine preservative is added within 4 hours. The sample is sent to the laboratory for testing. If not tested immediately, the sample is placed in a 2–8 C refrigerator. If not tested within 24 hours, the sample is stored frozen at ≤ –20 C. Fresh or thawed samples are centrifuged at 1000 rpm for 15 minutes before running the test.

Final result of 1,805 pg 11dhTxB2/mg creatinine is forwarded to the physician. Because the patient has been taking 81mg of ASA and had some risk factors for cardiovascular disease, the physician adjusted the daily dose of ASA to 162 mg to bring the 11dhTxB levels to ≤1500 pg 11dhTxB2/mg creatinine. Physician will then request retesting to see if patient is benefiting from adjusted ASA dose.

84590   Vitamin A

(Vitamin B-1, use 84425)

(Vitamin B-2, use 84252)

(Vitamin B-6, use 84207)

(Vitamin B-12, use 82607)

(Vitamin B-12, absorption (Schilling), see 78270, 78271)

(Vitamin C, use 82180)

►(Vitamin D, see 82306, 82652)◄

(Vitamin E, use 84446)

Rationale

In support of the deletion of code 82307, the cross-reference following code 84590 directing users to code for Vitamin D tests has been revised with the removal of code 82307.

Hematology and Coagulation

85004   Blood count; automated differential WBC count

85018   hemoglobin (Hgb)

(For other hemoglobin determination, see 83020-83069)

(For immunoassay, hemoglobin, fecal, use 82274)

►(For transcutaneous hemoglobin measurement, use 88738)◄

Rationale

A cross-reference has been added following code 85018 directing users to code 88738 for transcutaneous hemoglobin measurement.

85576   Platelet, aggregation (in vitro), each agent

►(For thromboxane metabolite[s], including thromboxane, if performed, measurement[s] in urine, use 84431)◄

Rationale

A cross-reference has been added following code 85576 directing users to code 84431 for urine testing of thromboxane metabolite(s).

Immunology

●**86305**   Human epididymis protein 4 (HE4)

Rationale

Code 86305 has been established to report testing used for assessment of ovarian masses of uncertain origin that utilizes human epididymis protein 4 (HE4) bio-marker for monitoring cancer.

 **Clinical Example (86305)**

The patient is a 68-year-old white female, gravida 4 para 4, who underwent cytoreductive surgery and staging for a stage IIIC poorly differentiated adenocarcinoma of the ovary. During surgery, all tumors larger than 2 cm in diameter were removed. It was decided to treat this patient with a 6-month course of monthly intraperitoneal chemotherapy. The baseline human epididymis protein 4 (HE4) level (obtained just prior to surgery) was 300 pM. After surgery and during the first course of chemotherapy, the HE4 level remained at 300 pM.

Description of Procedure (86305)

The HE4 level was obtained monthly during the chemotherapy encounter. On postoperative week 8, the HE4 level fell to 110 pM. The fall in the HE4 level continued. By the fourth month the HE4 level had decreased to 15 pM and remained at this level following the completion of the chemotherapy course. At that time, the patient was asymptomatic, and on abdominal and pelvic examination no tumor was palpated. Imaging confirmed the findings of no evidence of tumor. Repeat monitoring with HE4 levels confirmed the patient's response to treatment and gave the physician assurance that the course of chemotherapy was effective.

●**86352**   Cellular function assay involving stimulation (eg, mitogen or antigen) and detection of biomarker (eg, ATP)

86353   Lymphocyte transformation, mitogen (phytomitogen) or antigen induced blastogenesis

(Malaria antibodies, use 86750)

▶(For cellular function assay involving stimulation and detection of biomarker, use 86352)◀

 Rationale

Code 86352 has been established to report the measurement of early response to immune system stimulation by determining the concentration of adenosine triphosphate (ATP) produced in CD4-positive cells selected from phytohemagglutinin-stimulated whole blood. This test can be used to gauge the toxicity of immunosuppressants by measuring the ATP levels in the blood.

An instructional parenthetical note has been added following code 86353, instructing users to report code 86352 for a cellular function assay involving stimulation and detection of biomarker.

 **Clinical Example (86352)**

During a routine follow-up visit after receiving a solid-organ transplant, a 50-year-old recipient has blood drawn to measure the level of calcineurin inhibitor and undergoes allograft function tests (eg, creatinine, AST/ALT). The patient's cellular immune system is activated using an assay of cellular function after stimulation in order to gauge the toxicity of the immunosuppressants, the status of the allograft, and the activation of the cellular immune system, respectively.

Description of Procedure (86352)

The assay detects CMI by measuring the concentration of adenosine triphosphate (ATP) from CD4 + cells following stimulation. This measurement is made on heparin anti-coagulated whole blood using a luminometer and luciferin/luciferase.

Whole blood is aseptically collected into a specimen collection tube containing sodium heparin. The sample must be tested within 30 hours of draw and maintained at room temperature. Whole blood is incubated with stimulant for 15–18 hours (concurrently, whole blood is incubated in the absence of stimulant to assess basal ATP activity). Anti-CD4 monoclonal antibody coated magnetic beads are added to immunoselect CD4 + cells from both the stimulated and non-stimulated wells. The selected CD4 + cells are washed on a magnet tray, and lysis reagent is added to release intracellular ATP. Addition of luminescent reagent produces light proportional to the concentration of ATP. A luminometer is used to measure the light produced in Relative Light Units (RLUs), and this data is converted using the calculator to determine the concentration of ATP present.

The characterization of the cellular immune response (strong, moderate, or low) of a specimen is made by comparing the ATP concentration for that specimen to fixed ATP level ranges.

▲**86592**　Syphilis test, non-treponemal antibody; qualitative (eg, VDRL, RPR, ART)

(For antibodies to infectious agents, see 86602-86804)

▲**86593**　　　quantitative

86710　Antibody; influenza virus

86778　Toxoplasma, IgM

●**86780**　Treponema pallidum

(86781 has been deleted)

(For syphilis testing by non-treponemal antibody analysis, see 86592-86593)

✍ Rationale

Code 86592 has been revised to add the term "non-treponemal antibody." Code 86593 has also been revised as a result of this change and has a revised symbol (▲) indicating this.

With the deletion of code 86781, code 86780 has been established to report Treponema pallidum. A cross-reference has been added directing users to codes 86592 and 86593 for non-treponemal pallidum antibody.

🩺 Clinical Example (86780)

A 23-year-old pregnant female presents for her initial prenatal examination. As part of her examination, blood is drawn for clinical laboratory tests including a syphilis test. The syphilis test is sent to a national reference laboratory for

　　⃠=Modifier 51 Exempt　⊙=Moderate Sedation　✚=Add-on Code　✗=FDA approval pending testing for the presence of treponemal antibodies immunoglobulin G (IgG) and immunoglobulin M (IgM) using an automated instrument.

Tissue Typing

●**86825** Human leukocyte antigen (HLA) crossmatch, non-cytotoxic (eg, using flow cytometry); first serum sample or dilution

✚●**86826**   each additional serum sample or sample dilution (List separately in addition to primary procedure)

▶Do not report 86825, 86826 in conjunction with 86355, 86359, 88184-88189 for antibody surface markers integral to crossmatch testing)◀

▶(For autologous HLA crossmatch, see 86825, 86826)◀

▶(For lymphocytotoxicity visual crossmatch, see 86805, 86806)◀

 Rationale

Code 86825 has been established to report new methodology used for cross matching donor tissue with a patient serum sample.

Code 86826 has been established as an add-on code to report each additional sample or sample dilution to code 86825.

An instructional parenthetical note and two cross-references have been added following code 86826. The instructional parenthetical note instructs users not to report codes 86825 and 86826 in conjunction with code 86355, 86359, or 88184-88189 for antibody surface markers integral to cross match testing. The two cross-references direct users to codes 86825 and 86826 for autologous HLA cross match and codes 86805 and 86806 for lymphocytotoxicity visual cross match.

 Clinical Example (86825, 86826)

A 47-year-old female with diabetes and hypertension has developed end-stage renal disease. She is currently on dialysis. She is referred by her nephrologist to the nearest kidney transplant program for evaluation. After evaluation, she is listed on the network waiting list for organ sharing. While waiting for transplant, monthly serum samples are collected from the patient and stored at −80°C. After four years on the wait list, she is offered a deceased donor kidney. The transplant physician accepts the kidney. Cross matching is requested.

Description of Procedure (86825, 86826)

Cross matching is requested. In addition to the cytotoxic cross match, a flow cytometric cross match is performed with donor lymph node tissue and a current serum sample from the patient as well as three archived serum samples. An auto flow cytometric cross match is performed using the same sera. The results of all cross match procedures are reviewed. The patient's transfusion history, prior transplant history, and gravidity are reviewed. The typing of the donor and recipient are compared, and the donor typing is compared with any previously identified antibodies to HLA antigens. The cross match results are interpreted with this information and provided to the transplant surgeon or his representative.

Microbiology

▶Presumptive identification of microorganisms is defined as identification by colony morphology, growth on selective media, Gram stains, or up to three tests (eg, catalase, oxidase, indole, urease). Definitive identification of microorganisms is defined as an identification to the genus or species level that requires additional tests (eg, biochemical panels, slide cultures). If additional studies involve molecular probes, nucleic acid sequencing, chromatography, or immunologic techniques, these should be separately coded using 87140-87158, in addition to definitive identification codes. The molecular diagnostic codes (eg, 83890-83914) are not to be used in combination with or instead of the procedures represented by 87140-87158. For multiple specimens/sites use modifier 59. For repeat laboratory tests performed on the same day, use modifier 91.◀

87001	Animal inoculation, small animal; with observation
87076	anaerobic isolate, additional methods required for definitive identification, each isolate
87077	aerobic isolate, additional methods required for definitive identification, each isolate
87081	Culture, presumptive, pathogenic organisms, screening only;
87084	with colony estimation from density chart
87106	Culture, fungi, definitive identification, each organism; yeast
87107	mold
87109	Culture, mycoplasma, any source
87118	Culture, mycobacterial, definitive identification, each isolate

 Rationale

The guidelines at the beginning of the Microbiology subsection, beginning with the second paragraph, were editorially revised to provide clarification regarding the use of new, revised, and exisiting microbiology codes. The guidelines in the second paragraph were revised to include nucleic acid sequencing in the instruction for additional studies. The reference to codes 87140-87158 was moved to properly identify the codes for these additional studies. The guidelines were further revised to instruct the user that molecular diagnostic codes should not be reported in conjunction with or instead of the procedures described by codes 87140-87158.

In accordance with the changes in the guidelines, the parenthetical notes following codes 87076, 87077, 87106, and 87118 have been deleted.

87140	Culture, typing; immunofluorescent method, each antiserum
87143	gas liquid chromatography (GLC) or high pressure liquid chromatography (HPLC) method
87147	immunologic method, other than immunofluoresence (eg, agglutination grouping), per antiserum

⊘=Modifier 51 Exempt ⊙=Moderate Sedation ✚=Add-on Code ✔=FDA approval pending

▲87149   identification by nucleic acid (DNA or RNA) probe, direct probe technique, per culture or isolate, each organism probed

(Do not report 87149 in conjunction with 83890-83914)

●87150   identification by nucleic acid (DNA or RNA) probe, amplified probe technique, per culture or isolate, each organism probed

▶(Do not report 87150 in conjunction with 83890-83914)◀

✍ Rationale

Code 87149 has been revised to clarify its meaning by adding the term "(DNA or RNA)" and "direct probe technique, per culture or isolate, each organism probed." An instructional parenthetical note has been added following code 87149 instructing users not to report code 87149 in conjunction with codes 83890-83914.

When a primary source specimen is used, CPT instructions are clear regarding the separate coding for each result reported for different species or strain of organisms. However, there has been some confusion as to whether the same coding logic applies to testing performed on secondary source specimens.

Code 87150 was established to report the amplified probe technique testing performed on secondary source specimens.

In accordance with the establishment of code 87150, an instructional parenthetical note has been added following code 87150, instructing users not to report code 87150 in conjunction with codes 83890-83914.

⚕ Clinical Example (87150)

A 68-year-old male presents with symptoms of a deep painful abscess on his right foot. The abscess has been draining yellowish fluid for 2 days and has been accompanied by a high fever. A specimen for a culture is obtained and sent to the laboratory for testing.

Description of Procedure (87150)

After positive results show on the culture, a subsequent test is performed from the culture specimen to diagnose the type of *Staphylococcus aureus* present in the patient's wound, using polymerase chain reaction, amplified probe technique.

87152   identification by pulse field gel typing

▶(Do not report 87152 in conjunction with 83890-83914)◀

●87153   identification by nucleic acid sequencing method, each isolate (eg, sequencing of the 16S rRNA gene)

87158   other methods

87177   Ova and parasites, direct smears, concentration and identification

(Do not report 87177 in conjunction . . .

(For direct smears from a primary . . .

(For coccidia or microsporidia exam, use . . .

(For complex special stain (trichrome, iron . . .

(For nucleic acid probes in cytologic . . .

87250   Virus isolation; inoculation of embryonated eggs, or small animal, includes observation and dissection

87255   including identification by non-immunologic method, other than by cytopathic effect (eg, virus specific enzymatic activity)

▶These codes are intended for primary source only. For similar studies on culture material, refer to codes 87140-87158. Infectious agents by antigen detection, immunofluorescence microscopy, or nucleic acid probe techniques should be reported as precisely as possible. The molecular diagnostic codes (eg, 83890-83914) are not to be used in combination with or instead of the procedures represented by 87470-87801. The most specific code possible should be reported. If there is no specific agent code, the general methodology code (eg, 87299, 87449, 87450, 87797, 87798, 87799, 87899) should be used. For identification of antibodies to many of the listed infectious agents, see 86602-86804. When separate results are reported for different species or strain of organisms, each result should be coded separately. Use modifier 59 when separate results are reported for different species or strains that are described by the same code.◀

🖎 Rationale

Following code 87152, a parenthetical note has been added, instructing users not to report code 87152 in conjunction with codes 83890-83914.

Code 87153 has been established to report culture-typing identification by nucleic acid sequencing method, each isolate.

The parenthetical note following code 87177, which directs users to codes 83890-83898 and 87470-87799 for molecular diagnotics has been deleted.

Following code 87255, additional guideline revisions were made after the third sentence, to instruct users that "The molecular diagnostic codes (eg, 83890-83914) are not to be used in combination with or instead of the procedures represented by 87470-87801."

🩺 Clinical Example (87153)

Following a puncture wound to the thenar eminence of the right hand, a 45-year-old male machinist experienced pain and minimal purulent drainage resolving spontaneously over several days. Two weeks later and continuing off and on for 6 months, persistent swelling of the second and then fourth fingers was variably diagnosed as carpal tunnel syndrome and rheumatoid arthritis and was treated with prednisone and hydroxyquinolone. No osteomyelitis or abscess was noted on radiographic studies. A tenosynovectomy with carpal tunnel release was performed 7 months after the initial incident; stains were positive for acid fast bacilli. Mycobacterial cultures grew at 2 weeks but were negative with molecular probes for tuberculosis, avian-intracellulare, and gordonae species. DNA isolated from one colony was PCR-amplified and sequenced for the 16S ribosomal RNA gene with results indicating Mycobacterium haemophilum. Based on literature review, ciprofloxacin was recommended for treatment.

87470   Infectious agent detection by nucleic acid (DNA or RNA); Bartonella henselae and Bartonella quintana, direct probe technique

87492   Chlamydia trachomatis, quantification

●**87493**   Clostridium difficile, toxin gene(s), amplified probe technique

✍ Rationale

Code 87798 used to report Clostridium difficile detection by nucleic acid (DNA or RNA) does not adequately identify the analyte being measured. Therefore, code 87493 has been established to report Clostridium difficile, amplified probe technique detection by nucleic acid (DNA or RNA).

Most studies of Clostridium difficile have focused on patients in acute care hospitals. Clostridium difficile is important for other patient populations as well. For some patients, such as those with inflammatory bowel disease who also receive antimicrobial agents, Clostridium difficile is more prevalently found in patients residing in long-term care facilities, where greater morbidity and mortality rates exist.

Clinical Example (87493)

A liquid or soft stool specimen is collected and transported to the laboratory from a 32-year-old male admitted to the observation unit from the emergency department after the patient presented with diarrhea and bloody stools for 2 days and a temperature of 103°F.

Description of Procedure (87493)

A sterile dry swab is dipped into the liquid or soft stool material and processed. For testing, the swab is eluted in sample buffer, and the specimen is lysed. An aliquot of the lysate is added to PCR reagents that contain the tcdB specific primers used to amplify the genetic target of Clostridium difficile, if present. The assay also includes an internal control (IC) to detect (polymerase chain reaction) PCR inhibited specimens and to confirm the integrity of assay reagents. Amplified targets are detected with hybridization probes labeled with quenched fluorophores (molecular beacons). The amplification, detection, and interpretation of the signals are done automatically by the software. The entire procedure takes about 75 to 90 minutes, depending on the number of specimens processed.

Surgical Pathology

▲**88312**   Special stains; Group I for microorganisms (eg, Gridley, acid fast, methenamine silver), including interpretation and report, each

▲**88313**   Group II, all other (eg, iron, trichrome), except immunocytochemistry and immunoperoxidase stains, including interpretation and report, each

(For immunocytochemistry and immunoperoxidase tissue studies, use 88342)

+▲88314   histochemical staining with frozen section(s), including interpretation and report (List separately in addition to code for primary procedure)

▶(Use 88314 in conjunction with 88302-88309)◀

 Rationale

Codes 88312 and 88313 have been editorially revised to remove the add-on status of these codes. These codes may be reported separately from surgical pathology or non-surgical pathology examination codes. Code 88314 has been editorially revised to add "including interpretation and report (List separately in addition to code for primary procedure)" to retain its add-on status.

An instructional parenthetical note has been added following code 88314 instructing users to report code 88314 in conjunction with codes 88302-88309.

88384   Array-based evaluation of multiple molecular probes; 11 through 50 probes

88385   51 through 250 probes

88386   251 through 500 probes

(For preparation of array-based evaluation, see . . .

(For preparation and analyses of less . . .

●88387   Macroscopic examination, dissection, and preparation of tissue for non-microscopic analytical studies (eg, nucleic acid-based molecular studies); each tissue preparation (eg, a single lymph node)

▶(Do not report 88387 for tissue preparation for microbiologic cultures or flow cytometric studies)◀

▶(Do not report 88387 in conjunction with 88388, 88329-88334)◀

+●88388   in conjunction with a touch imprint, intraoperative consultation, or frozen section, each tissue preparation (eg, a single lymph node) (List separately in addition to code for primary procedure)

▶(Use 88388 in conjunction with 88329-88334)◀

▶(Do not report 88387 or 88388 for tissue preparation for microbiologic cultures or flow cytometric studies)◀

 Rationale

Code 88387 and add-on code 88388 have been established to report services performed prior to ancillary diagnostic testing currently applicable to molecular studies.

In support of the establishment of code 88387, two instructional parenthetical notes have been added. The first instructional parenthetical note instructs users not to report code 88387 for tissue preparation for microbiologic cultures or flow cytometric studies. The second instructional parenthetical note instructs users not to report code 88387 in conjunction with codes 88388, 88329-88334.

In support of the establishment of add-on code 88388, two instructional parenthetical notes have been added. The first instructional parenthetical note instructs users to use code 88388 in conjunction with codes 88329-88334. The second

---

⊘=Modifier 51 Exempt   ⊙=Moderate Sedation   ✚=Add-on Code   ✗=FDA approval pending

instructional parenthetical note instructs users not to report code 88387 or 88388 for tissue preparation for microbiologic cultures or flow cytometric studies.

 Clinical Example (88387)

A female patient is diagnosed with breast cancer. The surgeon performs a sentinel lymph node biopsy.

Description of Procedure (88387)

The pathologist receives the specimen fresh and uses sterile technique and careful dissection to examine for nodal tissue. The pathologist finds a 1.0 cm. lymph node and carefully dissects it from the surrounding fat. Because molecular studies may be done on the lymph node tissue, special precautions are taken for the handling and processing of the nodal tissue. Each lymph node is handled on a sterile surface to avoid contamination with breast tissue or primary tumor that can yield false positive assay results on subsequent molecular studies. If more than one sentinel node is obtained, these are also processed separately to avoid a positive node contaminating a negative node.

The pathologist then sections cleaned nodal tissue and does not see tissue suspicious for cancer. The node is parsed by the pathologist into subparts each approximately 2 mm in thickness. To further assess the node, alternating 2-mm subparts (in total one half the node) are tested using a molecular assay that targets a marker specific to breast tissue. First, the pathologist labels the nodes with the patient's identification number and with the node number. This is done for all sentinel nodes while keeping the tissue from each node in separate containers. Next, the tissue is carefully prepared for molecular analysis.

 Clinical Example (88388)

A female patient is diagnosed with breast cancer. The surgeon performs a sentinel lymph node biopsy and requests a frozen section or touch imprint in addition to further analytic studies.

Description of Procedure (88388)

The pathologist receives the specimen fresh. Because molecular studies will need to be performed on this specimen, the pathologist cannot use the typical frozen section protocol when initiating examination of the tissue.

Instead, the pathologist prepares the dissection area by using a sterile dissection field. This means the use of a sterile cutting board. The pathologist uses sterile technique and careful dissection to examine for nodal tissue. The pathologist finds a 1.0-cm lymph node and carefully dissects it from the surrounding fat. Because molecular studies may be done on the lymph node tissue, special precautions are taken for the handling and processing of the nodal tissue. Each lymph node is handled on a sterile surface to avoid contamination with breast tissue or primary tumor that can yield false positive assay results on subsequent molecular studies. If more than one sentinel node is obtained, these are also processed separately (each on its own dissection board) to avoid a positive node contaminating a negative node.

The pathologist then sections cleaned nodal tissue and does not see tissue suspicious for cancer. The node is parsed by the pathologist into even numbers of subparts of approximately 2 mm in thickness.

At this point the pathologist performs a frozen section or touch imprint and finds no malignant cells.

In Vivo (eg, Transcutaneous) Laboratory Procedures

●**88738**   Hemoglobin (Hgb), quantitative, transcutaneous

▶(For in vitro hemoglobin measurement, use 85018)◀

Rationale
Code 88738 has been established to report transcutaneous detection of hemoglobin (Hgb) and allow differentiation between transcutaneous Hgb measurement and invasive Hgb measurement performed on whole blood, in vitro. The transcutaneous method for accurately detecting Hgb without drawing blood is noninvasive while Hgb measurement performed on whole blood is invasive. A cross-reference has been added directing users to code 85018 for in vitro hemoglobin measurement.

A cross-reference has been added following code 85018 directing users to code 88738 for transcutaneous hemoglobin measurement.

Clinical Example (88738)
A 65-year-old male has recent onset exertional dyspnea, lethargy, tachycardia. Patient reports blood in stool. Transcutaneous hemoglobin evaluation is requested.

Reproductive Medicine Procedures

89300   Semen analysis; presence and/or motility of sperm including Huhner test (post coital)

89321   sperm presence and motility of sperm, if performed

▶(To report Hyaluronan binding assay [HBA], use 89398)◀

Rationale
With archiving of Category III code 0087T, a cross-reference has been added following code 89321 directing users to code 89398 for Hyaluronan binding assay (HBA).

89335   Cryopreservation, reproductive tissue, testicular

(For cryopreservation of embryo[s], use 89258. For cryopreservation of sperm, use 89259)

▶(For cryopreservation, ovarian reproductive tissue, oocytes, use 89240)◀

✍ Rationale

A cross-reference has been added following code 89335 directing users to code 89240 for cryopreservation of ovarian reproductive tissues.

89352	Thawing of cryopreserved; embryo(s)
89353	sperm/semen, each aliquot
89354	reproductive tissue, testicular/ovarian
89356	oocytes, each aliquot
●**89398**	Unlisted reproductive medicine laboratory procedure

✍ Rationale

Code 89398 has been established to report an unlisted testing procedure for reproductive medicine testing.

Medicine

A significant number of the revisions for the CPT® 2010 codebook are in the Medicine section. Among these revisions are
additions of codes to the vaccine coding section, revisions in
the ear, nose, and throat section (otorhinolaryngologic
services), and changes within the cardiovascular section.
An extensive amount of the changes that occurred in the
cardiovascular section were made within the codes related to
Implantable and Wearable Cardiac Device Evaluations. Many
of the changes have been made to reflect the need to clarify
the use of certain codes or to combine certain procedures that
are commonly performed together. In addition, some of the
changes also reflect deletions of codes, which represent
services that are no longer performed.

Medicine

▶Immune Globulins, Serum or Recombinant Products◀

▶Codes 90281-90399 identify the serum globulins, extracted from human blood; or recombinant immune globulin products created in a laboratory through genetic modification of human and/or animal proteins. Both are reported in addition to the administration codes 96365-96368, 96372, 96374, 96375 as appropriate. Modifier 51 should not be reported with this section of products codes when performed with another procedure. The serum or recombinant globulin products listed here include broad-spectrum anti-infective immune globulins, antitoxins, various isoantibodies, and monoclonal antibodies.◀

90281   Immune globulin (Ig), human, for intramuscular use

▲90378   Respiratory syncytial virus, monoclonal antibody, recombinant, for intramuscular use, 50 mg, each

▶(90379 has been deleted)◀

 Rationale

Code 90378 was editorially revised to categorize the product to represent a laboratory prepared monoclonal antibody rather than a human immune globulin. In concert with this revision, the introductory notes and section title have been expanded to encompass the full scope of products that are contained in this section including both serum and recombinant products. Currently, this section includes codes representing products intended for therapeutic immunity, however, future expansion of this section for other disease entities (eg, cancer) will occur as new products become available.

Code 90379 was deleted, as the product represented in the code is no longer manufactured or available.

Immunization Administration for Vaccines/Toxoids

Please note that the establishment of code 90470 and the revision of code 90663 will *not* be published in the *CPT 2010* codebook. These changes were made after the publication of the codebook.

In response to concerns related to the need for national vaccination efforts for H1N1 and to assist health plans with their commitment to cover the cost for vaccine administration, the CPT® Editorial Panel acted upon this urgent matter with the establishment of a new vaccine administration code, 90470, specific to the H1N1 virus, and to revise existing code 90663 for specificity to the H1N1 virus. Code 90663 is specific only to the H1N1 virus and is appropriate for either the intranasal or intramuscular formulations. The American Medical Association (AMA) expedited the publication of the new and revised codes to the AMA web site on Monday, September 28, 2009 for these codes to become immediately effective on that date.

The codes are as follows:

● **90470**   H1N1 immunization administration (intramuscular, intranasal), including counseling when performed

▲ **90663**   Influenza virus vaccine, pandemic formulation, H1N1

The use of the Current Procedural Terminology (CPT) codes 90470 and 90663 will help to efficiently report and track immunization and counseling services related to the H1N1 vaccine throughout the health care system, and will streamline the reporting and reimbursement procedure for physicians and health care providers, who are expected to administer nearly 200 million doses of the H1N1 vaccine in the United States.

For additional information on the use of these codes, please consult the *CPT Assistant*, October 2009 issue.

Vaccines, Toxoids

To assist users to report the . . .

The CPT Editorial Panel, . . .

Codes 90476-90748 identify the vaccine product . . .

If a significantly separately identifiable Evaluation . . .

To meet the reporting requirements of . . .

▶The "when administered to" age" descriptions included in CPT vaccine codes are not intended to identify a product's licensed age indication. The term "preservative free" includes use for vaccines that contain no preservative and vaccines that contain trace amounts of preservative agents that are not present in a sufficient concentration for the purpose of preserving the final vaccine formulation. The absence of a designation regarding a preservative does not necessarily indicate the presence or absence of preservative in the vaccine. Refer to the product's prescribing information (PI) for the licensed age indication before administering vaccine to a patient.◀

Separate codes are available for combination . . .

(For immune globulins, see codes 90281-90399, . . .

90476   Adenovirus vaccine, type 4, live, for oral use

🖉 Rationale

Similar vaccine products for the same indication are often represented in a single code versus multiple CPT vaccine product codes. Such is the case of the intramuscular influenza virus vaccines in which multiple products are represented by a single code (eg, 90656) even though these products differ in the amount of "preservative" they contain. Some vaccine products may contain only trace amounts of preservative agents, while in others no preservative is present.

To clarify this coding convention, the introductory language of the vaccine section has been modified to indicate that distinctions regarding the preservative status of vaccine product will not necessarily appear in all code descriptors, as both preservative-free and preservative-reduced vaccines can be adequately reported using the current coding structure. Further, the code descriptor included in CPT should not be used to determine the vaccine formulation or the licensed age indicator, but the information provided by the manufacturer (eg, product packaging insert containing the prescribing information or PI) should be utilized instead.

▲**90669**   Pneumococcal conjugate vaccine, 7 valent, for intramuscular use

✗ ●**90670**   Pneumococcal conjugate vaccine, 13 valent, for intramuscular use

📣 Rationale

Code 90670 has been established to report a new vaccine product code for a 13 valent pneumococcal conjugate vaccine (PCV-13) which, when approved by the US Food and Drug Administration (FDA), will be indicated for active immunization of infants and children for the prevention of invasive pneumococcal disease and otitis media. In concert with this addition, code 90669, commonly referred to as *PCV-7*, was revised to replace the term *polyvalent* with the term *7 valent*. Because these two similarly conjugated pneumococcal vaccine products, codes 90669 and 90670, are anticipated to be on the market simultaneously, identification of the valency in the code descriptors will aid to differentiate the two vaccines.

The new 13 valent pneumococcal conjugate vaccine, code 90670, will include 6 new serotypes in addition to those included in the existing 7 valent vaccine, code 90669. Code 90732 also exists for a 23-valent polysaccharide pneumococcal vaccine (PPV23), but this vaccine is not part of the routine childhood immunization schedule.

The age indicator "when administered to children younger than 5 years" was removed from code 90669 and excluded from code 90670 to limit any confusion when the vaccine is administered outside of the Advisory Committee on Immunization Practices (ACIP)–recommended age for universal immunization but still consistent with the FDA approved dosage.

Code 90670 will appear in the CPT codebook with the US Food and Drug Administration (FDA) approval pending symbol (✗). Updates on the FDA status of these codes will be reflected on the AMA CPT web site under Category I Vaccine Codes (www.ama-assn.org/ama/pub/category/10902.htlm) and in subsequent CPT publications.

Clinical Example (90670)

The typical patient would most likely include children up to the age of 5 years unless contraindiction exists (**Note:** it is unknown what the ACIP or the FDA will recommend.).

Description of Procedure (90670)

Patient undergoes vaccination in accordance with the recommended schedule or FDA indications, as appropriate to the patient.

▲**90738**　Japanese encephalitis virus vaccine, inactivated, for intramuscular use

🖎 **Rationale**

The vaccine product described in code 90738 for immunization to protect against Japanese encephalitis virus was approved by the US Food and Drug Administration (FDA) and thus will be listed in CPT codebook without the FDA approval pending symbol (✗). This update was also posted to the AMA CPT web site under Category I Vaccine Codes (www.ama-assn.org/ama/pub/category/10902.htlm) in Spring of 2009 when notification of FDA acceptance was received.

Ophthalmology

Special Ophthalmological Services

92120　Tonography with interpretation and report, recording indentation tonometer method or perilimbal suction method

　▶(For measurement of ocular blood flow, use Category III code 0198T)◀

🖎 **Rationale**

A parenthetical note to reference the new Category III code 0198T for the measurement of ocular blood flow utilizing a pneumotonometer probe has been added following code 92120.

Special Otorhinolaryngologic Services

Vestibular Function Tests, With Recording (eg, ENG)

●**92540**　Basic vestibular evaluation, includes spontaneous nystagmus test with eccentric gaze fixation nystagmus, with recording, positional nystagmus test, minimum of 4 positions, with recording, optokinetic nystagmus test, bidirectional foveal and peripheral stimulation, with recording, and oscillating tracking test, with recording

　▶(Do not report 92540 in conjunction with 92541, 92542, 92544, or 92545)◀

92541   Spontaneous nystagmus test, including gaze and fixation nystagmus, with recording

    ▶(Do not report 92541 in conjunction with 92542, 92544, 92545)◀

92542   Positional nystagmus test, minimum of 4 positions, with recording

    ▶(Do not report 92542 in conjunction with 92541, 92544, 92545)◀

92544   Optokinetic nystagmus test, bidirectional, foveal or peripheral stimulation, with recording

    ▶(Do not report 92544 in conjunction with 92541, 92542, 92545)◀

Rationale

Code 92540 was established to report a number of services that have been combined from the Special Otorhinolaryngologic Services under the heading "Vestibular Function Tests, With Recording (eg, ENG)." This code has been added to combine a number of services located in this specific section, which include spontaneous nystagmus testing (92541), positional nystagmus testing (92542), optokinetic nystagmus testing (92544), and oscillating tracking testing (92545). To allay confusion, an exclusionary parenthetical note has been added following codes 92540, 92541, 92542, and 92544 to preclude reporting these codes with any other service code included in this section during the same session.

Nystagmus in patients is a condition, which identifies an involuntary, rapid, rhythmic movement of the eyeball. Each of the codes included in the Vestibular Function Tests, With Recording (eg, ENG) section is specific to a particular type of nystagmus testing. Spontaneous nystagmus testing identifies nystagmus that occurs without specific stimulation of the vestibular system. Positional nystagmus testing identifies nystagmus that is produced due to a change in position of the head (which also includes an alteration in the form or intensity of the experienced condition). Optokinetic nystagmus testing studies normal nystagmus, which occurs when the patient views objects that pass across their field of vision, such as movement that may be observed from the motion of a moving car or train. Oscillating nystagmus identifies movement of the eyes in even patterns of movement (direction, rate, type of movement).

Clinical Example (92540)

A 67-year-old male presents with a 3-month history of spontaneous spells of incapacitating vertigo that last from 1 to 4 hours and occur 1 to 2 times per month. He reports the near simultaneous onset of fluctuating hearing loss in the left ear and left-sided tinnitus. He has a documented hearing loss in his left ear that varies over time.

Description of Procedure (92540)

The intraservice work begins with preparing the skin and applying electrodes that will record the nystagmus. After the electrodes are affixed to the skin with conducting gel or paste, they must be monitored for a short time to allow the impedance to stabilize. After the electrodes are applied and stabilized, calibration of the nystagmus must be performed by measuring the eye movements while tracking a light stimulus that moves across a predetermined arc to constitute a specified number of degrees in each direction. The health care provider then proceeds to the test battery, which consists of four successive procedures: (1) evaluation for spontaneous nystagmus, (2) positional nystagmus testing, (3) optokinetic nystagmus testing, and (4) oscillating tracking.

For evaluation for spontaneous nystagmus, the qualified health care professional monitors eye movements with a recording system while the patient views targets in the center and eccentric positions to the right, left, up, and down. The monitoring is then repeated with the eyes in similar positions but with visual fixation removed.

For evaluation of positional nystagmus, the qualified health care professional moves the patient into a series of specific positions while recording the eye movements that occur once the position is achieved. The number of positions varies but a minimum of four is routine.

For evaluation of optokinetic nystagmus, the qualified health care professional presents a large visual field stimulus typically composed of stripes or random dots that are set into motion to generate an optokinetic nystagmus that is recorded and analyzed for the speed of the eye referenced to the speed of the target.

To test oscillating tracking, the qualified health care professional records eye movements while the patient views a target that moves in the patient's visual field in a sinusoidal oscillatory profile.

Once the testing is completed, the necessary calculations are performed to determine the magnitude and direction of nystagmus under each test condition. The data are reviewed to ensure the absence of artifacts that could adversely influence the results and interpretation. The nystagmus recordings are printed for archival documentation, and a report of the diagnostic results and interpretation is prepared.

Audiologic Function Tests

The audiometric tests listed below require the use of calibrated electronic equipment, recording of results and a report with interpretation. Hearing tests (such as whispered voice, tuning fork) that are otorhinolaryngologic Evaluation and Management services are not reported separately. All services include testing of both ears. Use modifier 52 if a test is applied to one ear instead of two ears. All codes (except 92559) apply to testing of individuals. For testing of groups, use 92559 and specify test(s) used.

(For evaluation of speech, language and/or hearing problems through observation and assessment of performance, use 92506)

●92550   Tympanometry and reflex threshold measurements

▶(Do not report 92550 in conjunction with 92567, 92568)◀

92551   Screening test, pure tone, air only

92567   Tympanometry (impedance testing)

92568   Acoustic reflex testing, threshold

▶(92569 has been deleted. For acoustic reflex decay testing performed in conjunction with tympanometry, use 92570)◀

● **92570**   Acoustic immittance testing, includes tympanometry (impedance testing), acoustic reflex threshold testing, and acoustic reflex decay testing

▶(Do not report 92570 in conjunction with 92567, 92568)◀

92571   Filtered speech test

✒️ Rationale

Code 92570 is used to identify acoustic immittance testing. This is a procedure that combines a number of tests including (1) tympanometry (identified by code 92567) and (2) acoustic reflex testing for threshold (identified by code 92568). To allay confusion, an exclusionary parenthetical note has been added following code 92570 to preclude reporting these services together with code 92570 during the same session. An additional parenthetical note has been included following deleted code 92569, to identify the appropriate code to use for acoustic reflex decay testing in conjunction with tympanometry services (92570), and to exclude use of code 92570 from use with code 92567 or 92568.

Codes 92550 has also been added to combine tympanometry impedance testing (92567) with acoustic reflex testing for threshold (92568).

🩺 Clinical Example (92550)

A 73-year-old female was referred for an audiologic evaluation with the chief complaint of bilateral tinnitus and a history of occupational noise exposure. No episodes of vertigo or imbalance were reported.

Description of Procedure (92550)

Intraservice work for tympanometry begins by seating the patient next to the acoustic immittance unit. The audiologist informs and instructs the patient regarding the tympanometry procedure, apprising the patient regarding what to expect and asking that the patient not swallow or speak once the procedure begins. Otoscopy is then performed to inspect the ear canals and to evaluate the diameter of each canal. From that inspection, a probe tip is selected that will permit a hermetic seal. The probe is inserted into the ear canal to a sufficient depth to permit a hermetic seal. Air is pumped into the ear canal to a level of +200 daPa. The air pressure is then decreased over a range from +200 daPa to −400 daPa with the resulting immittance changes recorded on the instrument's screen. After the first ear is completed, the probe is switched to the opposite ear, and the process is repeated. The audiologist examines the data screen for the configuration of the tympanogram, the static compliance and gradient measurements, and equivalent volume of the ear canal.

The patient is instructed regarding the measurement of acoustic reflex thresholds and informed that she will hear loud sounds of approximately 1 second each. The probe is re-seated into the ear canal to again obtain a hermetic seal. An insert or supra-aural earphone is seated on the opposite ear to provide acoustic stimulation to elicit the reflexes. The audiologist must then ensure that the pressure in the ear canal corresponds to the maximum tympanic membrane compliance pressure for greatest recording sensitivity. A 500-Hz tone is presented at a level of 100 dB to the ear opposite the probe. The audiologist observes the waveform tracing on the unit screen to determine if there was evidence of a middle ear muscle contraction. If contraction was seen, the intensity of the tone is decreased in 10-dB steps until the reflex contraction is no longer observed. The stimulus intensity is then increased in 5-dB steps until the reflex is recorded once again. The lowest intensity necessary to evoke a middle ear muscle reflex is considered reflex threshold. If a reflex contraction was not observed with the initial stimulation of 100 dB, the intensity of the tone is increased to 105 dB and then 110 dB. This procedure is repeated for the ear contralateral to the probe for 1000 Hz, 2000 Hz, and 4000 Hz. Without adjusting the headset, the machine is reconfigured to provide the stimulation and record the response through the probe. A similar procedure is employed for the frequencies of 500 Hz, 1000 Hz, and 2000 Hz. After recording acoustic reflexes for contralateral and ipsilateral stimulation for the first ear, the probe is removed, the headset is reversed, the probe is reinserted into the opposite ear, and the procedure is repeated. A total of 14 frequencies (4 right contralateral stimulation, 3 right ipsilateral, 4 left contralateral, and 3 left ipsilateral) are used to evaluate the reflex threshold patterns diagnostically. The tympanogram findings are printed, and the test results are synthesized into other aspects of the audiological evaluation. Test outcomes are recorded in a written report for the patient's medical record.

⚕ Clinical Example (92570)

A 73-year-old female was referred for an audiologic evaluation with the chief complaint of progressive hearing loss and tinnitus in her right ear. No episodes of vertigo or imbalance were reported.

Description of Procedure (92570)

Intraservice work for tympanometry begins by seating the patient next to the acoustic immittance unit. The audiologist informs and instructs the patient regarding the tympanometry procedure, apprising the patient regarding what to expect and asking that the patient not swallow or speak once the procedure begins. Otoscopy is then performed to inspect the ear canals and to evaluate the diameter of each canal. From that inspection a probe tip is selected that will permit a hermetic seal. The probe is inserted into the ear canal to a sufficient depth to permit a hermetic seal. Air is pumped into the ear canal to a level of +200 daPa. The air pressure is then decreased over a range from +200 daPa to −400 daPa with the resulting immittance changes recorded on the instrument's screen. After the first ear is completed, the probe is switched to the opposite ear, and the process is repeated. The audiologist examines the data screen for the configuration of the tympanogram, the static compliance and gradient measurements, and equivalent volume of the ear canal.

The patient is instructed regarding the measurement of acoustic reflex thresholds and informed that she will hear loud sounds of approximately 1 second each. The probe is re-seated into the ear canal to again obtain a hermetic seal. An insert or supra-aural earphone is seated on the opposite ear to provide acoustic stimulation

⊘=Modifier 51 Exempt   ⊙=Moderate Sedation   ✦=Add-on Code   ✗=FDA approval pending

to elicit the reflexes. The audiologist then ensures that the pressure in the ear canal corresponds to the maximum tympanic membrane compliance pressure for greatest recording sensitivity. A 500-Hz tone is presented at a level of 100 dB to the ear opposite the probe. The audiologist observes the waveform tracing on the unit screen to determine if there was evidence of a middle ear muscle contraction. If contraction was seen, the intensity of the tone is decreased in 10-dB steps until the reflex contraction is no longer observed. The stimulus intensity is then increased in 5-dB steps until the reflex is recorded once again. The lowest intensity necessary to evoke a middle ear muscle reflex is considered reflex threshold. If a reflex contraction was not observed with the initial stimulation of 100-dB, the intensity of the tone is increased to 105-dB and then 110 dB. This procedure is repeated for the ear contralateral to the probe for 1000 Hz, 2000 Hz, and 4000 Hz. Without adjusting the headset, the equipment is reconfigured to provide the stimulation and record the response through the probe. A similar procedure is employed for the frequencies of 500 Hz, 1000 Hz, and 2000 Hz. After recording acoustic reflexes for contralateral and ipsilateral stimulation for the first ear, the probe is removed, the headset is reversed, the probe is reinserted into the opposite ear, and the procedure is repeated. A total of 14 frequencies (4 right contralateral stimulation, 3 right ipsilateral, 4 left contralateral, and 3 left ipsilateral) are used to evaluate the reflex threshold patterns diagnostically.

For reflex decay determination, the audiologist informs the patient to expect to hear several very loud, possibly uncomfortable, sounds that will each have durations of 10 seconds. After the reflex threshold measurements have been completed, the audiologist re-sets the frequency of stimulation to 500 Hz and through the contralateral earphone presents a tone at a level 10 dB above the reflex threshold (typically between 100 dB and 115 dB HL) for 10 seconds. The acoustic immittance unit records the waveform trace of the strength of muscle contraction for the stimulus duration. The audiologist must examine the trace to determine if an amplitude decrement of 50% or more is present. After the 10-second stimulation, the audiologist must wait at least 30 seconds to permit the ear to recover from the extremely loud stimulus. This procedure is repeated for 1000 Hz with the same headset arrangement. The headset/probe assembly will be reversed to test the opposite ear in the contralateral stimulation paradigm for a total of four recordings. The tympanogram findings are printed for acoustic reflex thresholds and reflex decay patterns, and the test results are synthesized into other aspects of the audiological evaluation. Test outcomes are recorded in a written report.

Cardiovascular

Therapeutic Services and Procedures

⊙**92960**   Cardioversion, elective, electrical conversion of arrhythmia; external

⊙**92961**   internal (separate procedure)

▶(Do not report 92961 in conjunction with 93282-93284, 93287, 93289, 93295, 93296, 93618-93624, 93631, 93640-93642, 93650-93652, 93662)◀

Rationale

Editorial revision to the parenthetical instructions following code 92961 for cardioversion were made to include the addition of codes 93284, 93287, and 93296 to preclude additional reporting for multiple lead cardioverter-defibrillator programming. In addition, code 93292 was deleted from this same parenthetical, because as a remote service, it could not be performed with cardioversion (eg, one would not wear an external defibrillator system and also have an internal cardiac defibrillator).

Cardiography

Codes 93040-93042 are appropriate when an . . .

Cardiovascular monitoring services are diagnostic medical . . .

***Attended surveillance* is the immediate...**

▶***Electrocardiographic rhythm derived elements:*** elements derived from recordings of the electrical activation of the heart including, but not limited to heart rhythm, rate, ST analysis, heart rate variability, T-wave alternans.◀

Mobile cardiovascular telemetry (MCT) continuously...

ECG rhythm derived elements are distinct . . .

For other services related to a . . .

(For echocardiography, see 93303-93350)

(For electrocardiogram, 64 leads or greater, . . .

93000 Electrocardiogram, routine ECG with at least 12 leads; with interpretation and report

93005   tracing only, without interpretation and report

93010   interpretation and report only

 Rationale

In accordance with the deletion of codes 0068T and 0070T, the cross-reference note following code 93010 directing users to codes 0068T and 0070T for acoustic heart sound recording has been deleted.

▶Implantable and Wearable Cardiac Device Evaluations◀

▶Cardiac device evaluation services are diagnostic medical procedures using in-person and remote technology to assess device therapy and cardiovascular physiologic data. Codes 93279-93299 describe this technology and technical/professional physician and service center practice. Codes 93279-93292 are reported per procedure. Codes 93293-93296 are reported no more than **once** every 90 days. Do not report 93293-93296 if the monitoring period is less than 30 days. Codes 93297, 93298 are reported no more than **once** up to every 30 days. Do not report 93297-93299 if the monitoring period is less than 10 days.

⊘=Modifier 51 Exempt   ⊙=Moderate Sedation   ✚=Add-on Code   ✗=FDA approval pending

A service center may report 93296 or 93299 during a period in which a physician performs an in-person interrogation device evaluation. A physician may not report an in-person and remote interrogation of the same device during the same period. Report only remote services when an in-person interrogation device evaluation is performed during a period of remote interrogation device evaluation. A period is established by the initiation of the remote monitoring or the 91st day of a pacemaker or implantable cardioverter-defibrillator (ICD) monitoring or the 31st day of an implantable loop recorder (ILR) or implantable cardiovascular monitor (ICM) monitoring and extends for the subsequent 90 or 30 days, respectively, for which remote monitoring is occurring. Programming device evaluations and in-person interrogation device evaluations may not be reported on the same date by the same physician. Programming device evaluations and remote interrogation device evaluations may both be reported during the remote interrogation device evaluation period.

For monitoring by wearable devices, see 93224-93272.◀

ECG rhythm derived elements are distinct . . .

For other services related to a . . .

Do not report 93012, 93014 when . . .

The pacemaker and ICD interrogation device . . .

The following definitions and instructions apply . . .

Attended surveillance: the immediate availability of . . .

Device, single lead: a pacemaker or . . .

Device, dual lead: a pacemaker or . . .

Device, multiple lead: a pacemaker or . . .

▶***Electrocardiographic rhythm derived elements:*** elements derived from recordings of the electrical activation of the heart including, but not limited to heart rhythm, rate, ST analysis, heart rate variability, T-wave alternans.◀

Implantable cardiovascular monitor (ICM): an implantable . . .

Implantable cardioverter-defibrillator (ICD): an implantable device . . .

Implantable loop recorder (ILR): an implantable . . .

▶***Interrogation device evaluation:*** an evaluation of an implantable device such as a cardiac pacemaker, implantable cardioverter-defibrillator, implantable cardiovascular monitor, or implantable loop recorder. Using an office, hospital, or emergency room instrument or via a remote interrogation system, stored and measured information about the lead(s) when present, sensor(s) when present, battery and the implanted device function, as well as data collected about the patient's heart rhythm and heart rate is retrieved. The retrieved information is evaluated to determine the current programming of the device and to evaluate certain aspects of the device function such as battery voltage, lead impedance, tachycardia detection settings, and rhythm treatment settings.◀

The components that must be evaluated . . .

Pacemaker: Programmed parameters,. . .

Implantable cardioverter-defibrillator: Programmed parameters,. . .

Implantable cardiovascular monitor: Programmed parameters...

Implantable loop recorder: Programmed parameters...

Pacemaker: Programmed parameters, lead(s), battery, capture . . .

Peri-procedural device evaluation and programming: an evaluation of an...

Physiologic cardiovascular data elements: data elements from...

▶*Programming device evaluation (in person):* a procedure performed for patients with a pacemaker, implantable cardioverter-defibrillator, or implantable loop recorder. All device functions, including the battery, programmable settings and lead(s), when present, are evaluated. To assess capture thresholds, iterative adjustments (eg, progressive changes in pacing output of a pacing lead) of the programmable parameters are conducted. The iterative adjustments provide information that permits the operator to assess and select the most appropriate final program parameters to provide for consistent delivery of the appropriate therapy and to verify the function of the device. The final program parameters may or may not change after evaluation.◀

The programming device evaluation includes all . . .

The components that must be evaluated . . .

Pacemaker: Programmed parameters, lead(s), battery, capture . . .

Implantable cardioverter-defibrillator: Programmed parameters, lead(s), battery, . . .

Implantable loop recorder: Programmed parameters and . . .

Transtelephonic rhythm strip pacemaker evaluation: service . . .

▲93279   Programming device evaluation (in person) with iterative adjustment of the implantable device to test the function of the device and select optimal permanent programmed values with physician analysis, review and report; single lead pacemaker system

(Do not report 93279 in conjunction with 93286, 93288)

▲93280   dual lead pacemaker system

(Do not report 93280 in conjunction with 93286, 93288)

▲93281   multiple lead pacemaker system

(Do not report 93281 in conjunction with 93286, 93288)

▲93282   single lead implantable cardioverter-defibrillator system

(Do not report 93282 in conjunction with 93287, 93289, 93745)

▲93283   dual lead implantable cardioverter-defibrillator system

(Do not report 93283 in conjunction with 93287, 93289)

▲93284   multiple lead implantable cardioverter-defibrillator system

(Do not report 93284 in conjunction with 93287, 93289)

▲93285   implantable loop recorder system

▶(Do not report 93285 in conjunction with 33282, 93279-93284, 93291)◀

Ⓢ=Modifier 51 Exempt   ◉=Moderate Sedation   ✚=Add-on Code   ✗=FDA approval pending

▲**93286** Peri-procedural device evaluation (in person) and programming of device system parameters before or after a surgery, procedure, or test with physician analysis, review and report; single, dual, or multiple lead pacemaker system

(Report 93286 once before and once after surgery, procedure, or test, when device evaluation and programming is performed before and after surgery, procedure, or test)

(Do not report 93286 in conjunction with 93279-93281, 93288)

▲**93287** single, dual, or multiple lead implantable cardioverter-defibrillator system

(Report 93287 once before and once after surgery, procedure, or test, when device evaluation and programming is performed before and after surgery, procedure, or test)

(Do not report 93287 in conjunction with 93282-93284, 93289)

 Rationale

The programming device evaluation codes 93279, 93280, 93281, 93282, 93283, 93284, and 93285; peri-procedural codes 93286 and 93287; and associated guidelines have been editorially revised to add the descriptor "in person" to clarify that these services are not performed remotely. Further instructions in the CPT codebook will be provided as remote programming technologies evolve.

Echocardiography

Echocardiography includes obtaining ultrasonic signals from . . .

▶A complete transthoracic echocardiogram without spectral or color flow Doppler (93307) is a comprehensive procedure that includes 2-dimensional and, when performed, selected M-mode examination of the left and right atria, left and right ventricles, the aortic, mitral, and tricuspid valves, the pericardium, and adjacent portions of the aorta. Multiple views are required to obtain a complete functional and anatomic evaluation, and appropriate measurements are obtained and recorded. Despite significant effort, identification and measurement of some structures may not always be possible. In such instances, the reason that an element could not be visualized must be documented. Additional structures that may be visualized (eg, pulmonary veins, pulmonary artery, pulmonic valve, inferior vena cava) would be included as part of the service.

A complete transthoracic echocardiogram with spectral and color flow Doppler (93306) is a comprehensive procedure that includes spectral Doppler and color flow Doppler in addition to the 2-dimensional and selected M-mode examinations, when performed. Spectral Doppler (93320, 93321) and color flow Doppler (93325) provide information regarding intracardiac blood flow and hemodynamics.◀

A follow-up or limited echocardiographic study . . .

In stress echocardiography, echocardiographic images are . . .

▶ When a stress echocardiogram is performed with a complete cardiovascular stress test (93015) (continuous electrocardiographic monitoring, physician supervision, interpretation and report), use 93351. Code 93350 is used to report the performance and interpretation of a stress echocardiogram only, with the components of the cardiovascular stress test reported separately using the appropriate codes (93016–93018).◄

When left ventricular endocardial borders cannot be adequately identified by standard echocardiographic imaging, echocardiographic contrast may be infused intravenously both at rest and with stress to achieve that purpose. Code 93352 is used to report the administration of echocardiographic contrast agent in conjunction with the stress echocardiography codes (93350 or 93351). Supply of contrast agent and/or drugs used for pharmacological stress is reported separately in addition to the procedure code.

Report of an echocardiographic study, whether . . .

Use of ultrasound, without thorough evaluation . . .

(For fetal echocardiography, see 76825-76828)

93303   Transthoracic echocardiography for congenital cardiac anomalies; complete

93350   Echocardiography, transthoracic, real-time with image documentation (2D), includes M-mode recording, when performed, during rest and cardiovascular stress test using treadmill, bicycle exercise and/or pharmacologically induced stress, with interpretation and report;

▶(Stress testing codes 93016-93018 should be reported, when appropriate, in conjunction with 93350 to capture the cardiovascular stress portion of the study)◄

▶(Do not report 93350 in conjunction with 93015)◄

Rationale

The Echocardiography guidelines have been editorially revised to indicate that codes 93306 and 93307 include selected M-mode examinations when they are performed. They also now clarify that codes 93016 through 93018 should be reported with code 93350, when appropriate, to capture the exercise portion of the study. An additional instructional note has been added instructing users not to report code 93350 with code 93015.

Noninvasive Physiologic Studies and Procedures

▲**93701**   Bioimpedance-derived physiologic cardiovascular analysis

▶(For left ventricular filling pressure indirect measurement by computerized calibration of the arterial waveform response to Valsalva, use 93799)◄

Code 93701 has been editorially revised to describe bioimpedance-derived physiologic cardiovascular analysis. Previously, code 93701 only described thoracic electrical bioimpedance in which electrodes are attached to the thorax for measurement. The revised code now allows for the reporting of cardiovascular analysis when measuring bioimpedance with electrodes attached to the wrist and ankle.

In accordance with the sundowning of Category III code 0086T, a cross-reference note has been added following code 93701 instructing users to report code 93799 for left ventricular filling pressure indirect measurement by computerized calibration.

⊘=Modifier 51 Exempt   ⊙=Moderate Sedation   ✚=Add-on Code   ✗=FDA approval pending

93745 Initial set-up and programming by a physician of wearable cardioverter-defibrillator includes initial programming of system, establishing baseline electronic ECG, transmission of data to data repository, patient instruction in wearing system and patient reporting of problems or events

(Do not report 93745 in conjunction with 93282, 93292)

●93750 Interrogation of ventricular assist device (VAD), in person, with physician analysis of device parameters (eg, drivelines, alarms, power surges), review of device function (eg, flow and volume status, septum status, recovery), with programming, if performed, and report

▶(Do not report 93750 in conjunction with 33975, 33976, 33979, 33981-33983)◀

Rationale

Code 93750 has been established to describe the in-person interrogation of a ventricular assist device (VAD). Code 93750 includes analysis of the device parameters by a physician and review of device function and programming, if performed. A report is also included in this service.

An instruction note has been added following code 93750, instructing users not to report code 93750 in conjunction with VAD insertion, removal, and replacement codes 33975, 33976, 33979, and 33981-33983.

Clinical Example (93750)

A 50-year-old patient is seen for regular, scheduled ventricular assist device (VAD) follow-up assessment. The VAD is interrogated.

Note: Evaluation and Management (E/M) is reported separately.

Description of Procedure (93750)

The physician disconnects the patient from the battery and attaches the outflow conduit to a cable, which in turn is connected to a non-portable VAD systems monitor that downloads information from the patient's VAD and performs a series of diagnostic checks (ie, VAD stroke rate, flow volume, pump rate, alarm history) to ensure the VAD is functioning within specified parameters. This real-time data are compared to recorded data to determine functioning as well as patient compliance with VAD operating instructions when the patient is engaged in activities of daily living.

Pulmonary

Other Procedures

Codes 94010-94799 include laboratory procedure(s) and . . .

94010 Spirometry, including graphic record, total and timed vital capacity, expiratory flow rate measurement(s), with or without maximal voluntary ventilation

⊙●94011 Measurement of spirometric forced expiratory flows in an infant or child through 2 years of age

⊙●**94012**   Measurement of spirometric forced expiratory flows, before and after bronchodilator, in an infant or child through 2 years of age

⊙●**94013**   Measurement of lung volumes (ie, functional residual capacity [FRC], forced vital capacity [FVC], and expiratory reserve volume [ERV]) in an infant or child through 2 years of age

⊘**94610**   Intrapulmonary surfactant administration by a physician through endotracheal tube

✎ Rationale

Pulmonary function test techniques that are designed for older children and adults are very difficult to apply to uncooperative infants. However, recent technology has been developed to accommodate the challenges presented in obtaining pulmonary function tests on infants. A technique known as *raised volume rapid thoracoabdominal compression (RVRTC)* allows the replication of standard forced expiratory flow measurements, functional residual capacity (FRC), forced vital capacity (FVC), and expiratory reserve volume (ERV) in infants. Using RVRTC involves the placement of an inflatable vest and a mask on the infant, and forced expiratory flow and lung volume measurements are then obtained in the usual manner. In order to apply the RVRTC technique, moderate sedation must be administered to the infant.

Due to the increased work and time involved in the performance of these procedures, codes 94011 through 94013 have been established. The moderate sedation symbol (⊙) has been added next to each code, because moderate sedation is an inclusive component of the procedures. Each code is reported for infants and children through 2-years of age. Code 94011 describes spirometric forced expiratory flow measurements using the RVRTC technique. Code 94012 describes spirometric forced expiratory flow measurements before and after administration of a bronchodilator using the RVRTC technique. Code 94013 describes functional residual capacity (FRC), forced vital capacity (FVC), and expiratory reserve volume (ERV) measurements using the RVRTC technique.

It is important to note that the preservice work for the infant pulmonary function test is different from the work of an evaluation and management (E/M) service during which the determination is made that spirometry is needed and is usually not provided on the same day as an infant pulmonary function test. Often, a different physician performs the spirometry rather than the provider ordering it.

🩺 Clinical Example (94011)

A 5-month-old infant with cystic fibrosis has a chronic cough. An infant pulmonary function test is ordered to determine if there are abnormalities in forced expiratory flows.

Description of Procedure (94011)

The infant is sedated following the sedation protocol. Paperwork is completed with a review of the medication list, the patient's vital signs, and a confirmation that the patient has not taken anything by mouth (npo). If the child awakens during the procedure, repeat sedation is administered. The mask is tightly sealed over the patient's nose and mouth. The patient is placed inside an airtight, transparent box. A series of measurements are made before, during, and after mechanically

⊘=Modifier 51 Exempt   ⊙=Moderate Sedation   ✚=Add-on Code   ✗=FDA approval pending

squeezing of the chest using a pneumatic vest. Repeated cycles are obtained to insure validity. Frequently the box must be opened and the patient repositioned in order to ensure a tight seal of the mask over the patient's face.

Clinical Example (94012)

A 4-month-old infant has a chronic cough. An infant pulmonary function test is ordered to determine if there are abnormalities in forced expiratory flows and if they are reversible by a bronchodilator.

Description of Procedure (94012)

The infant is sedated following the sedation protocol. Paperwork is completed with a review of the medication list, the patient's vital signs, and confirmation that the patient has not taken anything by mouth (npo). The mask is tightly sealed over the patient's nose and mouth. The patient is placed inside an airtight, transparent box. A series of measurements are made before, during, and after mechanically squeezing of the chest using a pneumatic vest. Repeated cycles are obtained to insure validity. Frequently the box must be opened and the patient repositioned in order to ensure a tight seal of the mask over the patient's face. A bronchodilator is administered after which the physician must wait to observe its effects. The procedure is then repeated. If the child awakens, repeat sedation is administered.

Clinical Example (94013)

A 9-month-old infant has survived perinatal lung surgery to remove a congenital cystic adenomatous malformation. Lung volumes are being assessed to determine compensatory growth.

Description of Procedure (94013)

The infant is sedated following the sedation protocol. Paperwork is completed with a review of the medication list, the patient's vital signs, and confirmation that the patient has not taken anything by mouth (npo). If the child awakens during the procedure, repeat sedation is administered. The mask is tightly sealed over the patient's nose and mouth. The patient is placed inside an airtight, transparent box. A series of measurements are made before, during, and after mechanically squeezing of the chest using a pneumatic vest. Repeated cycles are obtained to insure validity. Frequently the box must be opened and the patient repositioned in order to ensure a tight seal of the mask over the patient's face. The infant's lungs are passively inflated to total lung capacity. The procedure is repeated with multiple measurements after passive inflation.

Neurology and Neuromuscular Procedures

Sleep Testing

(Report with modifier 52 if less than 6 hours of recording or in other cases of reduced services as appropriate)

(For unattended sleep study, use 95806)

▲**95806**   Sleep study, unattended, simultaneous recording of, heart rate, oxygen saturation, respiratory airflow, and respiratory effort, (eg, thoracoabdominal movement)

(Do not report 95806 in conjunction with 93012, 93014, 93041-93227, 93228, 93229, 93230-93272, 0203T, 0204T)

(For unattended sleep study that measures heart rate, oxygen saturation, respiratory analysis, and sleep time, use 0203T)

(For unattended sleep study that measures heart rate, oxygen saturation, and respiratory analysis, use 0204T)

 ## Rationale

In support of the establishment of Category III codes 0203T and 0204T to report unattended sleep study testing services, Category I sleep study code 95806 has been revised to create consistent terminology within the family of codes and to report unattended sleep study testing measuring heart rate, oxygen saturation, respiratory airflow, and respiratory effort. Following code 95806, an instructional note and two cross-references have been added to (1) instruct the user not to report code 95806 with ECG monitoring services or new codes 0203T and 0204T; (2) direct the user to report Category III code 0203T for an unattended sleep study that measures heart rate, oxygen saturation, respiratory analysis, and sleep time; and (3) direct the user to report Category III code 0204T for an unattended sleep study that measures heart rate, oxygen saturation, and respiratory analysis.

Nerve Conduction Tests

▶ The following applies to nerve conduction tests (95900-95904): Codes 95900-95904 describe nerve conduction tests when performed with individually placed stimulating, recording, and ground electrodes. The stimulating, recording, and ground electrode placement and the test design must be individualized to the patient's unique anatomy. Nerves tested must be limited to the specific nerves and conduction studies needed for the particular clinical question being investigated. The stimulating electrode must be placed directly over the nerve to be tested, and stimulation parameters properly adjusted to avoid stimulating other nerves or nerve branches. In most motor nerve conduction studies, and in some sensory and mixed nerve conduction studies, both proximal and distal stimulation will be used. Motor nerve conduction study recordings must be made from electrodes placed directly over the motor point of the specific muscle to be tested. Sensory nerve conduction study recordings must be made from electrodes placed directly over the specific nerve to be tested. Waveforms must be reviewed on site in real time, and the technique (stimulus site, recording site, ground site, filter settings) must be adjusted, as appropriate, as the test proceeds in order to minimize artifact, and to minimize the chances of unintended stimulation of adjacent nerves and the unintended recording from adjacent muscles or nerves. Reports must be prepared on site by the examiner, and consist of the work product of the interpretation of numerous test results, using well-established techniques to assess the amplitude, latency, and configuration of waveforms elicited by stimulation at each site of each nerve tested. This includes the calculation of nerve conduction velocities, sometimes including specialized F-wave indices, along with comparison to normal values, summarization of clinical and electrodiagnostic data, and physician or other qualified health care professional interpretation.

Code 95905 describes nerve conduction tests when performed with preconfigured electrodes customized to a specific anatomic site.◀

⊘**95900**   Nerve conduction, amplitude and latency/velocity study, each nerve; motor, without F-wave study

⊘**95903**   motor, with F-wave study

⊘**95904**   sensory

(Report 95900, 95903, and/or 95904 only once when multiple sites on the same nerve are stimulated or recorded)

⊘●**95905**   Motor and/or sensory nerve conduction, using preconfigured electrode array(s), amplitude and latency/velocity study, each limb, includes F-wave study when performed, with interpretation and report

▶(Report 95905 only once per limb studied)◀

▶(Do not report 95905 in conjunction with 95900-95904, 95934-95936)◀

📝 Rationale

Code 95905 has been established to report the performance of motor and sensory nerve conduction using pre-configured arrays. New introductory language to assist in differentiating nerve conduction studies performed with individually placed stimulating electrodes from tests performed with preconfigured electrode arrays has also been added. Code 95905 may be reported only once per limb studied and cannot be used in conjunction with codes for nerve conduction (95900, 95903, 95904) or codes for H-reflex studies (95934, 95936), as indicated in the parenthetical notes following code 95905. Similar to codes 95900, 95903 and 95904, a modifier 51 exempt symbol "⊘" designation has been added to code 95905, as this procedure is usually performed with other services, and thus the pre- and post-service activities in this service are minimal and already reflect a reduced relative value unit (RVU). The Modifier 51 Exemption – Inclusion/Exclusion Criteria were introduced in the *CPT 2008* codebook as outlined in *CPT® 2008 Changes.*

🩺 Clinical Example (95905)

A 42-year-old female data entry clerk reported that, although she had had no injuries and during the day she felt okay, she woke in the middle of each night for the past 2 weeks with a numb, aching, burning feeling in her right hand that was relieved by holding her hand down and shaking it, rubbing it, and running cold water over it. Physical examination reveals weakness of right thumb abduction; wasting of the right thenar eminence; numbness of the palmar aspects of the right thumb, index finger, and middle finger; and a Tinel's sign over the right median nerve at the carpal tunnel. (History and exam are reported separately with evaluation and management [E/M] codes.) Nerve conduction testing using preconfigured arrays for the right arm is performed.

Description of Procedure (95905)

The physician reviews a summary of electrodiagnostic data from each nerve tested and assesses it in the context of comparison to normal values and the patient's history and physical examination.

Hydration, Therapeutic, Prophylactic, Diagnostic Injections and Infusions, and Chemotherapy and Other Highly Complex Drug or Highly Complex Biologic Agent Administration

Physician work related to hydration, injection, . . .

If a significant, separately identifiable Evaluation . . .

If performed to facilitate the infusion . . .

a. Use of local anesthesia

b. IV start

c. Access to indwelling IV, subcutaneous . . .

d. Flush at conclusion of infusion

e. Standard tubing, syringes, and supplies

(For declotting a catheter or port, . . .

When multiple drugs are administered, report . . .

When administering multiple infusions, injections or . . .

▶In order to determine which service should be reported as the initial service when there is more than one type of service, hierarchies have been created. These vary by whether the physician or a facility is reporting. The order of selection for physicians is based upon the physician knowledge of the clinical condition(s) and treatment(s). The hierarchy that facilities are to use is based upon a structural algorithm. When these codes are reported by the physician, the "initial" code that best describes the key or primary reason for the encounter should always be reported irrespective of the order in which the infusions or injections occur.

When these codes are reported by *the facility*, the following instructions apply. The initial code should be selected using a hierarchy whereby chemotherapy services are primary to therapeutic, prophylactic, and diagnostic services which are primary to hydration services. Infusions are primary to pushes, which are primary to injections. This hierarchy is to be followed by facilities and supersedes parenthetical instructions for add-on codes that suggest an add-on of a higher hierarchical position may be reported in conjunction with a base code of a lower position. (For example, the hierarchy would not permit reporting 96376 with 96360, as 96376 is a higher order code. IV push is primary to hydration.)◀

When reporting codes for which infusion . . .

⊘=Modifier 51 Exempt   ⊙=Moderate Sedation   ✚=Add-on Code   ⁄=FDA approval pending

Rationale

In order to clarify the relation of certain parenthetical instructions to the overriding guidelines for the Hydration, Therapeutic, Prophylactic, Diagnostic Injections and Infusions, and Chemotherapy and Other Highly Complex Drug or Highly Complex Biologic Agent Administration subsection, the guidelines were revised to clarify that the hierarchy structure for infusions is sequential and does not pertain to the level of difficulty. The guidelines were further refined to clarify appropriate reporting of the hierarchy structure by facilities.

Photodynamic Therapy

+▲96570   Photodynamic therapy by endoscopic application of light to ablate abnormal tissue via activation of photosensitive drug(s); first 30 minutes (List separately in addition to code for endoscopy or bronchoscopy procedures of lung and gastrointestinal tract)

+▲96571   each additional 15 minutes (List separately in addition to code for endoscopy or bronchoscopy procedures of lung and gastrointestinal tract)

Rationale

The photodynamic therapy codes 96570 and 96571 have been editorially revised to expand and include endoscopic application of gastrointestinal tract therapy. The procedure previously described endoscopic light application to a single region (esophagus) of the gastrointestinal tract. However, other areas of the gastrointestinal tract (eg, oral cavity, biliary tract) are also treated using endoscopic application of light (photodynamic therapy). Therefore, codes 96570 and 96571 have been revised to allow reporting of photodynamic therapy of the gastrointestinal tract.

Clinical Example (96570)

A 74-year-old male with a history of smoking and alcohol use complains of extreme difficulty with swallowing. Endoscopic examination is performed and reveals esophageal cancer. A computed tomography (CT) scan shows adjacent lymph node and celiac involvement. A determination is made that the patient is not a candidate for surgical resection. The patient receives radiation therapy and chemotherapy. Subsequently, the patient develops recurrent complaints of dysphagia. Reassessment reveals that the tumor has progressed and is surgically nonresectable. Therapy of the patient's dysphagia using photodynamic therapy is performed.

Description of Procedure (96570)

A diffuser tip is inserted, the endoscopic laser light source is activated, and the laser light is applied to the tumor. (Two-and-a-half minutes of endoscopic laser light using a diffusing fiberoptic endoscope are required for every 5 mm of tumor length.) During each application, the light source is periodically turned off so that the position of both the endoscope and the diffuser may be checked. At the completion of the procedure, the light application is turned off and the endoscope with the diffuser tip is withdrawn.

A 74-year-old male with a history of smoking and alcohol use complains of extreme difficulty with swallowing. Endoscopic examination is performed and reveals esophageal cancer. A computed tomography (CT) scan shows adjacent lymph node and celiac involvement. A determination is made that the patient is not a candidate for surgical resection. The patient receives radiation therapy and chemotherapy. Subsequently, the patient develops recurrent complaints of dysphagia. Reassessment reveals that the tumor has progressed and is surgically nonresectable. Therapy of the patient's dysphagia using photodynamic therapy is performed.

In the same session additional therapy of the patient's dysphagia using photodynamic therapy is performed.

Description of Procedure (96571)

Because of the size of the tumor, the treatment session lasts an additional 15 minutes beyond the initial 30 minutes assigned to CPT code 96570. (Two-and-a-half minutes of endoscopic laser light using a diffusing fiberoptic endoscope are required for every 5 mm of tumor length.) During each application, the light source is periodically turned off so that the position of both the endoscope and the diffuser may be checked. At the completion of the procedure, the light application is turned off and the endoscope with the diffuser tip is withdrawn.

Special Dermatological Procedures

96920   Laser treatment for inflammatory skin disease (psoriasis); total area less than 250 sq cm

96921   250 sq cm to 500 sq cm

96922   over 500 sq cm

▶(For laser destruction of premalignant lesions, see 17000-17004)◀

▶(For laser destruction of cutaneous vascular proliferative lesions, see 17106-17108)◀

▶(For laser destruction of benign lesions, see 17110-17111)◀

▶(For laser destruction of malignant lesions, see 17260-17286)◀

Rationale

Cross-references have been added to direct users to various laser dermatology procedures in the Integumentary section of the *CPT 2010* codebook.

Other Services and Procedures

99183   Physician attendance and supervision of hyperbaric oxygen therapy, per session

(Evaluation and Management services and/or procedures [eg, wound debridement] provided in a hyperbaric oxygen treatment facility in conjunction with a hyperbaric oxygen therapy session should be reported separately)

▶(99185, 99186 have been deleted)◀

 Rationale

Codes 99185 and 99186 describing regional and total body hypothermia were deleted from the *CPT 2010* codebook. Codes 99185 and 99186 were outdated and not specific to the type of technology used, thus making it difficult to adequately determine the procedure performed.

Category II Codes

This section continues to be the fastest growing section of the CPT® codebook, with the addition of 98 codes for quality improvement measures, 9 new clinical conditions, and 46 revised clinical conditions.

Category II Codes

▲**0519F**   Planned chemotherapy regimen, including at a minimum: drug(s) prescribed, dose, and duration, documented prior to initiation of a new treatment regimen (ONC)[1]

▲**0520F**   Radiation dose limits to normal tissues established prior to the initiation of a course of 3D conformal radiation for a minimum of 2 tissue/organ (ONC)[1]

Rationale

Two code revisions were made to existing codes included within the **Oncology (ONC)** Measure Set. Code 0519F was revised to utilize language that more accurately reflects the intent for use of this code. The phrase " . . . a new treatment regimen" has replaced " . . . course of treatment . . . " to note that the intent for use of this code is to identify documentation of a planned chemotherapy regimen prior to initiation of a *new* treatment regimen (ie, no need to provide planning during the course of treatment if planning occurred prior to the new treatment regimen). Code 0520F was revised to (1) to specify documentation of *radiation dose limits* for normal tissues, (2) to eliminate the reference to treatment days as the means of identifying the time frame in which documentation of dose limits must occur, and (3) to note that the measure specifications apply to two tissues or organs. The language in the measure (**Radiation Dose Limits to Normal Tissues**[1]) was revised to reflect these changes, as the measure specifications were also revised to specify this intent and capture these elements in both the code reference and the measure. In addition, the measure snapshot included in the Appendix H document was revised to note use of the code for pancreatic and lung cancer patients.

●**0528F**   Recommended follow-up interval for repeat colonoscopy of at least 10 years documented in colonoscopy report (End/Polyp)[5]

●**0529F**   Interval of 3 or more years since patient's last colonoscopy, documented (End/Polyp)[5]

Rationale

Codes 0528F and 0529F are both newly developed codes for the **Endoscopy and Polyp Surveillance (End/Polyp)** measure set. Though each code is included in a separate measure, the codes have a similar purpose as each code is included to prevent overuse of services. Code 0528F is included as part of the **Appropriate follow-up interval for normal colonoscopy in average risk patients**[5] measure, which is used to identify whether or not the patient aged 50 years and older receiving a screening colonoscopy without biopsy or polypectomy had a recommended follow-up interval of at least 10 years for repeat colonoscopy documented in the colonoscopy report. Code 0529F is used for the **Surveillance Colonoscopy Interval for Patients with a History of Colonic Polyps - Avoidance of Inappropriate Use**[5] measure to note whether or not the patient aged 18 years and older receiving a surveillance colonoscopy with a history of a prior colonic polyp in a previous colonoscopy finding had a follow-up interval of 3 or more years since their last colonoscopy documented in the colonoscopy report. Both of these measures are intended to ensure that a specific amount of time has elapsed prior to providing the service again. Inappropriate interval recommendations can result in overuse of resources and can lead to significant patient harm. Performing colonoscopy too often not only increases patients' exposure to procedural harm, but also drains resources that could be more effectively used to adequately screen those in need. The most common serious complication of colonoscopy is post-polypectomy bleeding.

●**0535F**   Dyspnea management plan of care, documented (Pall Cr)[5]

✑ Rationale

Code 0535F is used to identify documentation of a plan of care for dyspnea management. It is included as part of the **Dyspnea Management**[5] measure (one of the measures included in the **Palliative/End of Life Care (Pall Cr)** measure set) and is used to identify documentation of a plan of care to manage dyspnea (shortness of breath). This code is intended to be reported dependent on use of a specific set of denominator codes, and as a result, is used only after the patient population has been separated according to a number of continually narrowing factors, which include:

(1) whether the patient has a substantial risk of death within one year (identified by use of code 1150F) or if the patient's goal of care is to prioritize comfort (identified by use of code 1152F),

(2) whether patients with a substantial risk of death or with a goal to prioritize comfort have moderate or severe dyspnea (identified by code 3451F), and

(3) if a dyspnea plan of care is documented for the patient specified according to the grouping noted above (0535F).

Due to this, code 0535F is only used for a specific population of patients in which these conditions/circumstances exist. To exemplify this to Category II code users, reporting instructions have been included to direct users regarding the appropriate denominators codes to report for specific circumstances. In addition, a definition for "documented plan of care" has also been included within the Appendix H measure "snapshot" to provide users with additional insight regarding the intended use for this code. Finally, the reporting instructions included with this measure listing note that there are no exclusions for this measure. Therefore, modifiers 1P, 2P, and 3P may not be used with code 0535F.

●**0540F**   Glucocorticoid Management Plan Documented (RA)[5]

    ⊘=Modifier 51 Exempt   ⊙=Moderate Sedation   ✚=Add-on Code   ⫫=FDA approval pending

✍️ Rationale

Code 0540F is used to report documentation of a glucocorticoid management plan for patients with rheumatoid arthritis (RA). The measure in which this code is used (**Glucocorticoid Management**)[5] is included as part of the **Rheumatoid Arthritis (RA)** measure set. The intent for use of this code is similar to the use of code 0535F because code 0540F is intended to be reported dependent on use of a specific set of denominator codes. As a result, code 0540F is used only after the patient population has been separated according to a set of specific factors that note whether the rheumatoid arthritis patient is receiving glucocorticoid therapy (identified by report of codes 4193F or 4194F) or if the patient is not receiving glucocorticoid therapy (identified by report of code 4192F). If the patient is receiving a daily amount of 10 mg or more of prednisone (or equivalent medication) for longer than 6 months and the patient's condition improves or there is no change in disease activity, then code 0540F may be reported if the health care professional also documents a glucocorticoid management plan. In addition to reporting instructions that note the specific circumstances in which use of code 0540F is appropriate (thus noting compliance with the measure specifications when the noted circumstance exist), the measure "snapshot" included in the **Glucocorticoid Management**[5] measure also defines "prednisone equivalents" for users to allow a complete understanding of the patient population that this measure is intended to address. A definition of *glucocorticoid management plan* has also been included for users. Finally, because medical exclusions exist for this measure, the reporting instructions note that modifier 1P may be reported with code 0540F if the appropriate medical exclusion exists (the appropriate medical exclusion "glucocorticoid prescription is for a medical condition other than RA" has been noted in the **Exclusion(s)** section of the measure and is the only medical exclusion that applies for this measure).

●**0575F**   HIV RNA control plan of care, documented (HIV)[5]

✍️ Rationale

Code 0575F is used to report documentation of a plan of care for control of HIV RNA (ie, control of viral replication of the HIV virus). It is included as part of the **HIV RNA Control for Patients After Six Months of Potent Antiretroviral Therapy**[5] measure (included within the HIV/AIDS measure set). Similar to previous codes discussed, this code is reported according to a specific patient population that is determined by use of denominator codes. Code 0575F is used only for patients (1) who have received potent antiretroviral therapy for 6 months or longer (identified by code 4270F), and (2) whose HIV RNA viral load is not below limits of quantification but a plan of care has been documented for HIV RNA control. If the patient has received less than 6 months of potent antiviral therapy (which includes receipt of no antiviral therapy), then code 4271F should be reported. If the patient has received 6 months of antiviral therapy and has an HIV RNA viral load that is below limits of quantification, then code 3502F should be reported. Use of either of these codes excludes use of code 0575F because the intent of the measure is to ensure that a documented plan of care for management of the condition has been developed for the patient. To assist users in identification of the correct codes to use to identify the care provided, a number of definitions have been provided. This includes (1) definitions for limits of quantification, (2) identification of what is included as part of an appropriate plan of care, and (3) a definition for potent antiretroviral therapy. The reporting instructions include a time frame that identifies the number of visits (2) and days (60) between each medical visit that should be included for measure calculations. (Reporting instructions direct users to the measure specifications for a definition of medical visit.) Finally, the measure notes no performance exclusions for report of the measure. As a result, modifiers 1P, 2P, and 3P may not be used for this measure.

Patient History

● **1150F**   Documentation that a patient has a substantial risk of death within 1 year (Pall Cr)[5]

● **1151F**   Documentation that a patient does not have a substantial risk of death within one year (Pall Cr)[5]

● **1152F**   Documentation of advanced disease diagnosis, goals of care prioritize comfort (Pall Cr)[5]

● **1153F**   Documentation of advanced disease diagnosis, goals of care do not prioritize comfort (Pall Cr)[5]

✍ Rationale

Codes 1150F through 1153F are used to report care for a number of measures included within the **Palliative/End of Life Care** measure set. These codes are used within the **Advance Care Planning**,[5] **Dyspnea Screening**,[5] and **Dyspnea Management**[5] measures. The codes are used to define the patient population in the same way for each measure. This includes: (1) documenting if a patient has a substantial risk of death within 1 year (1150F or 1151F), and (2) noting if the documentation for the advance disease diagnosis prioritizes care (1152F or 1153F). Dependent on which of these codes is used, the Reporting Instructions for each of the three noted measures directs users toward report of a specific code that notes compliance with the measure specifications for that measure or eliminates that particular patient from consideration for the measure. Use of either code 1151F or 1153F eliminates the patient from consideration as the intent for each of these measures is to provide a reporting mechanism for treatment of patients who have a substantial risk of death within 1 year **or** who have a diagnosis in which the goal is comfort. Therefore, if code 1150F or 1152F is reported, then an additional coding is necessary to identify compliance with the measure being considered. For the **Advance Care Planning**[5] measure, code 1123F is used to identify the fact that an Advance Care Planning was discussed with the patient and/or family and that an advance care plan or surrogate decision maker was documented in the medical record. For the **Dyspnea Screening**[5] measure, use of code 1150F or 1152F necessitates report of code 3450F (which notes that the dyspnea screen reveals an absence of dyspnea or presence of mild dyspnea) to identify compliance with the measure. Use of code 1150F or 1152F in the **Dyspnea Management**[5] measure necessitates use of additional denominator codes to determine whether or not the patient should be considered for measurement. Use of code 3450F or

⊘=Modifier 51 Exempt   ⊙=Moderate Sedation   ✚=Add-on Code   ✗=FDA approval pending

3452F eliminates the patient from consideration for measurement. If the patient has moderate or severe dyspnea, then code 0535F is reported if there is a dyspnea management plan of care documented in the medical record. (For more information regarding documentation of a dyspnea management plan of care, see **Rationale** for code 0535F.) Special reporting instructions have been included for these measures directing users to reference the ICD-9 codeset for specifications for patients with incurable cancer, organ system failure, or severe progressive neurological conditions. In addition, the **Reporting Instructions** section provided for each measure provides instruction regarding the appropriate codes to use for each of the patient populations noted. Finally, because none of the three measures included in the **Palliative/End of Life Care** measure set includes performance exclusions, modifiers 1P, 2P, and 3P may not be reported with any of the codes included within these measures.

●**1157F** Advance care plan or similar legal document present in the medical record (COA)[2]

●**1158F** Advance care planning discussion documented in the medical record (COA)[2]

●**1159F** Medication list documented in medical record (COA)[2]

●**1160F** Review of all medications by a prescribing practitioner or clinical pharmacist (such as, prescriptions, OTCs, herbal therapies and supplements) documented in the medical record (COA)[2]

●**1170F** Functional status assessed (COA)[2] (RA)[5]

✍ Rationale

Codes 1157F-1160F and 1170F are all included as part of three separate measures within the **Care for Older Adults (COA)** measure set. These include the measure for **Advance Care Planning**,[2] the measure for **Annual Medication Review**,[2] and the measure for **Functional Status Assessment**.[2]

Codes 1157F and 1158F are included within the **Advance Care Planning**[2] measure and are used to note whether or not a patient aged 65 years or older had advance care planning during the measurement year. Code 1157F notes the presence of an advance care plan or a similar legal document in the medical record. Code 1158F identifies discussion regarding advance care planning that is documented in the medical record. In addition, the **Reporting Instructions** note that code 1123F or 1124F may alternatively be used because these codes represent documentation that exceeds the requirements of the numerator for this measure and, when submitted, will count toward compliance with the specifications of the numerator. The reporting instructions also note that code 1157F or 1158F should be reported at least once during the measurement year. This measure does not allow for performance exclusions. As a result, none of the performance exclusion modifiers (1P, 2P, or 3P) may be reported with the codes included for the measure.

Codes 1159F and 1160F are included within the **Annual Medication Review**[2] measure. These codes are used to report separately specified services for this measure. Namely, these codes are used to determine (1) whether or not a patient aged 65 years and older had at least one medication review conducted by a prescribing practitioner or a clinical pharmacist during the measurement year and (2) whether or not the presence of a medication list exists in the medical record for the patient. Because these are two separately required services, separate codes have been developed to identify compliance with both aspects of the measure specification. Therefore, to comply with this measure, **both codes must be reported**. Code 1159F notes that a medication list has been documented in medical record by the physician/health care professional, and code 1160F identifies that a review of all medications has been done by the prescribing practitioner or clinical pharmacist and that this review has been documented in the medical record. A definition of medication review has been included within the measure "snapshot" included in the Appendix H listing. A definition of a "medication list" has also been included to direct users regarding the intent of the measure and the use of the codes included in this listing. To provide additional insight regarding the intent of the use of the codes, a note has been included in the **Reporting Instructions** that indicates that codes 1159F and 1160F do not need to be reported during the same visit. In addition, the instructions prohibit use of modifiers 1P, 2P, or 3P with the codes included in this measure as medical, patient, and system exclusions do not exist for this measure.

Code 1170F is used to identify assessment of the functional status of the patient as part of the similarly named **Functional Status Assessment**[2] measure. The measure determines whether or not a patient aged 65 years or older had a functional status assessment during the measurement year. To provide more insight for use of the code included in the measure listing, a definition of functional status assessment has been included in the measure. In addition, no exclusions are identified for use with this measure, and modifiers 1P, 2P, and 3P may not be used with code 1170F for this measure.

A measure called **Functional Status Assessment**[5] is also included in the **Rheumatoid Arthritis (RA)** measure set. Code 1170F is used in this measure to report whether or not the patient aged 18 years or older with a diagnosis of rheumatoid arthritis (RA) has a functional status assessment performed at least once within a 12-month reporting period. The measure listing in Appendix H includes instruction regarding what should be included as a "documentation of an assessment." In addition, because this measure does not allow for performance exclusions, modifiers 1P, 2P, and 3P may not be reported for this measure.

●**1180F**   All specified thromboembolic risk factors assessed (AFIB)[1]

 Rationale
Code 1180F is used to identify assessment of all specified thromboembolic risk factors and is included as part of the **Assessment of Thromboembolic Risk Factors**[1] measure **(Atrial Fibrillation (AF) and Atrial Flutter (AFIB) measure set)**. It is used to determine whether or not the patient aged 18 years and older with a diagnosis of non-valvular atrial fibrillation or atrial flutter had an assessment of all of the specified thromboembolic risk factors documented during the 12-month reporting period. A definition of thromboembolic risk factors to

be assessed is also included. In addition, examples of medical exclusions for not assessing risk factors are provided, including whether the patient has a transient or reversible cause for the atrial fibrillation (such as the existence of fibrillation due to pneumonia or hyperthyroidism), post-operative patients, pregnant patients, the existence of a warfarin allergy, and the risk of bleeding. Existence of any of these exclusions or another reason identified by the physician allows for use of the modifier 1P with code 1180F for medical exclusion identification.

●**1220F** Patient screened for depression (SUD)[5]

 Rationale

Code 1220F is used to identify patient screening for depression. It is presently used as part of a single measure within the **Substance Use Disorder (SUD)** measure set. This code is used as part of the **Substance Use Disorders (SUD) Screening for Depression Among Patients With Substance Abuse or Dependence**[5] measure and is used to determine whether or not the patient aged 18 years and older with a diagnosis of current substance abuse or dependence was screened for depression within the 12-month reporting period. The measure specifications allow for medical exclusions when reporting this code. As a result, modifier 1P may be appended to code 1220F when medical exclusions exist.

Physical Examination

●**2050F** Wound characteristics including size AND nature of wound base tissue AND amount of drainage prior to debridement documented (CWC)[5]

 Rationale

Code 2050F is used to report documentation of wound characteristics. The measure in which this code is used denotes whether or not the patient aged 18 years and older with a diagnosis of chronic skin ulcer who is undergoing debridement had documentation of wound characteristics (including at a minimum size AND nature of the wound base tissue, AND the amount of drainage) prior to debridement. Because the **Reporting Instructions** included for use of this code note that no exclusions exist for this measure, modifiers 1P, 2P, and 3P may not be used with this code.

Diagnostic/Screening Processes or Results

●**3016F** Patient screened for unhealthy alcohol use using a systematic screening method (PV)[1]

 Rationale

Code 3016F is one of the first codes included in the CPT codeset that specifically addresses alcohol use. This code is included in the **Unhealthy Alcohol Use:**

Screening[1] measure as part of the **Preventive Care and Screening (PV)** measure set. It is used to determine whether or not the patient aged 18 years and older was screened for unhealthy alcohol use using a systematic screening method. To clarify intent regarding use of the code for this measure, a definition has been included for unhealthy alcohol use. In addition, users are referred to measure specifications for examples of systematic screening methods. Finally, because medical exclusions are identified for this measure, the **Reporting Instructions** direct users to report code 3016F with the 1P modifier to identify medical exclusions that may exist for the patient.

●**3018F**   Pre-procedure risk assessment AND depth of insertion AND quality of the bowel prep AND complete description of polyp(s) found, including location of each polyp, size, number and gross morphology AND recommendations for follow-up in final colonoscopy report documented (End/Polyp)[5]

✍ Rationale

Code 3018F is used to identify documentation of a number of important factors for colonoscopy. Specifically, this code is used to identify (1) the pre-colonoscopy risk assessment; (2) the depth of insertion (of the colonoscope); (3) the quality of the bowel preparation; (4) the complete description of polyp(s) found, which includes the location of each polyp, polyp sizes, the number of polyps, and gross morphology of each polyp; and (5) the inclusion of a recommendation for follow-up in the final colonoscopy report. Factors important for the final colonoscopy report are also included in the numerator description to provide users insight regarding what should be included in that report. Because the measure does not allow for exclusions, none of the performance exclusion modifiers may be used with this code.

●**3250F**   Specimen site other than anatomic location of primary tumor (PATH)[1]

✍ Rationale

Code 3250F is used to identify a particular patient population within the **Pathology (PATH)** measure. This code is included as part of two separate measures in this measure set performing the same purpose for each measure. It notes whether the specimen under consideration is from a site other than the anatomic location of the primary tumor for breast cancer or colon cancer patients. When this is the case, then code 3260F is used identifying the histological grade for resections provided for cancer reporting for both breast (**Breast cancer resection pathology reporting-pT category (primary tumor) and pN (regional lymph nodes) with histologic grade**[1]) and colorectal cancer (**Colorectal cancer resection pathology reporting-pT category (primary tumor) and pN category (regional lymph node) with histologic grade**[1]) measures. Because the intent of each measure is to identify information regarding the *primary tumor site*, the addition of code 3250F allows users the ability to identify circumstances when the tissue sampled is *not* from the anatomic location of the primary tumor and not part of the target population. As a result, **Reporting Instructions** direct users to report only code 3250F if the specimen is not primary breast or colorectal tissue (eg, if

⊘=Modifier 51 Exempt   ☉=Moderate Sedation   ✚=Add-on Code   ⋏=FDA approval pending

the specimen is a liver biopsy). The instructions included further note that these measures should be reported each time that a breast or colorectal biopsy resection pathology report is prepared. Finally, users are directed to report code 3260F with the modifier 1P if a medical exclusion exists for not providing documentation in the pathology report of the pT and pN categories and the histological grade of the specimen.

▶(Codes 3302F-3312F have been deleted)

(To report measures for cancer staging, see 3321F-3390F)◀

✍ Rationale

A parenthetic note has been included to note the deletion of codes 3302F-3312F, which were formerly used to identify cancer staging. A separate note has been included to direct users to the appropriate codes to use for cancer staging. For more information regarding changes for the cancer staging codes, see **Rationale** for codes 3321F, 3322F, and 3370F-3390F.

▲**3319F** 1 of the following diagnostic imaging studies ordered: chest X-ray, CT, Ultrasound, MRI, PET, or nuclear medicine scans (ML)[5]

✍ Rationale

Code 3319F is used to identify overuse of imaging for Stage 0 or IA melanoma patients. It is included as part of the **Over utilization of Imaging Studies in Stage 0-IA Melanoma**[5] measure. Because this is an overuse measure, the codes included for this measure separate the patients according to whether the patient has Stage 0 or IA cancer or if a higher melanoma stage is involved. If the patient has a Stage 0 or IA melanoma, then either code 3319F (noting that an imaging procedure was provided) or 3320F is used (noting compliance with the non-use of imaging for patient). If medical or system reasons exist for providing the imaging procedure, then code 3319F may be used with the exclusionary modifier 1P or 3P to identify the specific exclusion that exists (as is noted in the **Reporting Instructions**).

●**3321F** AJCC Cancer Stage 0 or IA Melanoma, documented (ML)[5]

●**3322F** Melanoma greater than AJCC Stage 0 or IA (ML)[5]

●**3370F** AJCC Breast Cancer Stage 0 documented (ONC)[1]

●**3372F** AJCC Breast Cancer Stage I: T1mic, T1a or T1b (tumor size ≤ 1 cm) documented (ONC)[1]

●**3374F** AJCC Breast Cancer Stage I: T1c (tumor size > 1 cm to 2 cm) documented (ONC)[1]

●**3376F** AJCC Breast Cancer Stage II documented (ONC)[1]

●**3378F** AJCC Breast Cancer Stage III documented (ONC)[1]

●**3380F** AJCC Breast Cancer Stage IV documented (ONC)[1]

- ●**3382F** AJCC colon cancer, Stage 0 documented (ONC)[1]

- ●**3384F** AJCC colon cancer, Stage I documented (ONC)[1]

- ●**3386F** AJCC colon cancer, Stage II documented (ONC)[1]

- ●**3388F** AJCC colon cancer, Stage III documented (ONC)[1]

- ●**3390F** AJCC colon cancer, Stage IV documented (ONC)[1]

✒ Rationale

The codes included for documentation of AJCC cancer staging have been revised, relocating and, in some instances, rewording the codes to eliminate stage information that is not germane to reporting (eg, Stage III cancer does not need further differentiation because there is no change regarding the appropriate code to use for Stage IIIA, IIIB, or IIIC codes). In other instances, other information has been added to specific codes noting factors important for use of the codes such as tumor size. These codes are included as part of two measures including the **Hormonal Therapy for Stage IC-IIIC, ER/PR Positive Breast Cancer**[1] measure (which utilizes codes 3370F, 3372F, 3374F, 3376F, 3378F, and 3380F), and the **Chemotherapy for Stage IIIA through IIIC Colon Cancer Patients**[1] measure (which includes use of codes 3382F, 3384F, 3386F, 3388F, and 3390F). Similar to the intent of use for the former codes used for cancer staging (3302F-3312F), these codes are used as **Denominator Codes** that separate the patient population according to directions included in the **Reporting Instructions** for each measure. Specifically, appropriate codes are used to identify the specific stage of cancer that has been documented for the patient. For breast cancer patients, if the patient is identified with Stage I cancer with a tumor size that is greater than 1 centimeter to 2 centimeters (code 3374F) or if Stage II (3376F) or Stage III (3378F) cancer is documented, then code 4179F may be reported to identify prescription of Tamoxifen or an aromatase inhibitor (AI). For colon cancer patients, if the patient is identified with Stage III cancer (code 3388F), then code 4180F may be used to identify referral, prescription, or previous receipt of adjuvant chemotherapy. Because report of both measures allows for medical, patient, and system exclusions, the **Reporting Instructions** for each measure directs users to report code 4179F or code 4180F with modifier 1P, 2P, or 3P to identify the appropriate exclusions when they exist.

- ●**3450F** Dyspnea screened, no dyspnea or mild dyspnea (Pall Cr)[5]

- ●**3451F** Dyspnea screened, moderate or severe dyspnea (Pall Cr)[5]

- ●**3452F** Dyspnea not screened (Pall Cr)[5]

✒ Rationale

Codes 3450F-3452F are included as part of the **Advance Care Planning,**[5] **Dyspnea Screening,**[5] and **Dyspnea Management**[5] measures within the Palliative/End of Life Care measure set. For more information regarding use of codes 3450F-3452F, see the **Rationale** for codes 1150F-1153F.

⊘=Modifier 51 Exempt   ⊙=Moderate Sedation   ✚=Add-on Code   ✗=FDA approval pending

●**3455F** TB screening performed and results interpreted within six months prior to initiation of first-time biologic disease modifying anti-rheumatic drug therapy for RA (RA)[5]

●**3470F** Rheumatoid arthritis (RA) disease activity, low (RA)[5]

●**3471F** Rheumatoid arthritis (RA) disease activity, moderate (RA)[5]

●**3472F** Rheumatoid arthritis (RA) disease activity, high (RA)[5]

●**3475F** Disease prognosis for rheumatoid arthritis assessed, poor prognosis documented (RA)[5]

●**3476F** Disease prognosis for rheumatoid arthritis assessed, good prognosis documented (RA)[5]

✍ Rationale

Code 3455F is used to identify the performance of screening and interpretation of results within 6 months prior to initiation of first-time biologic disease modifying anti-rheumatic drug therapy for RA. It is included as part of the Tuberculosis screening[5] measure and is used to note compliance with the measure specifications. Denominator codes 4195F and 4196F are used to separate the patient population according to those who are receiving the treatment from those who are not receiving the treatment (who, therefore, should not be included as part of the patients under consideration). If code 4195F is reported and the screening and results interpretation have been provided, then code 3455F should also be reported to identify compliance with the measure specifications. Medical exclusions for this measure note the ability to utilize the 1P modifier with code 3455F when the appropriate medical exclusions exist.

Codes 3455F, 3470F-3472F, and 3475F-3476F are all included as part of the **Rheumatoid Arthritis** measure set. Codes 3470F-3472F are used as part of the **Periodic Assessment of Disease Activity**[5] measure and identify whether or not the patient aged 18 years and older with a diagnosis of rheumatoid arthritis (RA) has an assessment and classification of disease activity at least once within 12 months. Use of any of these codes notes compliance with the measure by noting whether RA disease activity is low (3470F), moderate (3471F), or high (3472F). A definition has been included as part of the numerator information, identifying standardized descriptive or numeric scales and/or composite indexes. In addition, because no exclusions have been included for report of this measure, performance exclusion modifiers (1P, 2P, and 3P) may not be used for this measure.

Codes 3475F and 3476F are used to identify disease prognosis for rheumatoid arthritis. These codes are included as part of the **Assessment and Classification of Disease Prognosis**[5] measure and note whether or not the patient aged 18 years and older with a diagnosis of Rheumatoid Arthritis (RA) has an assessment and classification of disease prognosis at least once within 12 months. Similar to codes 3470F-3472F, use of either code notes compliance with the measure specifications. To assist users with the intended use for these codes, instruction regarding prognostic classification has been included with the numerator information for these codes. In addition, to provide additional instruction regarding the intended use for these codes, instruction regarding prognostic classification has been included with the measure information listing. Finally, performance exclusions are not identified for report of this measure, and modifiers 1P–3P may not be used for these codes.

● **3490F**   History of AIDS-defining condition (HIV)[5]

● **3491F**   HIV indeterminate (infants of undetermined HIV status born of HIV-infected mothers) (HIV)[5]

● **3492F**   History of nadir CD4+ cell count <350 cells/mm³ (HIV)[5]

● **3493F**   No history of nadir CD4+ cell count <350 cells/mm³ AND no history of AIDS-defining condition (HIV)[5]

● **3494F**   CD4+ cell count <200 cells/mm³ (HIV)[5]

● **3495F**   CD4+ cell count 200 – 499 cells/mm³ (HIV)[5]

● **3496F**   CD4+ cell count ≥500 cells/mm³ (HIV)[5]

● **3497F**   CD4+ cell percentage <15% (HIV)[5]

● **3498F**   CD4+ cell percentage ≥15% (HIV)[5]

● **3500F**   CD4+ cell count or CD4+ cell percentage documented as performed (HIV)[5]

● **3502F**   HIV RNA viral load below limits of quantification (HIV)[5]

● **3503F**   HIV RNA viral load not below limits of quantification (HIV)[5]

● **3510F**   Documentation that tuberculosis (TB) screening test performed and results interpreted (HIV)[5]

● **3511F**   Chlamydia and gonorrhea screenings documented as performed (HIV)[5]

● **3512F**   Syphilis screening documented as performed (HIV)[5]

● **3513F**   Hepatitis B screening documented as performed (HIV)[5]

● **3514F**   Hepatitis C screening documented as performed (HIV)[5]

● **3515F**   Patient has documented immunity to Hepatitis C (HIV)[5]

● **3550F**   Low risk for thromboembolism (AFIB)[1]

● **3551F**   Intermediate risk for thromboembolism (AFIB)[1]

● **3552F**   High risk for thromboembolism (AFIB)[1]

● **3555F**   Patient had International Normalized Ratio (INR) measurement performed (AFIB)[1]

● **3570F**   Final report for bone scintigraphy study includes correlation with existing relevant imaging studies (eg, x-ray, MRI, CT) corresponding to the same anatomical region in question (NUC_MED)[1]

● **3572F**   Patient considered to be potentially at risk for fracture in a weight-bearing site (NUC_MED)[1]

● **3573F**   Patient not considered to be potentially at risk for fracture in a weight-bearing site (NUC_MED)[1]

✍ Rationale

Codes 3490F, 3492F, and 3493F are all used as denominator codes to define the appropriate patient population for the **Adolescent and Adult Patients with HIV/ AIDS who are Prescribed Potent Antiretroviral Therapy**[5] measure. They are used to determine whether a patient with a diagnosis of HIV/AIDS and nadir CD4+ cell count <350 cells/mm³ or a history of an AIDS-defining condition, or is pregnant, had potent antiretroviral therapy prescribed. Code 3493F is used to identify patients who have no history of nadir CD4+ cell count that is < 350 cells/mm³ and who have no history of AIDS-defining condition. These patients are outside the scope of the measure and therefore are not included as part of the measurable population. Codes 3490F and 3492F are used to identify patient populations that have a history that is within the scope of the measure and therefore should be measured. For those patients, if a potent antiviral therapy is prescribed, then code 4276F should be reported to identify the prescription of the potent antiviral therapy. A special note has been included in the **Reporting Instructions** indicating that the physician providing ongoing HIV care is the individual who is anticipated to report the service. In addition, because no performance exclusions are identified for the measure, modifiers 1P, 2P, and 3P may not be used with these codes.

Code 3491F is included as part of the ***Pneumocystis jiroveci* pneumonia (PCP) Prophylaxis – Infants ≥6 Weeks to <12 Months**[5] measure. It is used as a denominator code and is the only denominator code used to identify the appropriate population for the measure—HIV indeterminate patients. Because the measure is used to determine whether or not the patient with a diagnosis of HIV/AIDS or who is HIV indeterminate had *Pneumocystis jiroveci* pneumonia (PCP) prophylaxis prescribed, use of this code (or an appropriate ICD-9 code that denotes that the patient has AIDS) are indicators of the measurable population and who, therefore, should have prophylaxis prescribed for *Pneumocycstis jiroveci* (identified by use of code 4279F). To assist users with the intent of use for the codes included with the measure, *HIV indeterminate* is defined as infants of undetermined HIV status born of HIV-infected mothers as determined by medical record review. Also included is information that notes who is anticipated to report the measure (ie, the physician providing ongoing HIV care). Users are also referred to the measure specifications for a definition of *medical visit* and other requirements for inclusion in measure calculation. Because there are no performance exclusions identified for this measure, modifiers 1P, 2P, and 3P may not be reported for this measure.

Codes 3494F-3498F are all used as denominator codes to separate the patient population for the ***Pneumocystis jiroveci* Pneumonia (PCP) Prophylaxis – Children 1–5 Years**[5] measure. This measure is used to determine whether or not the patient with a diagnosis of HIV/AIDS and a CD4+ cell count <500 cells/mm3 or a CD4+ cell percentage <15% had *Pneumocystis jiroveci* pneumonia (PCP) prophylaxis prescribed within 3 months of the low CD4+ cell count or low percentage. Three of these codes (3494F-3496F) are also used within the ***Pneumocystis jiroveci* Pneumonia (PCP) Prophylaxis – Adults and Children ≥6 Years**[5] measure. This measure identifies whether or not the patient with a diagnosis of HIV/AIDS and who had a CD4+ cell count <200 cells/mm3 had *Pneumocystis jiroveci* pneumonia (PCP) prophylaxis prescribed within 3 months of low CD4+ cell count. The measures differ according to the age of the patient and the cell count or percentage for CD4+ cells. As a result, the codes used to identify compliance for each measure differ due to specifications noted in each measure. The denominator codes listed within each measure should be reported each time that a CD4+ cell count is performed. Therefore, one of the codes (3494F-3496F) should be reported for both measures, and code 3497F or 3498F should be reported for CD4+ cell percentages. In addition, if a prophylaxis for *Pneumocystis jiroveci* pneumonia is prescribed within 3 months of the determination of the low CD4+ cell count or cell percentage, then code 4280F should also be reported to identify compliance with the measure specifications. Both measures only cite medical exclusions when reporting CD4+ cell counts/percentages. As a result, only the 1P modifier may be used to identify performance exclusions for this measure. Because specific medical exclusions are listed in the **Reporting Instructions** for these measures, only the noted examples are valid for use of the 1P modifier. (That is, the only medical exclusions that exist for these measures are those that note that CD4+ cell counts or percentages rose above the thresholds noted in the measure and code descriptors within 3 months of the original cell count/percentage determination and therefore indicate that the patient no longer need the prophylaxis.)

Code 3500F is used to report documentation of the performance of a CD4+ cell count or cell percentage. The measure in which this code is used is conveniently named **CD4+ Cell Count**[5] and is used to determine whether or not the patient with an HIV/AIDS diagnosis had a CD4+ cell count or CD4+ cell percentage performed at least once every 6 months. This code is the only code used to note both compliance with the measure and inclusion of the patient as part of the target population. This is due to the fact that the measure is intended for all patients aged 6 months and older with a diagnosis of HIV/AIDS. As a result, **Reporting Instructions** have been included in the Appendix H listing noting (1) that code 3500F is reported each time a CD4+ cell count or percentage is performed, and (2) that no performance exclusions exist for the measure (and therefore use of 1P, 2P, or 3P is not allowed for this code). The **Reporting Instructions** provide additional instructions that note which patients should be included for measurement/calculation (ie, patients who have at least two medical visits during the measurement year, with at least 60 days between each visit) and that direct users to the measure specifications for a definition of medical visit.

Codes 3502F and 3503F are used to report HIV RNA viral load quantification. Use of these codes separates the target population (ie, all patients aged 13 years and older with a diagnosis of HIV/AIDS who have received potent antiretroviral therapy for at least 6 months) into patients who will need a plan of care for HIV RNA control (identified 3503F) from those who do not (identified by use of code 3502F). These codes are included as part of the **HIV RNA Control for Patients After Six Months of Potent Antiretroviral Therapy**[5] measure and are reported in conjunction with two denominator codes (4270F and 4271F) and a code that notes compliance with the measure's specifications (0575F). For more regarding the intended use for codes 3502F and 3503F, see the **Rationale** for code 0575F.

Codes 3210F-3212F are used to identify codes that note screening for particular disease that may be contracted by patients with HIV/AIDS. Each code is included as part of a separate measure with separate specifications to note compliance. In addition, the intent for use of each measure may be due to gaps in care for screening of these opportunistic conditions or due to low rates of screening. As a result, the specifications for each measure vary and appropriate reporting for each condition is dependent on the specifications noted for each measure.

⊘=Modifier 51 Exempt   ⊙=Moderate Sedation   ✚=Add-on Code   ⊮=FDA approval pending

Code 3510F is used to report documentation of the performance and interpretation of the results of a tuberculosis screening test for HIV patients. The measure (**Tuberculosis (TB) Screening**)[5] is used to determine whether or not the patient with a diagnosis of HIV/AIDS has documentation of a tuberculosis (TB) screening test performed and results interpreted at least once since the diagnosis of HIV infection. Use of this single code notes compliance with the measure and does not require use of other codes for the measure. The measure does note performance exclusions that may exist when reporting this service, listing medical and patient exclusions for the measure. As a result, the 1P and 2P modifiers may be reported with code 3510F for patients with medical exclusions (such as patients who are already being treated for TB) or patient exclusions (patients who refuse testing).

Code 3511F is used to report documentation of the performance of a chlamydia and gonorrhea screening. The measure in which this code is included (**Sexually Transmitted Diseases – Chlamydia and Gonorrhea Screenings**)[5] notes whether or not the patient with a diagnosis of HIV/AIDS has chlamydia and gonorrhea screenings performed at least once since the diagnosis of HIV infection. Only patient exclusions are noted for this measure. As a result, only the 2P modifier may be reported with code 3511F to identify performance exclusions for this measure.

Code 3512F is used to report documentation of performance of a syphilis screening. Similar to the previously noted measures for opportunistic diseases that may be contracted concurrent with the HIV/AIDS condition, the measure in which this code is used (**Sexually Transmitted Diseases – Syphilis Screening**)[5] notes whether or not the patient with a diagnosis of HIV/AIDS has a syphilis screening performed. It too notes only the use of patient reasons for performance exclusions and therefore may only reflect exclusions via use of the 2P modifier with code 3512F.

Codes 3513F, 3514F, and 3515F are all used to report hepatitis B screening and hepatitis C screening for patients with HIV/AIDS. Code 3513 is used as part of the measure called **Other Infectious Diseases – Hepatitis B Screening**[5] and is used to identify whether or not the patient with a diagnosis of HIV/AIDS had a hepatitis B screening performed at least once since the diagnosis of HIV was made or whether the patient has documented immunity for hepatitis B. This code is reported with a code that currently exists in the CPT codebook—code 3516F. This code identifies that the patient has a documented immunity to hepatitis B. Use of either code identifies compliance with the measure. In addition, code 3513F may be reported with the 2P modifier to note any patient reasons for not performing the screening (such as the refusal of the patient to allow screening for the condition). Codes 3514F and 3515F are used in a similar manner for the **Other Infectious Diseases – Hepatitis C Screening**[5] measure, as these codes note whether or not the patient with a diagnosis of HIV/AIDS had a hepatitis C screening performed at least once since the diagnosis of HIV infection (identified by code 3514F) or if the patient has a documented immunity to hepatitis C (3515F).

Codes 3550F, 3551F, and 3552 are all included as part of the **Atrial Fibrillation and Atrial Flutter (AFIB): Chronic Anticoagulation Therapy**[1] measure. These codes are used to determine the level of risk of thromboembolism and whether or not Warfarin therapy was prescribed within a 12-month period for patients aged 18 years and older with a diagnosis of non-valvular atrial fibrillation or atrial flutter. These 3 codes are used as denominator codes within the **Atrial Fibrillation and Atrial Flutter (AFIB): Chronic Anticoagulation Therapy**[1] measure, separating the patients according to those who have a high risk of thromboembolism (3552F) from those who do not (3550F, 3551F). For those patients who do have a high risk, the measure notes that Warfarin therapy is appropriate and therefore code 4012F should be reported for those patients who have a high risk and were prescribed Warfarin therapy. To ensure that the appropriate patients are identified for therapy, the measure listing included in Appendix H notes definitions that clarify what is considered to be low, medium, and high risk for thromboembolism. In addition, both medical (1P) and patient (2P) performance exclusions exist for this measure. As a result, modifier 1P or 2P may be used to identify exclusions for compliance with this measure.

Code 3555F is used to report that a patient had an International Normalized Ratio (INR) measurement performed. It is includes as part of the **Monthly International Normalized Ratio (INR) Measurement Therapy**[1] measure (within the **Atrial Fibrillation/Atrial Flutter [AFIB]** measure set) and assists in determining if patients 18 years or older with a diagnosis of non-valvular atrial fibrillation or atrial flutter who are also receiving Warfarin therapy have at least one INR performed. Patient noncompliance with provider instructions is a factor in determining whether the specifications for this measure can be followed. As a result, the exclusions noted for this measure list an example for patient noncompliance. Since patients at high risk for thromboembolism are the only patients who should be included in the measure's denominator when calculating performance, codes 4300F and 4301F are used as denominator codes to separate the patients who are receiving Warfarin therapy (4300F) from those who are not (4301F). Use of code 3555F notes performance of the International Normalized Ration measurement. The modifiers 2P and 3P are used to indicate performance exclusions for patient and system reasons that exist.

Code 3570F is used to report correlation of bone scintigraphy with existing relevant imaging studies (such as X-rays and MRIs) for the same anatomical region. This code is included as part of the **Nuclear Medicine (NUC_MED): Correlation With Existing Imaging Studies for All Patients Undergoing Bone Scintigraphy**[1] (part of the **Nuclear Medicine [NUC_MED]** measure set) and is used to identify the physician's correlation of the scintigrapy study with other imaging performed. This is important because cross-referencing this imaging study with other available studies that have been provided will help the diagnostic process and treatment for the patient. As a result, only system reasons exist for not correlating the results of the scintigraphy with other imaging procedures (such as the absence of imaging procedures that have already been performed). The 3P modifier is used in this instance to note the system exclusions that exists for the measure.

Codes 3572F and 3573F are both used to identify whether a patient is considered to be at risk for developing a fracture in a weight-bearing site. These codes are included as part of the **Nuclear Medicine (NUC_Med)** measure for

⊘=Modifier 51 Exempt ⊙=Moderate Sedation ✛=Add-on Code ✗=FDA approval pending

Communication to Referring Physician of Patient's Potential Risk for Fracture for All Patients Undergoing Bone Scintigraphy.[1] These codes are used as denominator codes separating the patient population into patients who have a significant risk for obtaining a fracture in a weight-bearing site (3572F) from those who do not (3573F). For those patients who have a significant risk, code 5100F is additionally reported if that potential risk for fracture is communicated to the referring physician. To provide further information regarding compliance, a definition of direct communication has been included following the **Numerator** statement. The 1P modifier is included to identify medical exclusions for the measure, identifying those circumstances in which performance measurement modification is appropriate.

Therapeutic, Preventive, or Other Interventions

▲**4011F**   Oral antiplatelet therapy prescribed (CAD)[1]

 Rationale

Code 4011F has been revised to eliminate the example noted in the parentheses included within the code descriptor. Because the information listed is simply an example of the type of therapy that can be prescribed, the change is identified as an editorial change and does not reflect a revision of the intended use for the code.

●**4148F**   Hepatitis A vaccine injection administered or previously received (HEP-C)[1]

●**4149F**   Hepatitis B vaccine injection administered or previously received (HEP-C)[1]

▶(Code 4152F has been deleted.)◀

▶(Code 4154F has been deleted.)◀

▶(Code 4156F has been deleted.)◀

Rationale

Codes 4148F and 4149F are both used to report the injection or previous receipt of hepatitis A (4148F) or hepatitis B (4149F) vaccine. They are used as part of separate measures but identify similar concepts for the two different measures. Code 4148F is included as part of the **Hepatitis A Vaccination**[1] measure and is used to identify whether or not the patient aged 18 years and older with a diagnosis of hepatitis C received at least one injection of hepatitis A vaccine. Code 4149F does the same thing for the **Hepatitis B Vaccination**[1] measure except that it notes whether or not the patient aged 18 years and older with a diagnosis of hepatitis C received at least one injection of hepatitis B vaccine. Both sets of **Reporting Instructions** for these measures include information that notes compliance with the measure if any of the following conditions are satisfied: (1) If the patient has received at least one injection of hepatitis A (for the **Hepatitis A Vaccination**[1] measure) or hepatitis B (for the **Hepatitis B Vaccination**[1] measure), which includes injection by the reporting physician/health care professional or record of a previous administration by a different provider (identified by use of code 4148F or 4149F respectively); or (2) if the patient has a documented immunity to the hepatitis condition specified in the measure (identified by use of code 3215F or 3216F accordingly). As a result, only medical exclusions exist for these measures, and the 1P modifier may be reported with code 4148F or 4149F if medical exclusions exist. In addition, the **Reporting Instructions** also note that if all 3 doses of the appropriate vaccine have been previously administered, then code 4155F (for hepatitis A) or 4157F (for hepatitis B) may be used to identify compliance with the measure as use of these codes exceeds each of the measurement requirements, due to the fact that each measure is intended to obtain compliance with administration of a single dose of vaccine. Codes 4155F and 4157F identify that 3 doses have been performed. As a user note, codes 4155F and 4157F have been retained within the Category II code set to allow identification of the 3-dose administration of hepatitis A and hepatitis B vaccine. These codes are not used anywhere else within the code set. To provide guidance regarding the measures for which these codes may be used, codes 4155F and 4157F still include the suffix references noting that these codes may be found within the hepatitis C (HEP-C) measure set.

As a result of the addition of codes 4148F and 4149F, codes 4152F, 4154F, and 4156F have been deleted, because the new codes include language that is more specific to the intent of the noted measures. (Codes 4148F and 4149F include language that notes that the vaccination was administered or previously received.)

▲**4158F**   Patient counseled about risks of alcohol use (HEP-C)[1]

 Rationale
Code 4158F was revised to reflect language that was more specific to the intent for use of this code—to identify *counseling* for risks of alcohol use. This identifies a higher level of involvement by the provider in attempting to change the undesirable behavior than was previously stated through use of the previous language noting "education regarding risk of alcohol consumption performed."

▲**4180F**   Adjuvant chemotherapy referred, prescribed, or previously received for Stage III colon cancer (ONC)[1]

 Rationale
Code 4180F is used to report referral, prescription, or previous receipt of adjuvant chemotherapy for Stage III cancer. The language in this code has been revised to remove additional stage information that differentiates Stage III (ie, rewording of the code by changing "Stage IIIA, IIIB, and IIIC" to list "Stage III"). The additional information is not germane to reporting as there is no change regarding the appropriate code to use for Stage IIIA, IIIB, or IIIC codes. The term *referred* has also been added to the descriptor to reflect the complete intent of the measure. For more information regarding code 4180F and its use within the measure, see the Rationale for AJCC codes 3321F through 3390F.

●**4192F**   Patient not receiving glucocorticoid therapy (RA)[5]

●**4193F**   Patient receiving <10 mg daily prednisone (or equivalent), or RA activity is worsening, or glucocorticoid use is for less than 6 months (RA)[5]

●**4194F**   Patient receiving ≥10 mg daily prednisone (or equivalent) for longer than 6 months, and improvement or no change in disease activity (RA)[5]

●**4195F**   Patient receiving first-time biologic disease modifying anti-rheumatic drug therapy for rheumatoid arthritis (RA)[5]

●**4196F**   Patient not receiving first-time biologic disease modifying anti-rheumatic drug therapy for rheumatoid arthritis (RA)[5]

Rationale

Codes 4192F-4196F are all included as part of the **Rheumatoid Arthritis** measure set. Three of the codes (4192F-4194F) are included as part of the **Glucocorticoid Management**[5] measure. The remaining codes (4195F and 4196F) are included as part of the **Tuberculosis Screening**[5] measure. These codes are all used to separate the patient population to identify the target patients for whom the measure's specifications are written. For more information regarding intended use for codes 4192F-4194F, see the **Rationale** for code 0540F; for codes 4195F and 4196F, see **Rationale** for code 3455F.

▲**4200F**   External beam radiotherapy as primary therapy to prostate with or without nodal irradiation (PRCA)[1]

▲**4201F**   External beam radiotherapy with or without nodal irradiation as adjuvant or salvage therapy for prostate cancer patient (PRCA)[1]

Rationale

Codes 4200F and 4201F are both included as part of a single measure—**Three-Dimensional Radiotherapy.**[1] Both codes have been revised to more closely reflect the intent of the measure by identifying the patient population more specifically. These changes were made to the codes to match the changes in the measure itself as the measure language now focuses on *prostate cancer patients who receive external beam radiotherapy as primary therapy* to the prostate instead of patients with prostate cancer who might be receiving external beam radiotheraphy for another reason. The code descriptors and measure language now include language that serve multiple purposes: (1) It separates patients who receive the therapy as an adjuvant or salvage therapy to treat the prostate from the target population (prostate patients who are receiving external beam therapy as a primary therapy), and (2) it identifies the prostate as the anatomic area of focus. These codes are still used as **Denominator Codes** for the measure, allowing use of existing code 4165F to identify compliance with the measure (ie, provision/receipt of the 3-dimensional conformal radiotherapy [3D-CRT] or intensity modulated radiation therapy [IMRT]).

▲4250F   Active warming used intra-operatively for the purpose of maintaining normothermia, OR at least 1 body temperature equal to or greater than 36 degrees Centigrade (or 96.8 degrees Fahrenheit) recorded within the 30 minutes immediately before or the 15 minutes immediately after anesthesia end time (CRIT)[1]

🖉 Rationale

Code 4250F was revised to reflect the change to the measure specifications. The code has been revised to reflect that active warming should be used or that a body temperature equal to or greater than 36 degrees centigrade (96.8 degrees Fahrenheit) should be recorded within 30 minutes immediately before or 15 minutes immediately after the anesthesia administration end time.

●4260F   Wound surface culture technique used (CWC)[5]

●4261F   Technique other than surface culture of the wound exudate used (eg, Levine/deep swab technique, semi-quantitative or quantitative swab technique) OR wound surface culture technique not used (CWC)[5]

●4265F   Use of wet to dry dressings prescribed or recommended (CWC)[5]

●4266F   Use of wet to dry dressings neither prescribed nor recommended (CWC)[5]

●4267F   Compression therapy prescribed (CWC)[5]

●4268F   Patient education regarding the need for long term compression therapy including interval replacement of compression stockings received (CWC)[5]

●4269F   Appropriate method of offloading (pressure relief) prescribed (CWC)[5]

🖉 Rationale

Codes 4260F-4261F and 4265F-4269F are all included as part of the **Chronic Wound Care (CWC)** measure set. Some of these codes are used individually within a single measure within the set and others are used as part of a set of codes to help identify measure compliance. The instructions included for each measure identify the intent for use of the code in question as well as codes that may be associated with them.

Codes 4260F and 4261F are both included for use within a single measure—**Use of Wound Surface Culture Technique in Patients with Chronic Skin Ulcers (Overuse Measure).**[5] The codes differentiate patients with a diagnosis of chronic skin ulcer for whom a wound surface technique was used (4260F) from those for whom a wound surface technique was not used (4261F). Compliance with the measure is identified by use of code 4261F. Compliance can also be identified by use of code 4260F with the modifier 1P, which identifies that a valid medical exclusion exists for the patients for whom the wound surface technique was used (such as surface culture for methicillin-resistant *Staphylococcus aureus* [MRSA] screening). The measure's intent is to specify that a surface swab for bacteria is not appropriate for determining the organism that is causing the chronic wound infection because the true culprit may be found within the tissue and not on the surface. As a result of this, the information included within the measure directs

⊘=Modifier 51 Exempt   ⊙=Moderate Sedation   ✛=Add-on Code   ✗=FDA approval pending

users by identifying special circumstances in which the numerator is met (compliance with the measure). Because medical exclusions exist for the measure, as was previously noted, the 1P modifier may be used to identify medical exclusions.

Codes 4265F and 4266F are used to identify the recommendation or prescription (or lack thereof) for use of wet to dry dressings for chronic skin ulcer patients. The measure **Use of Wet to Dry Dressings in Patients with Chronic Skin Ulcers** (Overuse Measure)[5] identifies patient visits for patients aged 18 years and older with a diagnosis of chronic skin ulcer without a prescription or recommendation to use wet to dry dressings. As a result, compliance with the measure is identified by a lack of providing a recommendation/prescription of use of wet to dry dressings via use of code 4266F. Because there are no exclusions cited for this measure, no performance exclusions may be reported and the 1P, 2P, and 3P modifiers should not be used to identify exclusions for this measure.

Codes 4267F, 4268F, and 4269F are all included for use with separate measures within the **Chronic Wound Care** measure set. Code 4267F is used to identify prescription of compression therapy within the **Use of Compression System in Patients with Venous Ulcers**[5] measure. This measure is used to identify whether or not the 18-year-old (or older) patient with a diagnosis of venous ulcer was prescribed compression therapy within the 12-month reporting period. Medical, patient, and system reasons for not prescribing the compression therapy exist, and the 1P, 2P, and 3P modifiers may be used to identify exclusions for compliance with this measure. Code 4268F is included as part of the **Patient Education Regarding Long Term Compression Therapy**[5] measure. This code identifies the receipt of patient education regarding the use of compression therapy for chronic wound patients. Compliance with the measure specifications is reported by use of code 4268F. In addition, exclusion modifiers should not be reported as performance exclusions do not exist for this measure. Code 4269F is used to identify that an appropriate method of offloading (or relief of pressure for the wound site) was prescribed. To direct users regarding the intent for reporting this service, a definition of *an appropriate method of offloading* has been included as part of the numerator definition. The **Reporting Instructions** also assist users, identifying that the 1P, 2P, and 3P modifiers may be used to identify performance exclusions for this measure.

●**4270F** Patient receiving potent antiretroviral therapy for 6 months or longer (HIV)[5]

●**4271F** Patient receiving potent antiretroviral therapy for less than 6 months or not receiving potent antiretroviral therapy (HIV)[5]

●**4274F** Influenza immunization administered or previously received (HIV)[5] (P-ESRD)[1]

●**4275F** Hepatitis B vaccine injection administered or previously received (HIV)[5]

●**4276F** Potent antiretroviral therapy prescribed (HIV)[5]

●**4279F** Pneumocystis jiroveci pneumonia prophylaxis prescribed (HIV)[5]

● **4280F**   Pneumocystis jiroveci pneumonia prophylaxis prescribed within 3 months of low CD4+ cell count or percentage (HIV)[5]

● **4290F**   Patient screened for injection drug use (HIV)[5]

● **4293F**   Patient screened for high-risk sexual behavior (HIV)[5]

✍ Rationale

Codes 4270F-4271F, 4274F-4280F, 4290F, and 4293F are all included as part of the HIV/AIDS measure set. Some of these codes are used individually within a single measure within the set and others are used as part of a set of codes to help identify measure compliance. The instructions included for each measure identify the intent for use of the code in question as well as codes that may be associated with them.

Codes 4270F and 4271F are both included for use with a single measure—**HIV RNA Control for Patients After Six Months of Potent Antiretroviral Therapy.**[5] Code 4270F is used for patients who have received potent antiretroviral therapy for 6 months or longer while code 4271F is used for patients receiving potent antiretroviral therapy for less than 6 months or who are not receiving potent antiretroviral therapy. These codes are denominator codes used to define the target population for the measure. For more information regarding use of these codes for this measure, see the **Rationale** for code 0575F.

Code 4274F is used to report the administration or previous receipt of influenza immunization. It is included within separate measures in separate measure sets. It is used within the **Influenza Immunization**[5] measure of the HIV/AIDS measure set and in the **Pediatric End Stage Renal Disease (P-ESRD) measure set** for the same reason: to identify compliance with influenza immunization. The measures differ according to the age of the patient population that is being treated as well as the time frame in which the immunization should be administered (for visits between November 1st and February 15th). Both measures note medical, patient, and system exclusions, and the 1P, 2P, and 3P modifiers may be used to identify exclusions that are allowed for report with this measure.

Code 4275F is used to identify the administration or previous receipt of a hepatitis B vaccine injection. It is used to note compliance with the measure specifications for the **Hepatitis B Vaccination**[5] measure and is used to note whether or not the patient with a diagnosis of HIV/AIDS has ever received at least one injection of hepatitis B vaccine or who has documented immunity for hepatitis B. The measure includes special instructions that specify patients who should be included for measurement as well as instructions that identify compliance outside of the use of code 4275F (ie, the use of code 4157F for 3-dose injections performed—see **Rationale** for code 4157F for more information regarding use of this code). In addition, medical and patient exclusions exist for this measure, and the 1P and 2P modifiers may be used to identify exclusions that are allowed for report with this measure.

Code 4276F is used to report that potent antiviral therapy was prescribed. It is included as part of the **Adolescent and Adult Patients with HIV/AIDS who are**

⊘=Modifier 51 Exempt   ⊙=Moderate Sedation   ✚=Add-on Code   ✗=FDA approval pending

Prescribed Potent Antiretroviral Therapy[5] measure. Use of this code notes compliance with the measure as there are other codes included within the measure listing that are denominator codes that separate the patient population. For more information regarding the intended use for code 4276F, see the **Rationale** for codes 3490F et al.

Code 4279F is used to identify *Pneumocystis jiroveci* pneumonia prophylaxis that was prescribed. It is used to note compliance for a single measure—**Pneumocystis jiroveci pneumonia (PCP) Prophylaxis – Infants ≥6 Weeks to <12 Months.**[5] Because there is a separate code with the measure listing that is used as a denominator code to separate the target population (code 3491F), instructions have been included with this code to direct users regarding how this code should be reported. More information regarding this measure and the use of code 3491F has been included in the **Rationale** included for that code.

Code 4280F is used to identify *Pneumocystis jiroveci* pneumonia prophylaxis that was prescribed within 3 months of the low CD4+ cell count or percentage. Although these codes have similar language, code 4280F differs from use of code 4279F in that code 4280F specifically notes that it should be used for prescription of the prophylaxis within 3 months of the low CD4+ cell count or percentage. Other instructions are also included to direct users regarding the intent of use for code 4280F. For more information regarding use of this code, see the **Rationale** for code 3490F et al.

Codes 4290F and 4293F are both used to identify screening procedures for undesirable behaviors for HIV/AIDS patients. Code 4290F is used to identify screening of patients for injection drug use, and code 4293F is used to identify screening for high-risk sexual behaviors. Both codes include a definition for screening and do not allow for performance exclusions. As a result, the 1P, 2P, and 3P modifiers may not be reported for either code.

●**4300F**   Patient receiving warfarin therapy for non-valvular atrial fibrillation or atrial flutter (AFIB)[1]

●**4301F**   Patient not receiving warfarin therapy for non-valvular atrial fibrillation or atrial flutter (AFIB)[1]

 Rationale

Codes 4300F and 4301F are both used as denominator codes to separate the patients who are receiving Warfarin therapy (4300F) from those who are not (4301F). They are included as part of a single measure—**Monthly International Normalized Ratio (INR) Measurement Therapy**[1]. For more information regarding use of these codes see the **Rationale** for codes 3490F et al.

●**4305F**   Patient education regarding appropriate foot care AND daily inspection of the feet received (CWC)[5]

 Rationale

Code 4305F is used to identify receipt of patient education for appropriate foot care and daily inspection of the feet. It is the only code used within the **Patient**

Education Regarding Diabetic Foot Care[5] measure (**Chronic Wound Care [CWC]** measure set). This measure notes whether or not the patient aged 18 years and older with a diagnosis of diabetes and foot ulcer received education regarding appropriate foot care AND daily inspection of the feet within the 12-month reporting period. A definition for appropriate foot care has been provided to allow a better understanding of the numerator for this measure noting that appropriate foot care may include self-inspection and surveillance, monitoring foot temperatures, appropriate daily foot hygiene, use of proper footwear, good diabetes control, and prompt recognition and professional treatment of newly discovered lesions. Because there are no exclusions for this measure, no performance exclusions modifiers (1P, 2P, or 3P) may be reported for this measure.

●**4306F** Patient counseled regarding psychosocial AND pharmacologic treatment options for opioid addiction (SUD)[1]

●**4320F** Patient counseled regarding psychosocial AND pharmacologic treatment options for alcohol dependence (SUD)[5]

✍ Rationale

Codes 4306F and 4320F are both used as part of the **Substance Use Disorders** measure set. They are reported as part of independent measures within this set identifying patient counseling regarding psychosocial AND pharmacologic treatment options for alcohol dependence (within the **Counseling Regarding Psychosocial and Pharmacologic Treatment Options for Alcohol Dependence**[5] measure set and patient **Counseling Regarding Psychosocial AND Pharmacologic Treatment Options for Opioid Addiction**. These are unrelated measures that have codes that serve a similar purpose: the compliance with the indicated measure for counseling for the specified addiction. In addition, the measure that addresses opioid addiction defines this term in context to information included in the DSM-IV classification of opioid dependence and directs users to this resource for additional understanding regarding that term. Because neither code allows for performance exclusions, codes 4306F and 4320F may not be reported with modifiers 1P, 2P, or 3P.

Follow-up or Other Outcomes

▲**5020F** Treatment summary report communicated to physician(s) managing continuing care and to the patient within 1 month of completing treatment (ONC)[1]

✍ Rationale

Code 5020F was revised to align with changes made to the measure specifications noting that the treatment summary report should be communicated to both the physician managing continuing care *and to the patient*.

○=Modifier 51 Exempt   ⊙=Moderate Sedation   ✚=Add-on Code   ⋀=FDA approval pending

●**5100F**   Potential risk for fracture communicated to the referring physician within 24 hours of completion of the imaging study (NUC_MED)[1]

Rationale

Code 5100F is used to report the communication of the potential risk of fracture to the referring physician within 24 hours of completion of the imaging study. It is included as part of the **Communication to Referring Physician of Patient's Potential Risk for Fracture for All Patients Undergoing Bone Scintigraphy**[1] measure. Use of this code identifies compliance with the measure specifications and is used in addition to code 3572F. The reporting instructions included for this measure note allowances for medical exclusions only. As a result, the modifier 1P may be reported with qualifying medical exclusions (such as the report of a previous lesion in same location with no evidence of progression or regression).

Patient Safety

▲**6030F**   All elements of maximal sterile barrier technique followed including: cap AND mask AND sterile gown AND sterile gloves AND a large sterile sheet AND hand hygiene AND 2% chlorhexidine for cutaneous antisepsis (or acceptable alternative antiseptics, per current guideline) (CRIT)[1]

Rationale

Code 6030F was revised to align with changes made within the code descriptor with those made to the measure specifications as the measure specifications now note that *acceptable alternative antiseptics, per current guideline.*

FOOTNOTES

[1] Physician Consortium for Performance Improvement® (PCPI), www.physicianconsortium.org
[2] National Committee on Quality Assurance (NCQA), Health Employer Data Information Set (HEDIS®), www.ncqa.org
[3] Joint Commission on Accreditation of Healthcare Organizations (JCAHO), ORYX Initiative Performance Measures, www.jcaho.org/pms
[4] National Diabetes Quality Improvement Alliance (NDQIA), www.nationaldiabetesalliance.org
[5] Joint measure from the Physician Consortium for Performance Improvement, www.physicianconsortium.org and National Committee on Quality Assurance (NCQA), www.ncqa.org
[6] The Society of Thoracic Surgeons, www.sts.org, National Quality Forum, www.qualityforum.org

Category III Codes

Revisions to this section include the addition of 11 new codes and the deletion of 22 codes. Of the code deletions, seven codes have been converted to Category I codes, including the codes for reporting programming and analysis of gastric neurostimulators, template guided saturation prostate biopsies, cervical artificial disc arthroplasty, and actigraphy testing. The remaining 15 deleted Category III codes have been archived, without meeting the criteria for conversion to Category I codes. To support deletion of the Category III codes, cross-references have been established directing users to the appropriate unlisted Category I code for each service as described.

Category III Codes

The following section contains a set . . .

The inclusion of a service or . . .

►Services/procedures described in this section make use of alphanumeric characters. These codes have an alpha character as the 5th character in the string, preceded by four digits. The digits are not intended to reflect the placement of the code in the Category I section of CPT nomenclature. Codes in this section may or may not eventually receive a Category I CPT code. In either case, in general, a given Category III code will be archived five years from its date of publication or revision in the CPT code book unless it is demonstrated that a temporary code is still needed. Services/procedures described by Category III codes which have been archived after five years, without conversion, may be reported using the Category I unlisted code. New codes in this section are released semi-annually via the AMA/CPT internet site, to expedite dissemination for reporting. The full set of temporary codes for emerging technology, services, and procedures are published annually in the CPT codebook. Go to www.ama-assn.org/go/cpt for the most current listing.◄

(0029T has been deleted)

✍ Rationale

The introductory guidelines of the Category III section have been revised to include the phrase "in general," to clarify that no time limitations are in place to limit the CPT Editorial Panel consideration of a request to convert a Category III code to a Category I code.

Beginning with CPT 2009 and included in the 2010 codebook, a parenthetical note directing users to the appropriate Category I unlisted code is now included in the Category III subsection.

Codes 0062T, 0063T, 0064T, 0066T, 0067T, 0068T-0070T, 0077T, 0084T, 0086T, 0087T, and related cross-references have been deleted, according to the provisions of the Category III code set guidelines. To support deletion of the Category III codes, cross-references have been established directing users to the appropriate unlisted Category I code for each service as described.

0050T   Removal of a ventricular assist device, extracorporeal, percutaneous transseptal access, single or dual cannulation

►(For replacement of a ventricular assist device, extracorporeal, percutaneous transseptal access, use 33999)◄

✍ Rationale

In accordance with the changes in the establishment of three new codes for ventricular assist device replacement in the Cardiovascular System section in the Surgery section, a cross-reference note has been added following code 0050T directing users to code 33999 for replacement of an extracorporeal ventricular assist device with percutaneous transseptal access.

▶(0062T, 0063T have been deleted)◀

▶(For percutaneous intradiscal annuloplasty, any method other than electrothermal, use 22899)◀

✍ Rationale

Codes 0062T and 0063T, which previously described percutaneous intradiscal annuloplasty, any method other than electrothermal, should be reported with unlisted code 22899.

▶(0064T has been deleted. To report, use 94799)◀

✍ Rationale

Code 0064T, which previously described spectroscopy, expired gas analysis (eg, nitric oxide/carbon dioxide test), should be reported with unlisted code 94799.

▶(0066T has been deleted)◀

▶(To report CT colon, screening, use 74263)◀

▶(0067T has been deleted)◀

▶(To report CT colon, diagnostic, see 74261-74262)◀

✍ Rationale

Codes 0066T and 0067T, which previously described CT colonography diagnostic and screening services, have been deleted. In support of the deletion of these codes, Category I codes 74261, 74262, and 74263 and parenthetical notes have been established. An introductory note has been added to the Digestive System/Rectum/Endoscopy guidelines to direct the use of codes 74261, 74263, and 74263 for CT colonography. The cross-references following codes 72194, 74170, 76376, and 76377 have been updated to reflect these new codes.

▶(0068T-0070T have been deleted)◀

▶(For acoustic heart sound recording and computer analysis, use 93799)◀

✍ Rationale

Codes 0068T, 0069T, and 0070T, which previously described acoustic heart sound recording and computer analysis, should be reported with unlisted code 93799.

▶(0077T has been deleted. To report, see 61107, 61210)◀

✍ Rationale

Category III code 0077T, which previously described cerebral thermal perfusion probe, including twist drill or burr hole, has been deleted. These services are now reported using codes 61107 and 61210, as indicated in the new cross-reference.

⊘=Modifier 51 Exempt   ⊙=Moderate Sedation   ✚=Add-on Code   ∕=FDA approval pending

▶(0084T has been deleted. To report, use 53855)◀

✎ Rationale

Category III code 0084T, which previously described insertion of a temporary prostatic urethral stent, was deleted. The procedure is now performed frequently enough to warrant Category I status. Category I code 53855 has been established to report insertion of a temporary prostatic urethral stent, including urethral measurement.

▶(0086T has been deleted. To report use, 93799)◀

✎ Rationale

Code 0086T, which previously described left ventricular filling pressure indirect measurement by computerized calibration of the arterial waveform response to Valsalva maneuver, should be reported with unlisted code 93799.

▶(0087T has been deleted. To report, use 89398)◀

✎ Rationale

Category III code 0087T, which previously described sperm evaluation, Hyaluronan sperm binding test, has been deleted. A cross-reference has been added directing users to report code 89398 for this test.

▶(0144T-0151T have been deleted. To report, see 75571-75574)◀

✎ Rationale

Codes 0144T-0151T, which previously described cardiac computed tomography (CT) and coronary computed tomographic angiography (CTA) have been deleted. These procedures are now performed frequently enough to warrant Category I status. Category I codes 75571, 75572, 75573, and 75574 have been established to report these services. A cross-reference has been added in the Category III section directing users to the new Category I codes.

▶(0170T has been deleted. To report, use 46707)◀

✎ Rationale

In accordance with the conversion of code 0170T to Category I code 46707, a cross-reference has been added to note the deletion of code 0170T and to direct users to code 46707. For more information regarding replacement code (46707), please see **Rationale** for code 46707.

+0173T Monitoring of intraocular pressure during vitrectomy surgery (List separately in addition to code for primary procedure)

▶(Use 0173T in conjunction with 67036, 67039-67043, 67108, 67112, 67113)◀

 Rationale

The parenthetical note following code 0173T has been revised to expand the usage of code 0173T to be used in conjunction with code 67113 (repair of complex retinal detachment). A third code, 66990, would be reported along with the repair code (67113) and monitoring code (0173T) if an operating endoscope is utilized.

0184T Excision of rectal tumor, transanal endoscopic microsurgical approach (ie, TEMS)

(For non-endoscopic excision of rectal tumor, see 45160, 45171, 45172)

 Rationale

In accordance with the establishment of codes 45171 and 45172, a cross-reference following code 0184T has been added, directing the user to the appropriate codes to report for non-endoscopic excision of rectal tumor.

0193T Transurethral, radiofrequency micro-remodeling of the female bladder neck and proximal urethra for stress urinary incontinence

▶(0194T has been deleted. To report procalcitonin, use 84145)◀

 Rationale

In accordance with the establishment of code 84145 to report procalcitonin, Category III code 0194T has been deleted. A cross-reference has been added directing users to code 84145 for this test.

● 0197T Intra-fraction localization and tracking of target or patient motion during delivery of radiation therapy (eg, 3D positional tracking, gating, 3D surface tracking), each fraction of treatment

Rationale

Code 0197T has been added to describe a new technology for reporting intra-fraction target tracking procedures/services. The existing codes for target localization rely on imaging technologies utilizing ultrasound, CT, or X-ray based techniques (76950, 77014, 77421). These codes do not accurately describe localization with non-imaging technology nor do they describe intra-fraction tracking of the target or patient motion during radiation treatment delivery.

Existing radiographic image guidance identifies the organ or target position prior to radiation delivery. Tumors within the body are subject to motion. Motion may be attributed to the respiratory cycle (eg, lung, liver) or changes in peristalsis of the GI track (eg, prostate). Therefore, conformal radiation delivery may miss the

---

target due to continuous target drift, transient and persistent excursions, and high frequency/high amplitude motion.

For this reason, Category III code 0197T has been established to describe intra-fraction localization and tracking of target or patient motion during delivery of radiation therapy. Code 0197T may be reported for each fraction of treatment. In support of the addition of code 0197T, a cross-reference note has been included in the Category I Radiation Treatment Delivery section, directing users to the appropriate code for intra-fraction localization and tracking of a target.

Clinical Example (0197T)

A 65-year-old male presents with adenocarcinoma of the prostate, a Gleason score of 6, prostate-specific antigen (PSA) level of 7.1, and a clinical stage of T2a. After consultation with a urologist and a radiation oncologist, the patient selects primary external beam radiation therapy as his definitive treatment. Due to daily random prostate motion during the delivery of radiation therapy, the physician prescribes real-time intra-fraction tracking with continuous monitoring in conjunction with the delivery of the external beam radiation therapy.

Clinical Example (0197T)

A 59-year-old female who smokes was found to have a 3.5-cm right upper lobe mass and right hilar adenopathy. Computed tomography–guided needle biopsy revealed adenocarcinoma. Mediastinoscopy revealed lymph nodes involved with tumor in the aortic-pulmonary window. The patient was diagnosed as stage IIIB and combined chemotherapy-radiation therapy was advised. The radiation oncology physician prescribes a course of radiation therapy with respiratory gating to deliver precision radiation to the tumor and mediastinal structures while optimally sparing normal lung tissue.

Description of Procedure (0197T)

The patient is set up for daily radiation treatment according to usual procedures. Tracking device(s) and/or apparatus is/are put in place. Stability of position, or cyclical motion, is documented for the baseline in the treatment room. Continuous monitoring occurs from outside the treatment room at the device console. Treatment is interrupted according to tracking rules; changes in treatment delivery are made, and treatment resumes. The tracking device is put away. The tracking record is prepared for physician review.

●0198T   Measurement of ocular blood flow by repetitive intraocular pressure sampling, with interpretation and report

Rationale

Code 0198T has been established to report a diagnostic test to evaluate and manage patients with and at risk for glaucoma. This test includes measurement of intraocular pressure (approximately 200 times per second) to calculate ocular blood flow utilizing a device consisting of a pneumotonometer probe. A parenthetical note following code 92120 has been added directing users to code 0198T for measurement of ocular blood flow, as the test described in code 92120 measures aqueous outflow, not ocular blood flow. The technical component of this test is usually performed by the technician, and the interpretation is performed by the physician. Ocular blood flow measurement is a unique diagnostic test that is separate and complementary to other tests such as visual fields (92081-92083), scanning computerized ophthalmic diagnostic imaging (92135), fundus photography (92250), gonioscopy (92020), and evaluation and management (E/M) services. Ocular blood flow measurement when done is not an incidental or bundled test with any of these additional services.

 ### Clinical Example (0198T)

A 65-year-old man presents with normal or borderline intraocular pressure and optic nerve cupping suspicious for glaucoma. Ocular blood flow analysis is performed.

Description of Procedure (0198T)

The patient is given a topical anesthetic eyedrop and then placed into the ocular blood flow analyzer by the physician or a qualified ancillary staff member. The device's pneumotonometer probe is placed in contact with the corneal surface generating real time data that is analyzed by the onboard computer to calculate ocular blood flow. The physician then reviews and interprets the data.

●0199T Physiologic recording of tremor using accelerometer(s) and/or gyroscope(s) (including frequency and amplitude), including interpretation and report

 ### Rationale

Code 0199T has been established to describe tremor recording using accelerometer(s) and gyroscope(s). Frequency and amplitude of the tremor are measured, which aids in determining the tremor's etiology. For example, essential tremor has a frequency between 4 and 7 hertz (Hz), and the amplitude varies. The hertz is the measurement of frequency per unit of time. Essential tremor is a common type of tremor and may be genetic. A cerebellar tremor has a frequency between 3 and 5 Hz. Cerebellar tremors may be caused by multiple sclerosis or stroke.

Code 0199T describing tremor recording is reported one time, regardless of the number of gyroscopes and/or accelerometers used. Interpretation and report of the data are included and not reported separately.

 ### Clinical Example (0199T)

A 70-year-old male presents with a history of tremor for the past 3 months. His mental status is intact, and he has no other motor symptoms. A full neurological history and exam are done to try to determine the probable cause; however, the cause of his tremor is still unclear. The patient requires a tremor analysis in order to ascertain the cause of the tremor and to establish a baseline by which the effectiveness of future interventions can be measured.

⊘=Modifier 51 Exempt ⊙=Moderate Sedation ✚=Add-on Code ✗=FDA approval pending

Description of Procedure (0199T)

Accelerometers and gyroscopes are placed by the clinician on the arm. The physician guides the patient through a series of simple tests known to elicit rest, postural, or action tremor that include resting, posture, and nose touching. Resting: The patient is instructed to rest with his hands in his lap for 20 seconds. Posture: The patient is instructed to hold his arms straight out in front of him for 20 seconds. **Nose Touching**: The patient is instructed to repeatedly extend his arm and touch his nose for 20 seconds.

The clinician ensures that the test results are adequate for interpretation and may ask for additional tasks based on the initial assessment. The clinician does not need to leave the room to interpret before deciding if more testing is needed. The recording device may be moved to another extremity and the series of tests may be repeated, if clinically appropriate. Data is then interpreted by the clinician for frequency, amplitude, and rhythmicity. The data is then processed into reports for clinicians that describe motor symptom severity.

⊙●**0200T** Percutaneous sacral augmentation (sacroplasty), unilateral injection(s), including the use of a balloon or mechanical device, when used, 1 or more needles

⊙●**0201T** Percutaneous sacral augmentation (sacroplasty), bilateral injections, including the use of a balloon or mechanical device, when used, 2 or more needles

▶(For radiological supervision and interpretation, see 72291, 72292)◀

▶(If bone biopsy is performed, see 20220, 20225)◀

📝 Rationale

Two Category III codes, 0200T and 0201T, have been established to report the treatment of compression or other sacral fractures due to osteoporosis or other etiologies using fluoroscopic guidance or CT guidance. Code 0200T is indented to report unilateral percutaneous sacral augmentation (sacroplasty) injection(s), including the use of a balloon or mechanical device (if utilized), using one or more needles; and code 0201T is intended to report a bilateral procedure, which uses two or more needles. Codes 0200T and 0201T include moderate sedation and so sedation should not be separately reported.

Prior to 2010, there was no CPT code that described percutaneous, minimally invasive, radiologically guided sacral augmentation (sacroplasty) to repair sacral fractures commonly associated with osteoporosis. In 2001, codes 22520-22525 were established to report vertebral augmentation (percutaneous vertebroplasty) that are specific to the treatment of thoracic and lumbar compression fractures. These codes are not adequate to report the performance of percutaneous vertebroplasty or augmentation for sacral fractures. The anatomy, approach, techniques, and potential complications in performing vertebroplasty or vertebral augmentation for sacral insufficiency fractures is different and unique compared to the treatment of thoracic and lumbar compression fractures. Similar insufficiency fractures can occur in the sacrum. Although these are usually unilateral lesions, occasionally they can occur bilaterally. Injection of bone cement for sacral fractures has increasingly been reported as a viable treatment option for these fractures.

Two cross-reference notes have also been added following codes 0200T and 0201T, directing users to codes 72291 and 72292 for radiological supervision and interpretation, and to codes 20220 and 20225 if bone biopsy is performed.

 ### Clinical Example (0200T)

A 69-year-old female with a history of osteoporosis fell 3 weeks ago suffering a left sacral insufficiency fracture. Her pain has been severe and poorly responsive to narcotic analgesics and rest. The patient has had significant limitations in mobility, transfers, and activities of daily living (ADL) due to her fracture and pain. A left-side sacroplasty has been recommended to treat her fractures and pain.

Description of Procedure (0200T)

The patient was admitted to the outpatient surgery center to undergo attempted sacroplasty for her left-sided sacral insufficiency fractures under fluoroscopic guidance. The patient gave written informed consent and an intravenous line was placed for access. Vital signs and continuous pulse oximetry were used throughout the procedure. The patient was sterilely prepared and draped in the prone position on a radiolucent table. Under fluoroscopic guidance, the skin and subcutaneous tissues were anesthetized with topical anesthetic. A large-bore needle was placed into the sacral vertebrae of S1 and S2, where the fractures were located, using a posterior approach. Once the needle(s) was/were in proper position, radio-opaque bone cement was injected. Careful visualization to rule out any vascular uptake or extravasation toward vital neural structures was performed with fluoroscopic guidance. The needle was removed, a bandage applied, and the patient was taken to a recovery area for approximately 30 minutes of monitoring prior to being discharged with instructions.

 ### Clinical Example (0201T)

A 69-year-old female with a history of osteoporosis fell 3 weeks ago suffering bilateral sacral insufficiency fracture. Her pain has been severe and poorly responsive to narcotic analgesics and rest. The patient has had significant limitations in mobility, transfers, and ADLs due to her fracture and pain. A bilateral sacroplasty has been recommended to treat her fractures and pain.

Description of Procedure (0201T)

The patient was admitted to the outpatient surgery center to undergo attempted sacroplasty under fluoroscopic guidance for her bilateral sacral insufficiency fractures. The patient gave written informed consent and an intravenous line was placed for access. Vital signs and continuous pulse oximetry were used throughout the procedure. The patient was sterilely prepared and draped in the prone position on a radiolucent table. Under fluoroscopic guidance, the skin and subcutaneous tissues were anesthetized with topical anesthetic. A large-bore needle was placed into the sacral vertebrae of S1 and S2, where the fractures were located, using a left-sided posterior approach. Once the needle(s) was/were in proper position, 10 cc of radio-opaque methylmethacrolate cement was injected. Careful visualization to rule out any vascular uptake or extravasation toward vital neural structures

⊘=Modifier 51 Exempt   ⊙=Moderate Sedation   ✚=Add-on Code   ✗=FDA approval pending

was performed with fluoroscopic guidance. The needle was removed, and the same procedure and technique was performed using a right-sided approach to treat the right-sided sacral fractures. Once that was complete, bandages were applied, and the patient was taken to a recovery area for approximately 30 minutes of monitoring prior to being discharged with instructions.

●**0202T** Posterior vertebral joint(s) arthroplasty (eg, facet joint[s] replacement), including facetectomy, laminectomy, foraminotomy, and vertebral column fixation, injection of bone cement, when performed, including fluoroscopy, single level, lumbar spine

▶(Do not report 0202T in conjunction with 22521, 22524, 22840, 22851, 22857, 63005, 63012, 63017, 63030, 63042, 63047, 63056 at the same level)◀

Rationale

Category III code 0202T has been established to report the performance of posterior placement of a motion preservation device to supply additional stability or sagittal balance in the facet of a complete facetectomy when performing a decompression for moderate to severe stenosis. There is currently no CPT codes to describe the replacement of a facet joint or any device which replicates and preserves facet-like motion.

The posterior vertebral joint arthroplasty procedure as described by code 0202T is performed at the involved level of the lumbar spine. The device, which replaces the diseased facets after their removal, is anchored in place through the vertebral column utilizing pedicle fixation. At this time, bone cement may or may not be used for further support of the pedicle fixation. The motion-preserving part of the device is then attached via the pedicle fixation. This replicates the motion of the anatomic facet joint allowing movement in axial rotation, lateral bending, flexion, and extension. Replacement of the facet joint thus averts the need for arthrodesis.

An exclusionary parenthetical note has been added to restrict the use of code 0202T with codes 22521, 22524, 22840, 22851, 22857, 63005, 63012, 63017, 63030, 63042, 63047, and 63056 performed at the same level.

Clinical Example (0202T)

A 55-year-old male presents with a history of bilateral lower extremity pain greater than low back pain. His symptoms have been refractory to a 6-month course of conservative care including medications, physical therapy, and injective procedures. Magnetic resonance imaging examination is consistent with moderate-to-severe spinal stenosis at the L4-L5 level as well as degenerative facet arthropathy. Decompression and facet joint arthroplasty has been recommended at the L4-L5 level.

Description of Procedure (0202T)

The patient was admitted to the hospital for total facet arthroplasty. After informed consent was obtained, the patient was brought to the operating room, and general endotracheal anesthesia was induced. The patient was placed prone on the radiolucent operating table, all bony prominences were well padded, and the abdomen was free and uncompressed. The patient was prepared and draped in a sterile fashion. A posterior midline incision was made down to the level of the lumbodorsal fascia. Subperiosteal dissection was performed. Decompression was performed via laminectomy and bilateral total facetectomy at the involved level. The pedicles were then identified and a guide was used to measure the acceptable range of angles compatible with the device. Trial instrumentation was used to ensure appropriate sizing and alignment. The pedicle fixation was then inserted via triangulating bicortical trajectories under fluoroscopic guidance. These were then cemented using bone cement. An alignment gauge was then used to adjust the pedicle fixation height for accurate placement of the facet arthroplasty device. The components of the facet arthroplasty device were then attached utilizing special calibrated instruments. Final biplanar fluoroscopic confirmation of the positioning of the device and pedicle fixation was obtained. The wound was closed in a standard layered fashion. A sterile dressing was applied. The patient was extubated and taken to the recovery room.

●0203T   Sleep study, unattended, simultaneous recording; heart rate, oxygen saturation, respiratory analysis (eg, by airflow or peripheral arterial tone) and sleep time

▶(Do not report 0203T in conjunction with 93012, 93014, 93041-93227, 93228, 93229, 93230-93272, 95803, 95806, 0204T)◀

▶(For unattended sleep study that measures a minimum of heart rate, oxygen saturation, and respiratory analysis, use 0204T)◀

▶(For unattended sleep study that measures heart rate, oxygen saturation, respiratory airflow, and respiratory effort, use 95806)◀

●0204T   minimum of heart rate, oxygen saturation, and respiratory analysis (eg, by airflow or peripheral arterial tone)

▶(Do not report 0204T in conjunction with 93012, 93014, 93041-93227, 93228, 93229, 93230-93272, 95806, 0203T)◀

▶(For unattended sleep study that measures heart rate, oxygen saturation, respiratory analysis and sleep time, use 0203T)◀

▶(For unattended sleep study that measures heart rate, oxygen saturation, respiratory airflow, and respiratory effort, use 95806)◀

✍ Rationale
Codes 0203T and 0204T have been established for reporting unattended sleep study testing services. Code 0203T is intended to describe unattended sleep study testing measuring heart rate, oxygen saturation, respiratory analysis, and sleep time. Code 0204T is intended to describe unattended sleep study testing measuring a minimum of heart rate, oxygen saturation, and respiratory analysis. In support of these new codes, Category I sleep code 95806 was editorially revised to create consistent terminology within the family of codes and to report unattended sleep study testing measuring heart rate, oxygen saturation, respiratory airflow, and respiratory effort.

⊘=Modifier 51 Exempt   ⊙=Moderate Sedation   ✚=Add-on Code   ✗=FDA approval pending

Following code 0203T, two cross-reference notes and one instructional note have been added to: (1) instruct users not to report ECG monitoring services, actigraphy, sleep study, or code 0204T separately; (2) direct users to report code 0204T for unattended sleep study that measures a minimum of heart rate, oxygen saturation, and respiratory analysis; and (3) direct users to report code 95806 for unattended sleep study that measures heart rate, oxygen saturation, respiratory airflow, and respiratory effort.

Following code 0204T, two cross-references and one instructional note have been added to: (1) instruct users not to report ECG monitoring services, unattended sleep study, or code 0204T separately; (2) direct users to report code 0204T for unattended sleep study that measure heart rate, oxygen saturation, respiratory analysis, and sleep time; and (3) direct users to report code 95806 for unattended sleep study that measures heart rate, oxygen saturation, respiratory airflow, and respiratory effort.

Clinical Example (0203T)

55-year-old man with fatigue, prominent snoring, complaints of difficulty sleeping and who has a BMI of 33 is evaluated with an unattended sleep study.

Clinical Example (0204T)

55-year-old man with prominent snoring, excessive daytime sleepiness, whose wife reports he has nocturnal gasping and who has a BMI of 33 is evaluated with an unattended sleep study.

+●0205T Intravascular catheter-based coronary vessel or graft spectroscopy (eg, infrared) during diagnostic evaluation and/or therapeutic intervention including imaging supervision, interpretation, and report, each vessel (List separately in addition to code for primary procedure)

▶(Use 0205T in conjunction with 92980, 92982, 92995, 93508, 93510-93533)◀

Rationale

Add-on Category III code 0205T has been established to report intravascular catheter-based coronary spectroscopy. Code 0205T should be used in conjunction with codes 92980, 92982, 92995, 93508, or 93510-93533 as directed in the instructional note following code 0205T.

In support of the addition of code 0205T, a cross-reference note has been added in the Medicine section following intravascular ultrasound code 92979, directing users to code 0205T for intravascular catheter–based coronary spectroscopy.

Clinical Example (0205T)

A 70-year-old male presents with a small non–S-T segment elevation myocardial infarction caused by a culprit lesion in the mid-circumflex coronary artery. The angiogram revealed an additional 80% proximal stenosis in the left anterior descending (LAD) coronary artery that is flow limiting. The interventional cardiologist performs intravascular spectroscopy to generate a scan of the LAD to detect the presence of lipid core plaque at sites with and without stenosis.

Description of Procedure (0205T)

Intravascular infrared spectroscopy is used to detect lipid core coronary plaques without the need to flush or occlude the artery. A fiber-optic catheter with a laser light source is used to interrogate plaques of interest. The imaging catheter is loaded onto a guidewire and then introduced through a guide catheter. Once the physician has determined the optimal position for scanning, the rotation and pullback device is activated, and the scan begins. The scan provides a digital color-coded map of the location and the intensity of the lipid core containing plaques of interest in the artery. This information is compiled to report a measure of the total amount of plaques in the artery.

The single vessel scan revealed the presence of a plaque at a non-stenotic site 10 mm proximal to the LAD 80% stenosis. The interventional cardiologist chose to place a longer stent than would have otherwise been selected to cover both the stenosis and the lipid core plaque. This would also avoid ending the stent in a lipid core.

●0206T   Algorithmic analysis, remote, of electrocardiographic-derived data with computer probability assessment, including report

▶(When a 12-lead ECG is performed, 93000-93010 may be reported, as appropriate)◀

 Rationale

Code 0206T has been established to report a new technology that remotely analyzes ECG-derived data to perform a computer probability assessment of the severity of a patient's illness. The information obtained from this assessment is used in determining the next steps of a patient's treatment. A cross-reference note has been added following code 0206T instructing users to also report the appropriate code from the 93000-93010 series as appropriate when an ECG is performed in conjunction with the assessment.

 Clinical Example (0206T)

A 68-year-old male with a history of hypertension controlled with medication, and increased BMI, with no prior history of coronary disease or a coronary event, presents with recent onset atypical chest pain/pressure, most of which is non-exertional, nonspecific ST-T changes on his resting ECG, and mild dyspnea on exertion. A complete physical examination reveals no specific cardiovascular abnormality. A resting two lead ECG (II and V5) is ordered to assess the likelihood of obstructive coronary disease (coronary stenosis >70%).

Description of Procedure (0206T)

The patient has a two-lead ECG (II and V5) tracing performed using equipment capable of transmitting the data digitally to an offsite location. The pattern is analyzed by comparing it to an extensive database of tracings with known probability of acute ischemia. A probability report is provided to the treating facility.

✍️ Rationale

Code 0207T has been established to report meibomian gland evacuation using thermal energy and pressure for dysfunctional or obstructive meibomian gland(s) resulting in dry eye syndrome. Traditionally, this procedure is accomplished with manual heat compresses. This newer technique utilizes an automated device system that emits heat and pressure into a disposable lid warmer and eye cup. Code 0207T is reported once for each affected eye treated as indicated in the "unilateral" designation included in the code descriptor.

Clinical Example (0207T)

A 66-year-old female presents to the ophthalmologist complaining of chronic redness and irritation of both eyes that has not been relieved with artificial tears. After appropriate diagnostic testing, it is determined that the patient suffers from dry eye secondary to meibomian gland disease.

Description of Procedure (0207T)

Insert the disposable lid unit around the patient's upper and lower eyelids so that the lid warmer is under the eyelids and the eyecup is outside the eyelids. Verify proper position by ensuring that the lid warmer is under both eyelids. Attach the disposable to the handheld control system (HCS). Once attached, verify that eyelids are closed and begin treatment by pressing the button on the HCS. To monitor the treatment, refer to the LED (Light Emitting Diode) bars for temperature and pressure status. When the temperature LED bars are green, therapeutic temperature is reached and the display begins timing the treatment. After the treatment is complete, remove the disposable items, being careful to avoid creating a corneal abrasion. Dispose the single use disposable set (including lid warmer, eye cup, tubing, electrical wire and connector).

Tabular Review
of the Changes

Section/Code	Added	Deleted	Revised	Grammatical Revision	Cross-reference

Evaluation and Management

Nursing Facility Services

Initial Nursing Facility Care

New or Established Patient

Section/Code	Added	Deleted	Revised	Grammatical Revision	Cross-reference
99304			X		
99305			X		
99306			X		

Subsequent Nursing Facility Care

Section/Code	Added	Deleted	Revised	Grammatical Revision	Cross-reference
99307			X		
99308			X		
99309			X		
99310			X		

Other Nursing Facility Services

Section/Code	Added	Deleted	Revised	Grammatical Revision	Cross-reference
99318			X		

Prolonged Services

Prolonged Physician Service Without Direct (Face-To-Face) Patient Contact

Section/Code	Added	Deleted	Revised	Grammatical Revision	Cross-reference
99358			X		
99359			X		

Anesthesia

Shoulder and Axilla

Section/Code	Added	Deleted	Revised	Grammatical Revision	Cross-reference
01632		X			

Surgery

Integumentary System

Repair (Closure)

Adjacent Tissue Transfer or Rearrangement

Section/Code	Added	Deleted	Revised	Grammatical Revision	Cross-reference
14300		X			
14301	X				X
14302	X				X

Section/Code	Added	Deleted	Revised	Grammatical Revision	Cross-reference
Breast					
Introduction					
19295			X		X
Musculoskeletal System					
Head					
Excision					
21011	X				
21012	X				
21013	X				
21014	X				
21015			X		
21016	X				
Neck (Soft Tissues) and Thorax					
Excision					
21552	X				
21554	X				
21555			X		
21556			X		
21557			X		
21558	X				
Back and Flank					
Excision					
21930			X		
21931	X				
21932	X				
21933	X				
21935			X		
21936	X				

⊘=Modifier 51 Exempt   ⊙=Moderate Sedation   ✦=Add-on Code   ✗=FDA approval pending

Section/Code	Added	Deleted	Revised	Grammatical Revision	Cross-reference
Spine (Vertebral Column)					
Vertebral Body, Embolization or Injection					
22520			X		
22521			X		
Abdomen					
Excision					
22900			X		
22901	X				
22902	X				
22903	X				
22904	X				
22905	X				
Shoulder					
Excision					
23071	X				
23073	X				
23075			X		
23076			X		
23077			X		
23078	X				
23200			X		
23210			X		
23220			X		
23221		X			
23222		X			
Humerus (Upper Arm) and Elbow					
Excision					
24071	X				
24073	X				
24075			X		

Section/Code	Added	Deleted	Revised	Grammatical Revision	Cross-reference
24076			X		
24077			X		
24079	X				
24150			X		
24151		X			
24152			X		X
24153		X			

Forearm and Wrist

Excision

25071	X				
25073	X				
25075			X		
25076			X		
25077			X		
25078	X				
25170			X		

Hand and Fingers

Excision

26111	X				
26113	X				
26115			X		
26116			X		
26117			X		
26118	X				
26250			X		
26255		X			
26260			X		X
26261		X			
26262			X		X

⃠=Modifier 51 Exempt   ☉=Moderate Sedation   ✚=Add-on Code   ⊁=FDA approval pending

Section/Code	Added	Deleted	Revised	Grammatical Revision	Cross-reference
Pelvis and Hip Joint					
Excision					
27043	X				
27045	X				
27047			X		
27048			X		
27049			X		
27059	X				
27075			X		
27076			X		
27077			X		
27078			X		
27079		X			
Femur (Thigh Region) and Knee Joint					
Excision					
27327			X		
27328			X		
27329			X		
27337	X				
27339	X				
27364	X				
27365			X		X
Leg (Tibia and Fibula) and Ankle Joint					
Excision					
27615			X		
27616	X				
27618			X		
27619			X		
27632	X				
27634	X				

Section/Code	Added	Deleted	Revised	Grammatical Revision	Cross-reference
27640			X		X
27641			X		X
27645			X		
27646			X		
27647			X		

Foot and Toes

Excision

Section/Code	Added	Deleted	Revised	Grammatical Revision	Cross-reference
28039	X				
28041	X				
28043			X		
28045			X		
28046			X		
28047	X				
28171			X		
28173			X		
28175			X		

Application of Casts and Strapping

Body and Upper Extremity

Strapping—Any Age

Section/Code	Added	Deleted	Revised	Grammatical Revision	Cross-reference
29220		X			

Lower Extremity

Strapping—Any Age

Section/Code	Added	Deleted	Revised	Grammatical Revision	Cross-reference
29581	X				X

Respiratory System

Nose

Destruction

Section/Code	Added	Deleted	Revised	Grammatical Revision	Cross-reference
30801			X		X
30802			X		X

⊘=Modifier 51 Exempt   ⊙=Moderate Sedation   ✚=Add-on Code   ✗=FDA approval pending

Section/Code	Added	Deleted	Revised	Grammatical Revision	Cross-reference
Trachea and Bronchi					
Endoscopy					
31622			X		
31626	X				X
31627	X				X
31641			X		
31643			X		
31645			X		
31646			X		
31656			X		
Lungs and Pleura					
Introduction and Removal					
32552	X				
32553	X				X
Destruction					
32560			X		X
32561	X				X
32562	X				X
Cardiovascular System					
Heart and Pericardium					
Pacemaker or Pacing Cardioverter-Defibrillator					
33216			X		
33217			X		X
33223			X		
Transposition of the Great Vessels					
33782	X				X
33783	X				
Cardiac Assist					
33981	X				

Section/Code	Added	Deleted	Revised	Grammatical Revision	Cross-reference
33982	X				
33983	X				

Arteries and Veins

Vascular Injection Procedures

Intra-Arterial—Intra-Aortic

36145		X			X
36147	X				X
36148	X				X

Venous

36481			X		

Hemodialysis Access, Intervascular Cannulation for Extracorporeal Circulation, or Shunt Insertion

36834		X			

Portal Decompression Procedures

37183			X		X

Ligation

37760			X		
37761	X				X

Digestive System

Pharynx, Adenoids, and Tonsils

Excision, Destruction

42894			X		X

Esophagus

Laparoscopy

43281	X				
43282	X				X

Stomach

Introduction

43761			X		

⊘=Modifier 51 Exempt ⊙=Moderate Sedation ✚=Add-on Code ⊮=FDA approval pending

Section/Code	Added	Deleted	Revised	Grammatical Revision	Cross-reference
Bariatric Surgery					
Laparoscopy					
43775	X				X
Rectum					
Excision					
45170		X			X
45171	X				
45172	X				X
Anus					
Excision					
46200			X		
46210		X			
46211		X			
46220			X		X
46221			X		
46230			X		
46250			X		X
46255			X		
46258			X		
46260			X		
46262			X		
46275			X		
46280			X		
46320			X		
46945			X		
46946			X		
Repair					
46707	X				
Destruction					
46937		X			

Section/Code	Added	Deleted	Revised	Grammatical Revision	Cross-reference
46938		X			

Liver

Other Procedures

47382			X		

Biliary Tract

Introduction

47525			X		

Abdomen, Peritoneum, and Omentum

Introduction, Revision, Removal

49411	X				X

Urinary System

Kidney

Excision

50200			X		

Bladder

Urodynamics

51726			X		
51727	X				
51728	X				
51729	X				X
51772		X			
51795		X			
51797			X		

Transurethral Surgery

Urethra and Bladder

52282			X		X

Urethra

Repair

53415				X	

⃠=Modifier 51 Exempt   ⊙=Moderate Sedation   ✛=Add-on Code   ⋀=FDA approval pending

Section/Code	Added	Deleted	Revised	Grammatical Revision	Cross-reference
Other Procedures					
53855	X				X

Male Genital System

Prostate

Section/Code	Added	Deleted	Revised	Grammatical Revision	Cross-reference
Other Procedures					
55873			X		
55876			X		

Female Genital System

Vagina

Section/Code	Added	Deleted	Revised	Grammatical Revision	Cross-reference
Endoscopy/Laparoscopy					
57426	X				X

Maternity Care and Delivery

Other Procedures

Section/Code	Added	Deleted	Revised	Grammatical Revision	Cross-reference
59897			X		

Nervous System

Spine and Spinal Cord

Section/Code	Added	Deleted	Revised	Grammatical Revision	Cross-reference
Neurostimulators (Spinal)					
63660		X			
63661	X				X
63662	X				
63663	X				X
63664	X				X

Extracranial Nerves, Peripheral Nerves, and Autonomic Nervous System

Introduction/Injection of Anesthetic Agent (Nerve Block), Diagnostic or Therapeutic

Section/Code	Added	Deleted	Revised	Grammatical Revision	Cross-reference
Somatic Nerves					
64470		X			
64472		X			
64475		X			

Section/Code	Added	Deleted	Revised	Grammatical Revision	Cross-reference
64476		X			

Paravertebral Spinal Nerves and Branches

Section/Code	Added	Deleted	Revised	Grammatical Revision	Cross-reference
64490	X				X
64491	X				
64492	X				X
64493	X				
64494	X				
64495	X				X

Radiology

Diagnostic Radiology (Diagnostic Imaging)

Spine and Pelvis

Section/Code	Added	Deleted	Revised	Grammatical Revision	Cross-reference
72291			X		
72292			X		X

Gastrointestinal Tract

Section/Code	Added	Deleted	Revised	Grammatical Revision	Cross-reference
74261	X				
74262	X				X
74263	X				X

Heart

Section/Code	Added	Deleted	Revised	Grammatical Revision	Cross-reference
75558		X			
75560		X			
75562		X			
75564		X			X
75565	X				X
75571	X				
75572	X				
75573	X				
75574	X				

Section/Code	Added	Deleted	Revised	Grammatical Revision	Cross-reference
Vascular Procedures					
Aorta and Arteries					
75790		X			
75791	X				X
Radiologic Guidance					
Fluoroscopic Guidance					
77003			X		X
Radiation Oncology					
Medical Radiation Physics, Dosimetry, Treatment Devices, and Special Services					
77338	X				X
Stereotactic Radiation Treatment Delivery					
77371			X		
Nuclear Medicine					
Diagnostic					
Cardiovascular System					
78451	X				
78452	X				
78453	X				
78454	X				
78460		X			
78461		X			
78464		X			
78465		X			
78478		X			
78480		X			

Pathology and Laboratory

Organ or Disease-Oriented Panels

80055			X		X

Section/Code	Added	Deleted	Revised	Grammatical Revision	Cross-reference
Chemistry					
82306			X		
82307		X			
82652			X		
82784			X		
82785			X		
82787			X		
83516			X		
83518			X		
83519			X		
83520			X		
83986			X		
83987	X				
84145	X				
84431	X				X
Immunology					
86305	X				
86352	X				
86592			X		
86593			X		
86780	X				
86781		X			
Tissue Typing					
86825	X				
86826	X				X
Microbiology					
87149			X		X
87150	X				X
87153	X				

Section/Code	Added	Deleted	Revised	Grammatical Revision	Cross-reference
87493	X				

Surgical Pathology

88312			X		
88313			X		
88314			X		X
88387	X				X
88388	X				X

In Vivo (eg, Transcutaneous) Laboratory Procedures

88738	X				X

Reproductive Medicine Procedures

89398	X				

Medicine

Immune Globulins, Serum or Recombinant Products

90378			X		
90379		X			

Vaccines, Toxoids

90669			X		
90670	X				
90738			X		

Special Otorhinolaryngologic Services

Vestibular Function Tests, With Recording (eg, ENG)

92540	X				X

Audiologic Function Tests

92550	X				X
92569		X			
92570	X				X

Section/Code	Added	Deleted	Revised	Grammatical Revision	Cross-reference
Cardiovascular					
Implantable and Wearable Cardiac Device Evaluations					
93279			X		
93280			X		
93281			X		
93282			X		
93283			X		
93284			X		
93285			X		X
93286			X		
93287			X		
Noninvasive Physiologic Studies and Procedures					
93701			X		X
93750	X				X
Pulmonary					
Other Procedures					
94011	X				
94012	X				
94013	X				
Neurology and Neuromuscular Procedures					
Sleep Testing					
95806			X		X
Nerve Conduction Tests					
95905	X				X
Photodynamic Therapy					
96570			X		
96571			X		

⃠=Modifier 51 Exempt   ⊙=Moderate Sedation   ✚=Add-on Code   ✗=FDA approval pending

Section/Code	Added	Deleted	Revised	Grammatical Revision	Cross-reference
Other Services and Procedures					
99185		X			
99186		X			

Category II Codes

Patient Management

0519F			X		
0520F			X		
0521F			X		
0528F	X				
0529F	X				
0535F	X				
0540F	X				
0575F	X				

Patient History

1091F				X	
1150F	X				
1151F	X				
1152F	X				
1153F	X				
1157F	X				
1158F	X				
1159F	X				
1160F	X				
1170F	X				
1180F	X				
1220F	X				

Physical Examination

2050F	X				

Section/Code	Added	Deleted	Revised	Grammatical Revision	Cross-reference
Diagnostic/Screening Processes or Results					
3016F	X				
3018F	X				
3077F				X	
3078F				X	
3079F				X	
3080F				X	
3250F	X				
3302F		X			
3303F		X			
3304F		X			
3305F		X			
3306F		X			
3307F		X			
3308F		X			
3309F		X			
3310F		X			
3311F		X			
3312F		X			
3319F			X		
3321F	X				
3322F	X				
3370F	X				
3372F	X				
3374F	X				
3376F	X				
3378F	X				
3380F	X				
3382F	X				
3384F	X				

⊘=Modifier 51 Exempt ⊙=Moderate Sedation ✚=Add-on Code ✗=FDA approval pending

Section/Code	Added	Deleted	Revised	Grammatical Revision	Cross-reference
3386F	X				
3388F	X				
3390F	X				
3450F	X				
3451F	X				
3452F	X				
3455F	X				
3470F	X				
3471F	X				
3472F	X				
3475F	X				
3476F	X				
3490F	X				
3491F	X				
3492F	X				
3493F	X				
3494F	X				
3495F	X				
3496F	X				
3497F	X				
3498F	X				
3500F	X				
3502F	X				
3503F	X				
3510F	X				
3511F	X				
3512F	X				
3513F	X				
3514F	X				
3515F	X				

Section/Code	Added	Deleted	Revised	Grammatical Revision	Cross-reference
3550F	X				
3551F	X				
3552F	X				
3555F	X				
3570F	X				
3572F	X				
3573F	X				

Therapeutic, Preventive, or Other Interventions

Section/Code	Added	Deleted	Revised	Grammatical Revision	Cross-reference
4000F				X	
4001F				X	
4006F				X	
4009F				X	
4011F			X		
4040F				X	
4070F				X	
4148F	X				
4149F	X				
4152F		X			X
4154F		X			
4156F		X			
4158F			X		
4171F				X	
4172F				X	
4180F			X		
4192F	X				
4193F	X				
4194F	X				
4195F	X				
4196F	X				

Section/Code	Added	Deleted	Revised	Grammatical Revision	Cross-reference
4200F			X		
4201F			X		
4250F			X		
4260F	X				
4261F	X				
4265F	X				
4266F	X				
4267F	X				
4268F	X				
4269F	X				
4270F	X				
4271F	X				
4274F	X				
4275F	X				
4276F	X				
4279F	X				
4280F	X				
4290F	X				
4293F	X				
4300F	X				
4301F	X				
4305F	X				
4306F	X				
4320F	X				

Follow-up or Other Outcomes

5020F			X		
5100F	X				

Patient Safety

6030F			X		

Section/Code	Added	Deleted	Revised	Grammatical Revision	Cross-reference
Category III Codes					
0062T		X			
0063T		X			X
0064T		X			
0066T		X			X
0067T		X			X
0068T		X			
0069T		X			
0070T		X			
0077T		X			
0084T		X			
0086T		X			
0087T		X			X
0144T		X			
0145T		X			
0146T		X			
0147T		X			
0148T		X			
0149T		X			
0150T		X			
0151T		X			
0170T		X			
Remote Real-Time Interactive Videoconferenced Critical Care Services					
0194T		X			
0197T	X				
0198T	X				
0199T	X				
0200T	X				
0201T	X				X

⊘=Modifier 51 Exempt ⊙=Moderate Sedation ✚=Add-on Code ⊿=FDA approval pending

Section/Code	Added	Deleted	Revised	Grammatical Revision	Cross-reference
0202T	X				X
0203T	X				X
0204T	X				X
0205T	X				X
0206T	X				X
0207T	X